NGOs at the Table

NGOs at the Table

Strategies for Influencing Policies in Areas of Conflict

EDITED BY MARI FITZDUFF AND CHEYANNE CHURCH

ROWMAN & LITTLEFIELD PUBLISHERS, INC.
Lanham • Boulder • New York • Toronto • Oxford

ROWMAN & LITTLEFIELD PUBLISHERS, INC.

Published in the United States of America
by Rowman & Littlefield Publishers, Inc.
A wholly owned subsidiary of The Rowman & Littlefield Publishing Group, Inc.
4501 Forbes Boulevard, Suite 200, Lanham, MD 20706
www.rowmanlittlefield.com

P.O. Box 317, Oxford OX2 9RU, UK

British Library Cataloguing in Publication Information Available

Library of Congress Cataloging-in-Publication Data Available

ISBN 0-7425-2848-0 (cloth : alk. paper)
ISBN 0-7425-2849-9 (pbk. : alk. paper)

Printed in the United States of America

♾™ The paper used in this publication meets the minimum requirements of American
National Standard for Information Sciences—Permanence of Paper for Printed Library
Materials, ANSI/NISO Z39.48-1992.

Contents

Abbreviations

ANC	African National Congress
BAT	Belfast Action Teams
CAABW	Council for the Advancement of Arab/British Understanding
CDC	Community Development Center
CEDAW	Convention on the Elimination of All Forms of Discrimination against Women
CIDCM	Center for International Development and Conflict Management
CMG	Conflict Management Group
CMG/NRC	Conflict Management Group/Norwegian Refugee Council
CNDD-FDD	Conseil national pour la defense de la democratie-Forces nationales de liberation
CNN	Cable News Network
CSIS	Center for Strategic and International Studies
DAW	Division for the Advancement of Women (UN)
DDA	Department for Disarmament Affairs
DFID	Department for International Development
DOD	Department of Defense (United States)
DOMU	Document of Mutual Understanding
DPI/NGO	Department of Public Information/Nongovernmental Organizations
DPKO	Department of Peacekeeping Operations
DRC	Democratic Republic of Congo
ECCG	European Center for Common Ground
EU	European Union
FCO	Foreign and Commonwealth Office (UK)

G-8	Group of Eight
GLPF	Great Lakes Policy Forum
GONGO	Government Organized Nongovernmental Organizations
IA	International Alert
IAWGDF	Interagency Working Group for Displaced Families
IBM	International Business Machines
ICRC	International Committee of the Red Cross
IGAD	Intergovernmental Authority on Development
IGO	Intergovernmental Organization
IOM	International Organization on Migration
JCC	Joint Control Commission
MADAM	Multi-Agency Delivery Action Mechanism
MOD	Ministry of Defence (UK)
MSF	Médicins sans Frontières
NGO	Nongovernmental Organization
NGO-WB	NGO-World Bank
NGOWG	NGO Working Group on Women Peace and Security
NIHE	Northern Ireland Housing Executive
NIO	Northern Ireland Office
NRC	Norwegian Refugee Council
NWHSSI	North-West Belfast Health and Social Services Trust
ODIHR	Office for Democratic Institutions and Human Rights
OSAGI	Office of the Special Advisor to the Secretary-General on Gender Issues and Advancement
PFA	Platform for Action
PKK	Workers Party of Kurdistan
PRIO	Peace Research Institute of Oslo
RTNB	Official Radio Station in Burma
RUC	Royal Ulster Constabulary
SAIS	School of Advanced International Studies
SFCG	Search for Common Ground
SIPRI	Stockholm International Peace Research Institution
SSA	Social Security Agency (UK)
TOBB	Turkish Union of Chambers of Commerce and Industry
TOSAM	Center for the Research of Societal Problems
TOSAV	Foundation for Research of Societal Problems
UMAC	U Managing Conflict
UN	United Nations

UNHCR/CIS	United Nations High Commission for Refugees/ Commonwealth of Independent States
UNICEF	United Nations Children's Fund
UNIFEM	United Nations Development Fund for Women
UNSRSG	United Nations Special Representative to the Secretary-General
USAID	U.S. Agency for International Development
WFP	World Food Program
WPC	Women's Peace Center

Foreword
A View from Another World—The Policymaker's Perspective

Ambassador John W. McDonald

It was not until 1967, when I was assigned to the State Department's Bureau for International (United Nations) Organizations Affairs after twenty years as a U.S. diplomat serving in Europe, the Middle East, and the United States, that I first heard the words nongovernmental organization (NGO). This was at my first United Nations World Conference on trade and development, held in New Delhi, India, in 1968. There were a handful of NGO representatives present at that ten-week conference, but little attention was paid to them. This, however, was soon to change.

In 1968, the then Swedish ambassador to the United Nations General Assembly proposed a two-week conference to be held in Stockholm, with a focus on the environment, to which I was appointed Secretary to the United States Delegation. The Stockholm Conference was unique because for the first time, environmentally concerned NGOs met in parallel sessions in an attempt to influence the policy crafting of the formal negotiations. This established a new model for the inclusion of NGO participation into the policymaking arena, as evidenced by at least twenty-five United Nations conferences echoing a similar organizational format since 1972. It was the first time that I heard the NGO community raise its voice and attempt to influence policy, and it was the first of many public struggles between NGOs and their governments about their respective roles at United Nations international conferences.

The four United Nations World Conferences on Women and Development—Mexico City in 1975, Copenhagen in 1980, Nairobi in 1985, and Beijing in 1995—subsequently saw an enormous and exciting growth in NGO participation; it was estimated that some thirty-five thousand women and some three thousand NGOs were in China at the United Nations Beijing Conference in 1995. At all of the United Nations Summit Conferences on the environment, there has also been a similar massive growth in NGO participation, with over twenty-four thousand NGO representatives at Johannesburg in 2002. Gradually, governments across the world began to change their attitudes toward the potential role of NGOs and, for their part, the diverse NGO community increasingly became more adept and skillful in utilizing United Nations and other intergovernmental organizational processes and procedures to their advantage. They have become more conscious of their potential in assisting governments to implement many of the recommendations that emerged from these global conferences.

Over the past few decades, NGOs have been incrementally gaining more access to the policymaking arena, resulting in the cultivation of various mutually beneficial collaborative relationships particularly at the intergovernmental level. One noteworthy example regards the change in perception of the United Nations Security Council in the broadening of its institutional approach toward addressing the complexities and intricacies in the field of conflict resolution. In 1997, senior representatives from CARE, Médicins sans Frontières (MSF), and Oxfam were invited to brief Security Council members on the grim situation in the Great Lakes region of East Africa. These NGO leaders pointed out that humanitarian assistance was being used as a substitute for political action. These informal, unofficial consultations still continue and are an outstanding example of how NGOs can impact positively at the elite global policy level by providing factual information not readily accessible to large policymaking institutions. Credibility, respect, and trust are the building blocks upon which successful collaborative relationships are established between these two worlds.

A further illustration of the persuasive influence of conflict NGOs on the intergovernmental stage occurred in 2000. Under the leadership of significant NGOs such as International Alert, Safer World, and the European Platform for Conflict Prevention, fifty-five international NGOs, including our own Institute for Multi-Track Diplomacy,[1] cosponsored a report for the group of Eight (G-8) Heads of State meeting in Okinawa on 21-23 July 2000 on the topic of conflict prevention. The G-8 communiqué following that meeting was most remarkable, as paragraphs 72 and 73, for the first time in the history of G-8 summits, talked forcefully about the need for measures directed toward conflict prevention and urged foreign ministers to continue to develop this work. Subsequently, the communiqué issued at the G-8 foreign ministers meeting in Rome on 18-19 July 2001 expanded on this theme. The world leaders articulated a new initiative on conflict prevention which focused on the contribution and role of women and the private sector in this area. Such developments illustrate the unique capacity of NGOs not only to postulate alternative avenues in conflict policy but also to persuade and affect the policy agenda at the highest level of both UN and U.S. policymaking.

However, it must also be remembered that governmental perspectives on the value of increasing NGO participation in the policymaking process are far from universally positive. Many diplomats, members of the military, and officials in the field of foreign affairs prefer to operate and work within the framework of governmental circles, and are reluctant to engage with NGOs, citing the differences in professional conduct, objectives, and tactics of NGOs as an impediment to productive cooperation. Many senior U.S. diplomats that I know have horror stories to tell about the ineptness of particular NGOs they have met, operating in conflict regions while lacking in knowledge of the particular culture, history, and language of the country. Anecdotes often present NGOs as being demanding, impatient, stubborn, and overly aggressive on their single issue. Diplomats repeatedly complain that NGOs ignore the depth and complexities of the wider political scene. Their independence and unwillingness to coordinate their activities with embassies has fueled tensions and damaged their perceived usefulness as partners in policy implementation. It must also be noted, however, that having now worked within NGOs for the past fifteen years, I have heard similar stories from NGO personnel who are equally critical of governmental and intergovernmental organizations (IGOs), indeed often using the same words and phrases to describe their frustrations at the inflexibility of the policy process.

While some of these mutual negative perceptions emanate from particular and true realities on both sides, many of them are based on a significant lack of communication and understanding between these diverse groups about the meaningful yet distinctive roles that each can play in their overall objective of building peace. For NGOs involved in the relatively new fields of conflict prevention and conflict resolution, communication, and cooperation between NGOs, governments, diplomats, and the military is an area which requires improvement. In recognizing these significant challenges, this volume attempts to explore and contribute to the institutional knowledge of how NGOs may effectively penetrate major policymaking organizations and engage with them on policy issues in the field of conflict resolution.

Having worked as a policymaker with such diverse organizations as the United States State Department, U.S. Agency for International Developmnent (USAID), the World Bank, and the International Labor Organization, and as NGO president of both the Iowa Peace Institute and the Institute for Multi-Track Diplomacy, I do believe it is possible for NGOs to affect very significant changes in the programs and institutional practices of policymakers, if one is strategic and astute. From my experience, I have noted a number of fundamental challenges and realities which NGOs must adapt to and accept when interacting with policymakers.

It is important to remember that most politicians usually have a particular political time frame in mind and often want to start and finish a successful initiative "on their watch" so they can receive the credit. Impatience and often a lack of realism in terms of feasibility of accomplishments are ever-present political pressures affecting both politicians and diplomats. Recognition by NGOs of such time pressures and the needs attendant with them is therefore critically important. If NGOs can help deliver on some "instant" successes for the politicians, they may gain support for longer-term measures.

Allied to the above is the need for NGOs to be creative about where and how to allocate credit for policy successes. Most policymakers have large egos, and they must be treated accordingly by being allowed to take glory and potential accolades. NGOs need to persuade and coax the policymaker into the change process, and give the policymaker all the credit they can when the change is successful.

I believe that letters and e-mails are always secondary to personal contacts. On whatever issue you want to deal, and at whatever level (local, national, or international), I have found the best way an NGO can hope to bring about change is through face-to-face meetings. Building personal relationships on a one-to-one basis can be pivotal, and these relationships are even more valuable than small group meetings. One-to-one contact enhances opportunities to explain and persuade, but it also allows an NGO representative to plant an idea in the mind of a policymaker which can easily be adopted and incorporated into the policymaker's thinking, making it easier for them to take the credit if the idea translates into a successful initiative.

NGOs must gain an understanding of how an organization functions to become familiar with the intricacies and peculiarities of the system they intend to target, and become adaptable to the particular environment upon which they intend to impact. It is often useful for them to get to know the personal assistant of the individual who they wish to meet and influence, and to remember that this person is the "gatekeeper." It could prove a costly mistake, or even one fatal to the work an NGO is undertaking, to unnecessarily antagonize or patronize these individuals who hold the key that unlocks access to the policymaker. It is also important to remember that bureaucracies approach change at a snail's pace. Therefore, to affect an evolution in institutional behavior, an NGO is advised to develop and cultivate relationships with personnel from all levels in an organization. Seek out sympathetic and visionary individuals who will be prepared to take risks in support of the long-term benefits of change.

It is essential to remember that political and diplomatic personnel operate in a fluid environment. Governmental personnel turnover is high compared with NGO consistency of philosophy and attitude. This can be a hindrance when policy allies are transferred or policy objectives alter. Time and effort spent building a cooperative trusting relationship can swiftly be undone with the stroke of a pen. For example, in post-Dayton Bosnia, the Organization for Security and Cooperation in Europe (OSCE) has a significant presence. In the early years, however, coordination with NGOs was severely undermined because OSCE personnel were in a constant state of flux, with headquarters rotating positions every six months or so. This situation has been remedied to a slight degree, with personnel now remaining for longer time periods, but it exemplifies the challenge for NGOs to remain alert to the reality of changing governmental personnel and to ensure that they remain flexible in attitude and approach in order to deal with the next person, who may have different needs, style, and so on.

An awareness and understanding of policymaking is crucial for an NGO to effectively articulate its perspectives on conflict issues at the governmental and intergovernmental level. NGOs will face many obstacles and challenges along the way. Just as there are no quick fixes or magic wands in the management and transformation of conflicts, neither is there a road map to guide NGOs through the briar patch of the policy process. This volume, in examining a variety of NGOs diverse in size, location, and financial means who have successfully influenced policy and program development in conflicts throughout the world, provides valuable insights into how these organizations have implemented their strategies and overcome formidable challenges in the process. In sharing the experiences outlined in this book, I hope the reader will see how NGOs can significantly expand their capacity to exert a meaningful influence on the policy process and thus help to bring about real and more successful changes to the conflicts of today's world.

Note

1. The Institute for Multi-Track Diplomacy takes a systems approach to peace. It focuses on the use of Track Two diplomacy, which involves dialogues that are non-governmental, citizen to citizen, informal, often risk-taking, and unofficial. It utilizes interaction between private citizens or groups of people within a country, or from different countries, who are outside the formal governmental power structure. Track Two diplomacy, a phrase coined by Joe Montville (Joseph Montville, "The Arrow and the Olive Branch: A Case for Track Two Diplomacy," in *Conflict Resolution: Track Two Diplomacy*, eds. J. McDonald and D. Bendahmane, [Washington, D.C.: Foreign Service Institute, United States Department of State, 1987.]), has as its objective the reduction or resolution of conflict within a country through the lowering of anger, tension, and fear, by means of improved communications and a better understanding by the parties to conflict of each other's point of view. See www.imtd.org.

Acknowledgments

The idea for this volume originated in the work that UNU/INCORE undertakes with policymakers, practitioners, and academics to facilitate mutual learning on issues of intercommunal conflict and coexistence. As part of that process, we sought to identify the most effective mechanisms for practitioners wishing to affect conflict policy processes. When our initial research on this issue identified a significant dearth of information on such mechanisms, we decided to produce a book that would build on the experiences of individuals working in the field, who had had direct experience of impacting the policy process. It is primarily to such individuals, and the institutions they represent, that we wish to extend our thanks. Many of them work in situations where conflict and violence are endemic, and it was often not an easy task for them to take the time out required by this book to reflect upon and specify the practices that they thought had been most effective in having a decisive impact on policymaking. The editors gratefully appreciated their support and patience. We hope that they, and the field that they represent, will agree with us that the exercise has been a worthwhile one, and one that will encourage many others working in the NGO and civic society field to further develop their capacity to more significantly impact upon the change processes that are needed in so many conflicts around the world today.

The editors also wish to express a deep debt of gratitude to the Alan B. Slifka Foundation without whose encouragement and financial assistance this book would not have been possible. Our thanks are also especially extended to Fiona Barr, Malin Brenk, and Chris O'Donnell for their diligence, commitment, and thoughtful commentary during the arduous editing process. In addition, grateful appreciation is also extended to the staff at UNU/INCORE for their efforts and assistance in producing this book—their support is, as always, greatly appreciated.

Chapter 1
Stepping Up to the Table: NGO Strategies for Influencing Policy on Conflict Issues

Mari Fitzduff and Cheyanne Church

- NGOs working in Afghanistan in 1997 had more resources than the United Nations. The total aid budget for Afghanistan was US$200 million, of which the NGO share was US$136 million.[1]
- In 1997, a consortium of over three hundred fifty NGOs succeeded in obtaining an international treaty against the use of land mines.[2]
- In December 2002, a working group sponsored by the U.S. Council on Foreign Relations recommended that NGOs be offered training on issues of weapons of mass destruction, and suggested that the U.S. government should issue licenses for NGOs to undertake assessment missions in Northern Iraq.[3]

As the above examples show, there is little doubt that the growth and confidence of NGOs working in coexistence and conflict resolution work has dramatically increased over the past three decades and that their influence on governments and IGOs is increasing.[4] As Canadian Foreign Minister Lloyd Axworthy has suggested, one can no longer relegate NGOs to simple advisory or advocacy roles in this process; they are now part of the way decisions have to be made (Axworthy, 1997). Despite the challenges posed by working closely with policymakers, NGOs are recognizing that such work is key to increasing their capacity for leverage and extending their power. For many, the real test of NGOs' policy usefulness now will be the quality of their policy contributions: how do they move from being critics of policy to playing the role of an informed and thoughtful source of viable policy alternatives (Draimin and Plewes, 1995: 66)?

Such a role in policymaking, which Bratton defines as "the process in which decision makers respond to existing and potential pressures in the political environment" (Bratton, 1990: 93), is still relatively new to most NGOs. Traditionally, NGOs have attempted to affect the policy process by criticizing and lobbying from outside the halls of power. This was for a good reason, as many NGOs were and still are wary of developing work which is specifically designed to influence policymaking. However, an increasing number are learning that in attempting to achieve specific objectives, their work can be hindered if they do not engage in such work with governments, diplomats, bureaucrats, and regional organizations, international organizations, and IGOs, so as to ensure effective and sustainable success.

Influencing policymaking requires an NGO to adopt different responsibilities, utilize assorted methodologies, and adapt their role in relation to the policymakers they wish to influence. This poses a significant philosophical question for many of them: how can they maximize their capacity to influence policy while simultaneously retaining their core characteristics? Such prized characteristics usually include independence of thought and action, flexibility, and the capacity to play a variety of roles such as advocate, bridge builder, or honest broker—many of which may not easily be retained if close partnerships are forged with policymakers.

This volume examines the experiences of a variety of NGOs who have sought to enhance their capabilities by attempting to successfully bridge the gap between the NGO and policy worlds in the field of conflict resolution. Recognizing the paucity of literature specifically engaging with advocacy strategies in conflict contexts, the book begins with two essential discussions. Mark Howard Ross first provides a useful grounding in the policymaking process and examines the effect of conflict on this process. Hizkias Assefa then addresses the conceptual and practical challenges that face NGOs who seek to engage at the conflict policy level. These two chapters offer a framework for the remainder of the book, which focuses on strategies that have been successfully utilized in conflict contexts to impact policy. Written with the realities of the conflict resolution practitioner particularly in mind, the six case studies articulate the strategies, tactics, and lessons learned from their experiences in the policy world. The final chapter attempts to encapsulate the collective learning of all of the authors in their endeavor to systematically alter and affect positive change via the building of productive relationships between conflict resolution practitioners and policymakers.

The Growth of a Sector: NGOs

The variety and scope of the case studies in this volume is an indication of the evolution of the NGO world, whose growth over the past few decades has been exponential. A critical mass has been reached, with some believing that NGOs are becoming the new "fifth estate" on issues of global governance, particularly since the business scandals that marked the beginning of the millennium. In a statement to the World Economic Forum, Richard Edelman said: "We believe

NGOs are now the Fifth Estate in global governance—the true credible source on issues related to the environment and social justice . . . even with global recession and the events of 9/11, NGOs have strengthened their position. Last year in the United States, business was alone at the top of the pyramid of influence. Now companies must communicate with multiple stakeholders, especially NGOs, with speed, transparency, and an offer of interactivity" (Edelman, 2002).[5]

As Ambassador McDonald notes in the Foreword to this volume, the growth of NGOs, particularly over the last decade, has been phenomenal. In 1993-1994, only one decade ago, the Union of International Associations listed over fifteen thousand NGOs (Weiss and Gordenker, 1996: 17), while in 1995, a United Nations report on global governance noted that nearly twenty-nine thousand NGOs were functioning at the international level (Economist, 2000: 25). Such has been their growth that their numbers are now almost beyond counting. In 2000, it was estimated that there were over two million NGOs in the United States alone. As state contexts shift, the number of NGOs is rapidly increasing in places where there previously were few. In Russia, there are now about sixty-five thousand in existence, most of them having developed since the end of the Cold War (Economist, 2000: 25). It is estimated that, since democratization, twenty-one thousand NGOs have been set up in the Philippines, and twenty-seven thousand have been established in Chile (Boutros-Ghali in Weiss and Gordenker, 1996: 7). In fact, in 1997, Smith and Weiss estimated that NGO capacity was so large that the value of assistance delivered by these organizations was greater than that provided by the United Nations system, excluding the World Bank and International Monetary Fund (Smith and Weiss, 1997: 614).

The explosion of NGO representatives attending world conferences on women is an example of this phenomenon. At the first United Nations World Conference on Women in Mexico City in 1975, two thousand government delegates and six thousand NGO delegates attended—a ratio of three to one. Five years later, eight thousand NGO delegates attended the 1980 women's conference in Copenhagen, Norway. In Nairobi in 1990, there were eleven thousand. In 1995, Beijing hosted the Fourth World Conference on Women, with forty thousand NGO delegates and only six thousand governmental delegates in attendance. Over the course of four conferences in twenty years, the number of government delegates in attendance had tripled while the number of NGOs had increased more than sixfold.[6]

Although there is sometimes a tendency to speak about NGOs as a collective, this is far from the reality. NGOs form a rich if untidy community, with members ranging across the spectrum from the huge international professional body to the local grassroots organization. They come in an array of shapes and sizes, focusing on distinct issues, with a range of expertise and approaches to achieving their goals. They differ among themselves in their analyses of problems and the interventions necessary to achieve their goals. Nevertheless, in the current world context, NGOs have, in many places, become significant political actors, and this heterogeneous group has made its presence felt at the local, national, and international level.

Along with their growth, NGOs are now showing marked signs of system-

atic engagement with the policymaking world, although this shift toward institutional engagement has not been free of criticism. As yet, many NGOs feel ill-
equipped and uncomfortable in this endeavor, for not only has it raised a series
of conceptual concerns regarding the role and legitimacy of NGOs in such policy
work, it has also generated significant resistance on the part of many established
policy players. Despite such criticisms and concerns, however, there is an increasing realization by many NGOs of the necessity to be involved in the development of policy, and to become mainstreamed as part of normal programmatic
decisions in order to enhance the long-term effectiveness of their work.

The Evolution of Conflict NGOs

This volume focuses particularly on NGOs whose mandates involve conflict
resolution or peacebuilding and whose growth has mirrored that of the sector as
a whole. In particular, there has been a significant increase in the number of
NGOs indigenous to developing and war-affected countries during the 1990s, as
identified by organizations such as the European Platform for Conflict Intervention and Transformation.[7] These NGOs of today are very different from their
predecessors, and their roles continue to evolve with each passing decade. The
history of NGOs can be traced to 1807, when Britain abolished the slave trade,
thus instigating a growth of organized, nonprofit-based movements whose mission was to address the plight of slaves and the existence of slavery itself. Rieff,
a vociferous critic of the axis between modern humanitarian NGOs and the major state powers, referred to this shift as a new kind of humanitarian colonialism
(Rieff, 2002). The subsequent one hundred fifty years witnessed the foundation
of some of the major NGO players in the world today. Henri Dunant set up the
International Committee of the Red Cross (ICRC) in 1864, which subsequently
became one of the foremost humanitarian organizations working in the field of
conflict. It radically altered attitudes toward the treatment of war victims and
prisoners of war, seeing itself as the custodian of the laws of war. More than
fifty years later, the American Friends Service Committee was set up, followed
by the Save the Children Fund in 1917. OXFAM joined the club when it was
founded in 1942. Initially, all of these organizations saw themselves a primarily
service-oriented, dedicated to addressing the consequences of war on its victims.

After World War II, a second generation of NGOs emerged; in many cases,
they tackled problems previously handled by missionary societies (Lissner,
1977: 91). The scope of operations of many of these agencies, such as the Salva-
tion Army, the YMCA and YWCA, and CARE, encompassed the globe in dealing with aid, war relief, and postwar reconstruction. The majority of these organizations were also service-oriented, and avoided involvement in the politics of
the regions in which they worked, as they perceived their work as distinct from
the politics of the conflict. Generally, they believed that the maintenance of "neutrality" on issues of conflict was vital—engaging in the policy arena, therefore,
was both beyond their mandate and possibly threatening to their very existence.[8]

Many of the generation of NGOs that were to follow in the 1960s and

1970s took a more radical approach to the problems they were addressing and often chose to deliberately abandon the supposed "neutrality" so jealously guarded by the ICRC. Instead, they adopted a more confrontational approach to the occurrence of war and other ills of the world. After long and difficult debates, these NGOs decided they had to address not only the ravages of famine and war but also their causes, through advocacy, campaigning, or lobbying.[9] This is best exemplified by the work of Amnesty International and MSF, and the debt relief work of organizations like Christian Aid and Oxfam. In refusing to avoid addressing issues of politics as the previous generation had, these NGOs became active and vocal critics of states and multilateral organizations and their positions on war and conflict.

The 1990s saw several further significant evolutionary steps in the evolution of NGOs. As indigenous and international NGOs began to multiply, a new kind of professional engagement began to emerge between NGOs and hitherto unacceptable "bedfellows" such as IGOs, governments, and business. Partnerships that were previously viewed with suspicion and derision began to be recognized as potentially beneficial. Some NGOs gradually began to develop tentative working relationships with such organizations, leading them to become increasingly integrated into the more formal policymaking structures.

These processes appear to be deepening and solidifying as the new millennium unfolds, and such partnerships are becoming increasingly important, whether in the delivery of aid, working on conflict issues, or both. With more and more bilateral governmental aid being channeled through NGOs, the number of emerging and long-established NGOs who are happy to take state contracts—and, indeed, to actively seek such contracts—has increased significantly. Many NGOs have also begun to form strategic alliances with businesses. CARE established an alliance with Cable and Wireless to produce emergency communication kits (West, 2001: 33), and the American Red Cross partnered with IBM and CNN on a website about disasters. For some, this shift was an obvious evolution—as Sadako Ogata, the former United Nations High Commissioner for Refugees, notes, "businesses and humanitarians are destined to become partners in helping those in need" (Ogata, 2000: 4). Others, however, have struggled more with the moral challenges of engaging with those organizations, who often operate from different assumptions and motives, as discussed in chapter 3 of this book.

Whatever the challenges, from the mid-1990s until the present day, these partnerships have become increasingly formalized and significant. In terms of multilaterals and intergovernmental agencies, such as the United Nations, joint projects are becoming increasingly frequent. For instance, in liaison with the United Nations, NGOs have run one of the most successful landmine clearances in Afghanistan (West, 2001: 27). Increasingly, the status of NGOs within the United Nations is being systematized through formal measures of integration. The establishment of the NGO working group of the United Nations Security Council in 1995 showed how far the influence of NGOs had developed. This working group was instituted as a mechanism for off-the-record dialogue between about thirty NGO and Security Council members to share perspectives on issues of conflict around the world, and signified a real shift in Security Council-NGO relationships.

A precursor to this move was the development of the Arria Formula in 1993. In a break from the normally closed formula of United Nations consultations, Ambassador Arria of Venezuela invited Security Council members to hear, over coffee, the views of a Bosnian priest on the crisis in the Balkans. This kind of informal consultation became known as the Arria Formula,[10] and its use at the United Nations helped break down the barriers between governments and NGOs.

Another formalized mechanism that has changed the role of NGOs is consultative status within the United Nations.[11] This gives agencies a recognized and legitimate place within many United Nations proceedings and their decision-making processes. As a result, many of these agencies are now officially participating in United Nations conferences as well as organizing their own shadow conferences. Some have access to United Nations documents or official passes allowing entry to United Nations buildings; all of this has increased the lobbying and policy leverage of these organizations considerably. As these relationships have deepened, there has been an increase in instances of NGOs being requested to attend United Nations briefings and strategy meetings on situations of conflict. The United Nations Secretary-General, Kofi Annan, in his address to the DPI/NGO fiftieth annual conference, recognized that the relationship today between the United Nations and NGOs is increasingly one of partnership. "Nongovernmental organizations are now seen as essential partners of the United Nations, not only in mobilizing public opinion, but also in the process of deliberation and policy formulation and—even more important—in the execution of policies, in work on the ground."[12]

It is not only the United Nations, however, that has recognized the capacity of NGOs to assist international institutions in delivering on their objectives. Other agencies, such as the World Bank, have also recognized the need for engagement. In the early 1980s, a global mechanism for policy dialogue between the World Bank and NGOs was established. The aims of this forum were to promote public consensus and local ownership for reforms and development strategies; to give a voice to stakeholders, particularly at the grassroots level; to bring new ideas and innovative solutions to the work of the Bank on local problems; and to promote public sector transparency and accountability, thus contributing to good governance. This NGO-World Bank Committee[13] enabled annual discussions on poverty reduction, participation, postconflict reconstruction, and other issues of mutual importance. This dialogue was subsequently decentralized in 1995, and regional and national-level NGO-World Bank Committees were established to consolidate and extend dialogue on World Bank policies, programs, and loans. In the United Kingdom, for instance, since the mid-1990s, the FCO (Foreign and Commonwealth Office), MOD (Ministry of Defence), and DFID (Department for International Development) have held regular meetings with British conflict and aid agencies to share analyses and address issues of common concern about conflicts around the world.[14]

As this decade progresses, NGOs are fast becoming a vital component of the international response to conflicts, going well beyond their traditional roles as service providers or distributors of food. Many believe that in the last few decades, they have also begun to change the world system through their increasingly powerful global networks (Kaldor, 1999: 4). Some argue that such networks are enhancing NGOs' ability to influence decisions and policymaking processes even at the global level: "Transnational civil society is a piece—an increasingly important piece—of global governance" (Florini and Simmons, 2000: 3).[15] According to Rice and Ritchie (cited in Koenig, 1996: 28), the emergence of NGOs is now paralleling the expanding role of the IGOs in the political sphere, and rapid globalization in the economic sphere.

Such a role has certainly been enhanced by the fact that NGOs are handling increasingly large budgets. CARE, for instance, during the fiscal year 2001, notched up almost US$380 million in program expenditure.[16] The revenue of Catholic Relief Services was US$334 million in 2001.[17] In 2002, World Vision raised US$1.032 billion in cash and goods in support for its mission in ninety countries worldwide.[18] In fact, there are now instances in which the total NGO budget for a crisis exceeds that of the United Nations. In Afghanistan in 1997, for example, NGOs received US$136 million of the US$200 million that constituted the total United Nations aid budget for the country. Even in Rwanda in 1994, where the United Nations ostensibly had the larger budget—50 percent of the US$1.29 billion given in aid was given to the United Nations, and only 20 percent to NGOs in the region—the United Nations subsequently subcontracted a substantial part of their Rwandan funds to the NGOs (West, 2001: chapters 5 and 6).

As a consequence of becoming more professional, engaging in formal and recognized ways with multilaterals and governments, and experiencing serious increases in budgets, NGOs are quickly losing their perceived "inferior" status (West, 2001: 211). They are no longer systematically relegated to the margins; the hierarchies restricting interaction between multilaterals, IGOs, governments, and NGOs have started to soften, permitting more formal and informal interaction. The cachet of the major NGOs is increasingly matching that of the IGOs, with employees moving easily between the two (West, 2001: 212).

Why Such Growth?

NGOs are rapidly expanding in number, budget, and credibility—but why has this sector grown with such rapidity, particularly over the last decade? Their growth has been attributed to a variety of factors including the end of the Cold War, an increase in subcontract opportunities, a growth in humanitarian norms, and a developing perception of NGOs as organizations who are more trustworthy than governments.

The ending of the Cold War had two direct consequences on NGO work in aid and conflict. Firstly, this shift in international political relations meant that the superpowers, who previously had attempted to retain and control issues of aid, development, and conflict to secure their own ends, were less worried about

other superpower influence on countries needing assistance. With this new freedom to operate, NGOs expanded their mandates. At the same time, increasing
democratization allowed new agencies to grow and develop.

Secondly, the nature of conflicts changed significantly, with most conflicts
now happening at a substate rather than an interstate level and arising between
opposing groups of an ethnic, religious, or cultural nature (SIPRI, 2002;[19]
Horowitz, 1985). Such conflicts, unless directly threatening to state interests, were
of significantly less concern to the majority of governments. Although states were
frequently still pressurized to assist in crises and conflict, the end of the Cold
War meant that they were often relatively happy to use humanitarian aid and conflict resolution support as a substitute for political action. In undertaking such
work, NGOs became increasingly important and became in many cases "the front
line troops for governments which prefer humanitarian help to political solutions"
(ICRC, 1995). One consequence of this is an increase in service contract opportunities that has resulted in a significant incentive for NGO development.

Another perspective suggests that the increasing number of NGOs in the
field is linked to the increasing importance of the human rights field in the development of humanitarian norms. Following World War II, human rights pros-
pered mainly because NGOs mobilized public opinion and leveraged states to
accept such norms. As the primary promoters of such norms were the NGOs,
their influence grew in turn as these norms became accepted at the national and
international level (West, 2001: 50).

Finally, Wuori (1997) has suggested that NGOs are not only considered the
clearest expression of the emerging transnational civil society, but are now often
regarded as the "keepers of conscience" of the emerging international moral
community. Consequently, present governmental and intergovernmental structures and processes that exclude or minimize the involvement of NGOs may be
seen as lacking in moral legitimacy despite the formal legal authority of
governments (Carroll and Vignard, 2002: 23). NGOs are thus increasingly seen
as demonstrating popular representation at work in the world. Former United
Nations Secretary-General Boutros Boutros-Ghali acknowledged this relationship when he said:

> Non-governmental organizations are a basic form of popular representa-
> tion in the present-day world. Their participation in international
> relations is, in a way, a guarantee of the political legitimacy of those
> international organizations. It is therefore not surprising that in a short
> space of time we have witnessed the emergence of many new non-
> governmental organizations.[20]

Becoming Full Players

Despite the rise in informal and formal mechanisms that are increasingly placing
NGOs in the room with policy actors, and the increase in contracts that allow

NGOs to enact many government and IGO policies, many NGOs argue that the "fifth estate" is not yet fully established. These NGOs claim that while NGO-United Nations shadow conferences, for instance, are a step in the right direction, they do not provide the level of access or degree of authority required to effect change. Cynics will go significantly further, citing these examples of policy inclusion as smoke screens that keep NGOs and the liberal elite occupied and away from the real processes, freeing the policy actors to get on with the business at hand.[21]

In addition, although certain governments do formally engage with NGOs, as in the case of the Canadian Peacebuilding Coordinating Committee Conference,[22] not all have been persuaded of the need to do so. Many NGOs, perhaps the majority, do not as yet feel they have the experience, skills, confidence, time, or resources to step away from their daily activities and engage in the policy arena. For some, this has led to a sense of powerlessness where official actors and the policy process are concerned, which inhibits their ability to strategize and engage effectively. The relative youth and small size of many conflict NGOs, particularly in comparison to the enormity of multilaterals and the complexity of government, also contribute to this sense of paralysis. There is also an apparent vacuum in literature which addresses this topic, and those professional organizations that possess advocacy or lobbying experience are often outside of the financial capacities of nonprofit institutions.

The field itself, however, is beginning to recognize the need for NGOs to increase their capacity to work with policymakers. In the past few years in Europe and North America, there has been a surge in the number of conferences, workshops, and meetings attempting to address the question of how aid and conflict NGOs can engage in more effective policymaking.[23]

Policymaker Concerns

A crucial inhibitor to NGO policy engagement is the fear held by some governments and IGOs of losing control of their own agendas (Jackson, 2000).[24] This loss of control is perceived to be caused by pressure focusing on singular interests, potential demands to alter historical or political structures and systems, and a possible increase in scrutiny of these structures and systems by external actors (in this case, NGOs).

States fear losing control over their agendas through the pressure of NGO special interests. These interests are perceived to make governmental decisions more difficult, as the representations made by these organizations often have rather narrow concerns as opposed to a government's obligation to balance a broader spectrum of concerns on the part of many stakeholders. This fear by states has been exacerbated by the ever-increasing ability of international NGOs to outweigh the voices of states in forcing agendas. It has been estimated by Spiro that "environmentalist and human rights NGOs collectively speak for many times over the numbers represented by even medium-size states in the UN, and that even narrowly defined NGOs would sometimes outrank the microstates in terms of numbers" (Spiro, 1996: 52).

Often, governments are also concerned that NGOs will introduce values or working practices, such as greater consultative democracy, that will erode the often narrower practices of the state. They fear that NGOs may question existing rules and suggest alternatives to the habitual traditions of governments. As Lawson suggests, "international public opinion, transnational NGOs, and revolutions in telecommunications and the mass media have all begun to erode the traditional boundaries and prerogatives of diplomatic praxis" (Lawson, 1998: 96). Governments worry that these additions will slowly force change to the political system, and this often causes official actors to resist cooperation with NGOs.

States also feel that they may face increased scrutiny by allowing NGOs to be privy to their decision-making discussions. Their discussions are usually private, in-house negotiations, with very little transparency or accountability. Governments are often fearful that NGOs may not respect such confidentiality, and this is indeed a problem for many NGOs, particularly those who are advocacy groups and who see themselves as primarily accountable to their members. Governments fear, therefore, that what are often seen as sensitive issues could be transmitted to the greater public through channels of mass media, and that the capacity of NGOs to utilize information technology will make it increasingly difficult for governments to monopolize information. As Price has suggested, the greater freedom NGOs enjoy often means that they can mobilize public or media opinion in a way that governments and IGOs cannot, and such access decreases the capacity of the state to monopolize information and increases the power of NGOs to create pressure on governments (Price, 1998: 107).

Concerns about the Role of NGOs

The work of NGOs is not without its critics. As NGOs become more powerful, they are coming under more scrutiny and are facing critical questions about their roles and the consequences of their work. They have been accused of being counterproductive in situations of conflict (Duffield, 1997), and critics like Stubbs (1997) have argued that NGOs in Yugoslavia, for instance, have caused the erosion of the middle classes and thereby caused the suspension of civil society activities, including policymaking activities, as a result of many of their actions. Eagen has suggested that in Mozambique, NGOs have caused the underdevelopment of local governments and inhibited the development of local participatory activities, which has adversely affected the sustainable recovery of Mozambique (Eagen, 1991). In other conflicts, NGOs have been accused of succumbing to government agendas. In Sri Lanka, for instance, NGOs are accused of getting more involved in longer-term activities in areas held by the government than in areas held by the The Liberation Tigers of Tamil Eelam (LTTE), against whom the government is waging a military campaign.

The criticism of many NGOs by the various United Nations peacekeeping forces in particular is also legendary, resulting in NGO proliferation not always being welcomed by all sections of the United Nations and other IGOs. Their complexity, freedom, and numbers often prove to be disconcerting to peacekeeping organizations who wish to develop collective and strategic approaches to the resolution of conflict and postconflict problems. Such forces often see some of the NGO agencies as naive, meddling, and with their own, often competing, agendas. There is also a view that NGOs can foul up delicate negotiations with their unreasonable demands and proposals (Carroll and Vignard, 2002: 1). An example of this was the much criticized role of International Alert (IA) in Sierra Leone (Duffield, 1997).

A more recent criticism of the role of NGOs is that the peacebuilding agenda can serve as a fig leaf for the political inaction of international actors, helping to mask the local and global political and economic dynamics that are in fact the driving forces of violent conflict in peripheral countries. This can be particularly true where peacebuilding programs do not take into account the local and international structural issues which are an integral part of many conflicts (Duffield, 1999; Keen, 1999). In addition, many people living in conflict situations, particularly in the developing South, see NGOs, despite their apparently neutral status, as inevitably laden with the agendas of their respective home countries. As Hizkias Assefa discusses in chapter 3, this is particularly true if the NGOs in question are in receipt of state funds and thus may become the implementers of donor policies (Smillie, 1997). Furthermore, many advocacy and human rights groups are seen by local people as not being at all neutral but as being supportive of particular political or group agendas. In some cases, NGOs have been accused of selectivity in their advocacy of human rights, a charge which has been leveled against Amnesty International over its condemnation of state violence in Northern Ireland without any parallel condemnation of the violence committed by paramilitaries (Fitzduff, 2002b).[25] Anderson (1999) suggests that, in the cases of Rwanda and Yugoslavia, widespread publicity about human rights abuses disseminated by some NGOs may have actually caused certain groups to harden their position in order to portray themselves more successfully as misunderstood or maligned by the international community; consequently, NGOs inadvertently reinforced the pursuit of war.

Governments and others have often voiced concerns about the accountability of NGOs. Unlike democratically elected governments and politicians, NGOs are not generally accountable to the wider public, only to their members or supporters or those who fund them. Assefa, in chapter 3 of this book, ponders the question of how the NGO community can be held accountable, arguing that NGOs often misrepresent who they are speaking for. In addition, transparency regarding issues such as funding or criteria for choice of activities is often optional for some independent NGOs.

Part of the difficulty here is also the tendency for some NGOs to operate in an unprofessional or disorganized manner. The squabbling and lack of cooperation that often appear where there is a high density of NGO activity is frequently cited as one of the factors that makes NGO policy engagement problematic. There are also severe tensions and conflicting views among NGOs themselves as to the best approaches to resolving conflict. As a result, governments or IGOs may be faced with several different policy proposals, all from agencies purporting to represent the same actors in the conflict. In addition, some NGOs are comfortable working with official institutions and states while others are not, and this can prevent cooperation on areas such as service delivery and joint leveraging of influence.

Furthermore, the process of engagement with official bodies usually involves only elite NGOs—those with sufficient finance, the loudest voice, and the better contacts in a region (Spiro, 1995: 52). This frequently means that smaller NGOs, commonly indigenous to the conflict region, will not have a voice at the policymaking table, and that their often valuable perspectives may not be included in the decision-making process. It has also been suggested that those NGOs that do achieve leverage and attention are not necessarily those whose values and assistance are most needed in a particular situation.

NGO Concerns about Engagement

It is evident therefore that the expansion of NGO activity into policy engagement should not be embarked upon without careful consideration of the potential negative ramifications. Although each situation has its own pitfalls and issues, there are general questions around independence, neutrality, and the freedom to act that NGOs should soberly consider and reflect upon before taking the decision to engage in close working liaisons with policymakers.

In the first place, NGOs need to consider the potential loss of independence that may result from cooperating too closely with officialdom and participating in its decision-making processes. Not only will the NGO have to abide by collective decisions and bear any negative repercussions emanating from such decisions, but also, as a consequence of such interaction, the NGO will almost certainly have to endure greater scrutiny of its activities by governmental agencies. Indeed, Gordenker and Weiss (1997: 451) question whether a move toward greater cooperation is in fact a step closer to increased regulation by government. Being answerable to government, rather than to their members or values and principles, may challenge the freedom and flexibility that are at the core of an NGO's existence. In addition, NGOs' capacity to be an effective opposition to official policies could decrease for one of two reasons. Close working relationships formed as a result of joint decision-making interaction could stimulate empathy on the part of the NGO to their new colleagues in the policy world. Also, NGOs could become dependent upon official bodies for funding and thus lose their ability to foster approaches, ideas, language, and values that run counter to official orthodoxy (Edwards and Hulme, 1996: 7).

Ultimately, NGOs must recognize that states are obliged to follow their own self-interest, which may or may not be the route that offers the most help in a situation of conflict. For many states, "relations are not solely governed by such considerations as generosity and solidarity between peoples; other constraints, such as security, diplomacy and economic interests, impose a definite limit to cooperation and partnership" (CCIC, 1988: 23). NGOs may not want to be limited or constrained by state or other official concerns, but the very process of joint decision making, and the relationships developed therein, may mean that NGOs find it increasingly difficult to criticize governments and others. As Jackson (2000) points out, NGOs "may have to compromise standards and values in order to accomplish their goals. This may even be necessary just to be included in the policymaking process." As a result, NGOs could lose their credibility as an independent and neutral actor in the eyes of those they are seeking to work with on the ground. This would be a significant loss, as trust and goodwill are the crucial features of an NGO's attractiveness to local people.

For most NGOs, policymaking is a relatively new role which must be aligned with their values and methodologies. In changing their role from that of critics to that of potential collaborators, there can be a number of pitfalls. While this new challenge presents the need for NGOs to develop policymaking skills, capacity, and expertise in order to be respected and effective in the formal policymaking process, some critics may see these qualities as incongruous with the unique NGO characteristics of informality, spontaneity, and flexibility. Nevertheless, if NGOs are to be valuable contributors to the formal policy process, more formalized techniques must be used to work effectively within the established system.

The Necessity to Be Involved

Despite the above concerns on both sides, there are valuable arguments for the engagement of NGOs in policymaking. By adopting such a strategy, conflict resolution NGOs can increase the depth and duration of their work far beyond what could be achieved simply by depending upon their own resources and processes. The leverage that an NGO can bring to bear upon a conflict situation is often limited unless the NGO can ensure sustained implementation and continuation of a project by official actors such as political parties, governmental agencies, or international organizations. As Anderson and Olson (2003) have found in their project assessing critical lessons for peace practitioners, the success of a conflict intervention is often determined by two factors: the number of people or groups at both a personal and societal/political level who can be brought to engage in the peacemaking agenda, and the capacity of those individuals or groups with the power to implement conflict interventions and agreements at the required regional, national, or international level. Thus, interventions that are to be effective often have to be woven into the formal infrastructure of states, either existing or under construction. Such mainstreaming of programs and processes will often determine whether or not such interventions are sustained for the duration required to be successful.

NGOs can bring contextually relevant, locally sourced knowledge to the policy table which is a necessary dimension to successful policymaking in divided and violent societies. Such interaction expands the democratic scope of the decision-making process by making it more representative and inclusive, thus increasing its chances of success. Policymakers often find it difficult to access and address local needs and conditions unless these are garnered for them in an identifiable vehicle, with the accompanying pressure to take such perspectives seriously. An illustration of this precise interaction can be found in chapter 5 of this volume. In this case, civil servants who sought to address the needs of communities from violent interface areas in Belfast agreed to a partnership with a local community organization in order to develop an effective policy to deal with a recurring crisis. Policies and programs that make tidy sense at the official level may have little chance of successful implementation if they are not adequately tailored to needs at the local community level.

NGOs can help find new and creative ways to reconceptualize conflicts and suggest possibilities for conflict intervention outside of the normal paradigms utilized by governments and official bodies. Official actors are often significantly more constrained in terms of their capacity to be innovative. This is either because they are part of the conflict process itself, and seen as such, or because they are nominally outside of the process but are not capable of creative thinking or permitted to undertake it, given their bureaucratic and conservative nature. NGOs, on the other hand, can often undertake initiatives which would spell political anathema to many governments. For instance, they can talk to paramilitaries and guerrilla fighters, as IA has done in Sri Lanka (see www.international-alert.org/fieldwork/srilanka.htm), as the Henri Dunant Center has done in Indonesia (see www.atimes.com/se-asia/BE24Ae01.html), and as many NGOs and civil society individuals have done in Northern Ireland (Fitzduff, 2002a), South Africa (Collin Marks, 2000), and the Middle East (Kelman, 1996). The capacity of NGOs for facilitating dialogue has few boundaries except that of courage.

Such creativity and flexibility, usually sorely needed in conflict situations, is often one of the defining characteristics of NGOs. "The institutions at the periphery of society, and not the government, have historically been the originators of new ideas" (Draimin and Plewes, 1995: 71). We see such innovation in the work carried out by Center for the Research of Societal Problems (TOSAM), discussed in chapter 9 of this volume, in which the organization catalyzed the reframing of the traditional, official perspective on the Kurdish conflict in Turkey. Hence, despite the challenges, there are many powerful reasons why NGOs should consider reviewing their capacity to impact upon a much wider range of significant and powerful organizations that can more effectively help them to deliver on optimum developments in conflict situations.

Influencing Policy in Conflict Situations

Before reviewing the strategies outlined in this book, it is important to consider some of the fundamental conceptual challenges to work of this nature. As Mark Howard Ross describes in chapter 2, the policy process in a conflict often features more chaos than clarity, and thus to claim a unilateral influence amongst the diversity and richness of actors involved is extremely difficult. What, then, does impact or influence actually mean? All the authors involved in this book grappled with the notion of impact. A general consensus would seem to suggest that to influence or impact policy means to play a significant role in affecting policy-related decision making and actions. This is not to say that successful impact necessarily means that the desired policy of the NGOs will be fully adopted, but it does mean one can perhaps be influential in the process without totally determining the final outcome. It is also important to remember that rarely is an NGO—or indeed any other organization—the sole cause of change, and all of the case studies under discussion recognize the usual multifaceted nature of influences in impacting on policy. While some of the projects in the book have undertaken formalized evaluations of their work, it is recognized that the evaluation of conflict interventions is as yet an underdeveloped phenomena. Nevertheless, such uncertainties should not negate the worth of the efforts illustrated in these pages—indeed, to be cognizant of the challenges in evaluating causality and outcome should enhance the critical reflections of this field rather than paralyze them (Church and Shouldice, 2002; 2003).

Strategies to Consider

There are six cases described in this volume, each differing in terms of strategy, size of organization, issues addressed, and the country or region involved. Due to the heterogeneous nature of this field, these differences were perceived as essential in producing a volume that spoke to the wide variety of circumstances and needs involved. Each case attempts to provide a practical understanding of the realities of implementing each strategy.

A useful way of considering the strategies outlined is through a popular advocacy dichotomy: insider versus outsider strategies. Broadly speaking, insider strategies are those that seek to work alongside the policymakers, often in partnership with their organizations, to influence decisions or guide their behavior. Outsider strategies, on the other hand, attempt to drive policy actors in specified directions by applying pressure from outside their organizations or groups. Both approaches have merit and use depending on context, resources, and policy issue. In terms of the six strategies outlined here, only two can be seen as adopting just one of these roles, with the other four adopting more mixed approaches. The cases are ordered so that they flow from one end of the spectrum to the other, starting with a pure insider strategy.

The most distinct insider strategy is Track One and a Half diplomacy, used by Conflict Management Group and the Norwegian Refugee Council (CMG/NRC) in the conflict between Georgia and South Ossetia. The latter had declared itself as an independent Soviet Republic separate from and in opposition to the wishes of Georgia, causing an armed struggle to erupt in 1990. With over a thousand killed and tens of thousands displaced, a peace deal was brokered by the Russians in 1991. By 1995, peace negotiations were stalled and beginning to deteriorate. In response to this situation, CMG/NRG devised a Track One and a Half strategy, bringing together key participants from the talks to learn new skills and techniques for handling the deadlock and providing a safe space to think outside official positions. After multiple workshops over five years, the project succeeded in transferring three main results from the unofficial to the official processes: improved relationships, improved processes, and concrete ideas.

This case study shows an excellent example of NGOs engaging at the highest political levels, right up to and including the President of Georgia. It examines in detail the criteria utilized to select participants which were felt to be instrumental in the subsequent success of the work. In addition, it discusses the issues relevant to adopting a partnership approach to influencing strategy.

Although the second case, that of the Community Development Centre (CDC) in Belfast, Northern Ireland, follows a mainly insider approach, those involved utilized outsider measures in order to increase the effectiveness of their strategy. In the summer of 1996, North Belfast, a community with a history of violence, experienced some of the worst sectarian violence in decades, at the end of which one hundred ten families had left their homes as a result of sectarian intimidation. The rapidity of this expulsion caught the authorities unawares, leaving families without access to many of the social services upon which they were dependent. The CDC stepped into this vacuum with a strategy to mainstream partnership approaches to crisis between the community and government agencies.

Primarily working within the halls of power, but also keeping press attention focused on the issue—a classic outsider tactic—the strategy bridged the gap between government agencies and the affected community through the establishment of an Interagency Working Group. This group, which had community representation, developed policies around crisis response. However, as time passed and stability appeared to strengthen, the importance placed on the working group by policy actors decreased, and so therefore did the ability of community groups to effectively engage these key policy actors. This highlights one of the key lessons to be learned from this case.

The third case illustrates the most ambitious of our examples in that it is a multifaceted global campaign that draws equally from both the insider and outsider domains. Led by IA in London, the campaign "Women Building Peace: From the Village Council to the Negotiating Table" was a reaction to the failure to implement the majority of security policies relating to women at the local, national, regional, and international levels. This failure left women vulnerable during conflicts and excluded from the determination of possible solutions to their problems. The campaign sought the inclusion of women in five critical areas of peacebuilding, and its ultimate goal was a United Nations Security Council resolution on women and security.

The strategy devised was multifaceted, integrated, international, and focused. Balancing the need to work with key policy actors while simultaneously raising public awareness and political pressure, the strategy was owned by over three hundred fifty organizations around the world. Activities ranged from systematic multiconstituency consultations intended to refine the critical areas, to a postcard campaign which resulted in over a hundred thousand signatures being presented to the Special Adviser on Gender to the United Nations Secretary-General. After an intensive eighteen-month campaign and a significant effort, the Security Council passed Resolution 1325, which incorporated all the themes highlighted by women's groups in the campaign. This case provides a multitude of lessons for those wishing to embark on the international campaign trail.

From an international campaign, the volume moves to a local initiative designed to implement community policing policy in South Africa. One of the essential features of the apartheid transition was a reframing of the security forces from a militarist, authoritarian body to one that was based on the premise of crime prevention and community participation. Although successive, progressive legislation was passed from 1995 to 1999, crime rates soared; society, including even former advocates for the community approach, clamored for the forceful police tactics of the past, which, despite their lack of success in curbing crime, nevertheless gave people a sense of security.

A local agency, U Managing Conflict (UMAC), which had been operational on security issues previous to the transition, decided to act upon its conviction that it was not a flawed approach but rather a flawed implementation that was at the root of the problem. On this basis, UMAC developed a strategy to pilot a community policing structure as a new way of operationalizing the existing legislation and developing a model that could then be implemented across the country. Through the strategic use of a feasibility study, its own reputation and conflict resolution process expertise, and a sound insider approach, UMAC was able to show the effectiveness of the idea of community policing. The lessons this case offers are valuable in a multitude of scenarios where implementation rather than formulation of policy is the problem in need of attention.

Our fifth case diverges slightly from the others in this series in that it advocates the inclusion of players in the policy process at the macrolevel while also seeking the advancement of a particular policy issue. In 1993, civil war raged in Burundi and the region struggled to prevent the kind of genocide that had happened in Rwanda. Search for Common Ground (SFCG), which had opened its first office in Burundi in 1995, became conscious of Burundi's lack of presence on the American foreign policy agenda. It was concerned, given the historical evidence of Rwanda, which indicated that without a presence on the international agenda, gross tragedy could develop unchecked in Burundi. SFCG wanted not only to place the issue of Burundi on the international agenda, but also to ensure that the voices and approaches of the NGO community could become regular players in the policy process.

An inclusion strategy was developed which answered both objectives and which materialized in the formation of the Great Lakes Policy Forum (GLPF) in Washington, and subsequently the European Great Lakes Forum in Brussels. The forums in Washington are regular, inclusive, and participatory, adding value to the debate on the region by providing a platform for diverse and current thinking. Through systematic recruitment, attendance at the forums reflects a wide range of stakeholders in this region, including embassy staff, State Department officials, Department of Defense, NGOs, and even the private sector. Now running for eight years, the GLPF is considered by many to be the prime arena for discussion on the region and a key vehicle for inserting new ideas into the policy domain. This case study offers a series of principles for this type of engagement as well as a number of lessons that have been learned over the years. It also offers an interesting case from the insider/outsider perspective in that it instigated a process to move NGOs as a whole from outsider status to inside players.

The final case study in this volume brings us to the opposite end of the spectrum with a classic illustration of an effective outsider strategy. Established in 1923, the Republic of Turkey has an ethnically mixed population and a state-centric government that exerts much effort in its attempts to control the country's diverse population. However, the country erupted into violent unrest, predominately between the Turkish identity groups and the Kurdish minority, in the mid-1980s. Since then this unrest, commonly referred to as the "Kurdish problem," remains unresolved, and has claimed tens of thousands of lives.

This issue embraces the entire nation and dominates thinking within the government and military. Attempting to inject new thinking into this policy dialogue is daunting; this is due not only to the scope of the issue, but also to the potential personal ramifications for the actors involved. What began as a social science research study on Kurdish attitudes launched an NGO which took up the challenge to reframe the Kurdish problem. The strategy involved a focused effort to define the perceived nature of the problem, facilitate further discussions to refine this understanding throughout Turkey, and finally take this understanding to the European Union (EU). The strategy was not implemented without significant hurdles, including the fact that the first NGO which was founded to take this reframing challenge forward was shut down by the government. The work continued, however, and has resulted in a series of valuable lessons for the NGO community as a whole.

The case studies in this volume provide a range of strategies that have been effective in the context in which they were developed. In many cases they will have relevance to other situations throughout the world, and such is the hope of this book. It must be borne in mind, however, that serious consideration should be given as to what is transferable to particular and unique conflict contexts, and that what is of value in each situation will need careful thought in relation to the particular conflict situation, policy issue, organizational capacity, or culture of the context. As the case studies themselves show, there are few easy answers for NGOs working on conflict-related issues. What they also show, however, is that where they so desire, and if they strategize well, NGOs can have a significant role in the policy process in conflict areas, and thus increase their positive influence in situations of conflict around the world.

Notes

1. West, 2001: chapter 5.
2. See www.kiwi-us.com/~selasj//jsc/english/network/asianet2.htm. Baker Institute, 2002.
3. NGOs are defined as those organizations which are outside the realm of gov-

ernment, distinct from the business community, and working either within a conflict, or on conflict issues. Such organizations are commonly characterized by their non-profit status and by a distinct value-based and humanitarian orientation (Hudcock, 2002: 1).

4. "Conflict resolution" is used in this book as an umbrella term to include the variety of nonmilitary activities that are implemented as a response to conflict, such as conflict prevention, resolution, management, transformation, peacebuilding, and so on. Each author uses the term in a way that is most appropriate for her or his context.

5. British Parliamentarian Edmund Burke coined the phrase "fourth estate," concluding that there were three estates within Parliament and that newspapers were the fourth estate. In recent times, the business community has been dubbed the "fifth estate." However, a recent survey of European and American opinion leaders conducted by Edelman PR Worldwide found that trust in NGOs to "do the right thing" remains strong in Europe and has risen in the United States. NGOs now challenge business as the credible source on issues such as social justice and the environment. See http://solidar.org/Document.asp?DocID=3598&tod=487

6. See www.rrojasdatabank.org/dp83-03.htm

7. See www.euconflict.org. An open information network of NGOs involved in the prevention and/or resolution of violent conflicts in the international arena.

8. The ICRC defines its neutrality thus: "In order to continue to enjoy the confidence of all, the Red Cross may not take sides in hostilities or engage at any time in controversies of a political, racial, religious or theological nature" (Roberts, 1966: 51).

9. Advocacy is usually defined as the pleading of a particular cause, generally on behalf of another or others; campaigning is defined as the development of an organized series of operations in the advocacy of a cause; and lobbying is defined as activities designed to persuade legislators or politicians to support a particular cause.

10. The Arria Formula was one of the mechanisms used by IA in bringing the gender and security issue to the attention of the Security Council (see chapter 6).

11. United Nations Resolution 1996/31 expanded the consultative remit and participation of NGOs at the United Nations Economic and Social Council (ECOSOC). It enables approved NGOs to attend United Nations conferences, designate participants in the General Assembly, and attend meetings of ECOSOC. Privileges range from circulating statements to speaking at meetings and proposing items for the agenda of some bodies.

12. Opening Address to the DPI/NGO, 10 September 1997. See www.globalpolicy.org/ngos/docs97/kofi997.htm.

13. See www.worldbank.org/devforum/forum_ngowg.html.

14. Inevitably, aid and conflict NGOs have recognized the need to work closely together on many issues, as conflict and the need for aid are often inextricably linked. See www.codep.org.uk.

15. While the definition of civil society varies from country to country, it is usually taken to mean all those organizations which are not part of government, such as NGOs, trade unions, businesses, and so on.

16. See www.careusa.org/newsroom/publications/annualreports/2001/15financial.pdf.

17. See www.catholicrelief.org/about_us/financial_information/summary.cfm

18. See www.wvi.org/home.shtml.

19. See www.sipri.se.

20. Boutros Boutros-Ghali, speech to the DPI Annual Conference, United Nations, New York, September 1995.

21. See particularly the work of Rieff (2002) on Bosnia, Rwanda, Kosovo, and Afghanistan.
22. See www.cpcc.ottawa.on.ca/about.htm.
23. See www.codep.org.uk.
24. This section has built upon the work of Heidi Jackson (2000).
25. See www.idha.ch/HNTC/REF/GR/Documents/hrd2-7.pdf.

References

Anderson, Mary. 1999. *Do No Harm: How Aid Can Support Peace—or War*. London: Lynne Rienner.
Anderson, M., and M. Olson. 2003. *Confronting War: Critical Lessons for Peace Practitioners*. Cambridge, MA: Collaborative for Development Action.
Axworthy, Lloyd. 1997 (10 September). "Notes for an Address by the Honourable Lloyd Axworthy, Minister of Foreign Affairs, to the Oslo NGO Forum on Banning Anti-Personnel Landmines." DFAIT Statement, Oslo.
Baker Institute Working Papers. 2002. "Guiding Principles for U.S. Post-Conflict Policy in Iraq." Report of an Independent Working Group Cosponsored by the Council on Foreign Relations and the James A. Baker III Institute for Public Policy of Rice University. www.rice.edu/projects/baker/Pubs/workingpapers/iraq/iraq_5.html.
Bratton, Michael. 1990. Non-governmental Organisations in Africa: Can they Influence Policy?" *Development and Change*, Vol 21: 87-118. London: Sage.
Canadian Council for International Cooperation (CCIC). 1988. *Mind If I Cut In? The Report of the CCIC Task Force on CIDA-NGO Funding Relationships*. Ottawa: CCIC.
Carroll, S., and K. Vignard. 2002. "NGOs as Partners: Assessing the Impact, Recognizing the Potential." *Disarmament Forum* 1 :31-35. www.unidir.ch/pdf/articles/pdf-art11.pdf.
Church, C., and J. Shouldice. 2002. *Framing the State of Play*. INCORE.
———. 2003. *The Evaluation of Conflict Resolution Interventions. Part II: Emerging Practice and Theory*.
Collin Marks, Susan. 2000. *Watching the Wind: Conflict Resolution during South Africa's Transition to Democracy*. Washington, D.C.: United States Institute of Peace.
Draimin, Tim, and Betty Plewes. 1995. "Civil Society and the Democratization of Foreign Policy." In *Canada among Nations: Democracy and Foreign Policy,* edited by Maxwell A. Cameron and Maureen Appel Molot. Ottawa: Carleton University Press.
Duffield, M. 1997. "Evaluating Conflict Resolution—Context, Models and Methodology." In *Evaluation of International Alert*. Oslo: Christian Michelson Institute.
———. 1999 (March). "Promoting Order or the Return to History: Globalisation and War Economies." Paper for the Development Studies Association Conference on Conflict.
Eagen, E. 1991. "Relief and Rehabilitation Work in Mozambique: Institutional Capacity and NGO Executional Strategies." *Development in Practice 1991*; 3:174-84.
Economist. 2000. (29 January-4 February). "Sins of the Secular Missionary."

Economist 25.

Edelman, Richard. 2002. Speech at the World Economic Forum in New York. www.nfn.org.au/pressrel/alert19.html.

Edwards, Michael, and David Hulme. 1996. "Introduction: NGO Performance and Accountability." In *Beyond the Magic Bullet: NGO Performance and Accountability in the Post-Cold War World,* edited by Michael Edwards and David Hulme. West Hartford, CT: Kumarian Press.

Fitzduff, M. 2002a. "Beyond Violence: Conflict Resolution Processes in Northern Ireland." In *UNU Policy Perspectives* 7. Tokyo and New York: Brookings Institution Press.

———. 2002b (Winter). "Principle versus Pragmatism." In *Human Rights Dialogue*: Carnegie Council, Series 2, No. 7.

Florini, A., and P. J. Simmons. 2000. "What the World Needs to Know." In *The Third Force: The Rise of Transnational Civil Society,* edited by A. Florini. Washington: Japan Center for International Exchange and Carnegie Endowment for International Peace.

Gordenker, Leon, and Thomas G. Weiss. 1997. "Devolving Responsibilities: A Framework for Analysing NGOs and Services." *Third World Quarterly* 18, no. 3: 443-455.

Horowitz, Donald L. 1985. *Ethnic Groups in Conflict.* London and Berkeley: University of California Press.

Hudcock, A. 2002. *NGOs and Civil Society: Democracy by Proxy?* London: Polity Press.

ICRC. 1995. *World Disasters Report.* Geneva, Switzerland.

Jackson, H. 2000 (January). "Reluctant Partners: Including NGOs in Conflict Management Policymaking." *e-merge: A Graduate Journal of International Affairs* 1. www.carleton.ca/e-merge/v1_art/v1_jack/v1_jac1.html.

Kaldor, Mary. 1999. *New and Old Wars: Organized Violence in a Global Era.* Stanford, CA: Stanford University Press.

Keen, D. P. 1999. "'Who's it Between?' 'Ethnic War' and Rational Violence." In *The Media of Conflict: War Reporting and Representations of Ethnic Violence,* edited by T. Allen and J. Seaton. London: Zed.

Kelman, Herbert. 1996. "The Interactive Problem-Solving Approach." In *Managing Global Chaos: Sources of and Responses to International Conflict,* edited by Chester A. Crocker and Fen Osler Hampson with Pamela Aall. Washington, D.C.: USIP.

Koenig, B. 1996. "The Management of International Non-governmental Organisations in the 1990s." *Transnational Associations* 2.

Lawson, Robert. 1998. "The Ottawa Process: Fast-Track Diplomacy and the International Movement to Ban Anti-Personnel Mines." In *Canada among Nations 1998: Leadership and Dialogue,* edited by Fen Osler Hampson and Maureen Appel Molot. Toronto: Oxford University Press.

Lissner, Jorgen. 1997. *Politics of Altruism—Study of the Political Behaviours of Voluntary Development Agencies.* Geneva: Lutheran World Federation.

Ogata, Sadako. 2000. "An Agenda for Business-Humanitarian Partnerships." *Washington Quarterly* 23, no. 1.

Price, Richard. 1998 (Spring). "International Norms and the Mines Taboo: Pulls Toward Compliance." *Canadian Foreign Policy* 5, no. 3: 105-123.

Rieff, D. 2002. *A Bed for the Night: Humanitarianism in Crisis.* London: Random House.

Smith, Edwin M., and Thomas G. Weiss. 1997. "UN Task-Sharing: Toward or Away from Global Governance." *Third World Quarterly* 18, no. 3: 595-619.

Spiro, Peter J. 1995 (Winter). "New Global Communities: Nongovernmental Organizations in International Decision Making Institutions." *Washington Quarterly* 18, no. 1: 45-56.

Stockholm International Peace Research Institute (SIPRI) website www.sipri.se.

Smillie, Ian. 1997. "NGOs and Development Assistance: A Change in Mind-Set?" *Third World Quarterly* 18, no. 3: 563-577.

Stubbs, P. 1997 (May). "The Role of NGOs in Social Reconstruction in Post-Yugoslav Countries." *Relief and Rehabilitation Network*, paper 8.

Weiss, T., and L. Gordenker, eds. 1996. *NGOs, the UN and Global Governance.* Boulder, CO and London: Lynne Rienner.

West, K. 2001. *Agents of Altruism. The Expansion of Humanitarian NGOs in Rwanda and Afghanistan.* London: Ashgate.

Wuori, M. 1997. "On the Formative Side of History: The Role of Non-governmental Organisations." In *International Governance on Environmental Issues*, edited by M. Rolen, H. Sjoberg, and U. Svedin. Dordrecht: Kluwer.

services to people. Many policies fit into more than one category and both their substantive impact and the feelings that their adoption and implementation produce need to be understood.[1] Conflicts occur over the substance of policy, but also around the process by which it is made and implemented, and, in societies where political access has been highly restricted or constrained in the past, issues of voice and empowerment can be especially divisive.

Underlying any policy are (often unarticulated) hypotheses about a social problem, including why the problem exists and specific proposals about how best to address the problem given the resources available. Considering policy proposals as hypotheses about how to solve problems is especially useful in encouraging policymakers to articulate their analyses of a problem and to spell out how a policy they propose is intended to produce specific results (Campbell, 1969; 1998). Engaging in such self-conscious thinking helps advocates to distinguish between their commitment to action and specific proposals that they, or others, offer.

Conflict permeates policy in divided societies, affecting both what governments and other agencies do substantively and how their actions are evaluated. Although conflicts of varying scope, intensity, and duration occur in all societies, and conflict is a normal aspect of human interaction, in some cases conflicts escalate to include violence and destruction. The conflict cycle is the course a conflict takes from the conversion of grievances into active complaints and explicit actions that escalate tensions and produce destructive interactions among the parties. Eventually, but not always quickly, de-escalation occurs as outcomes are produced that may be destructive or constructive to the parties and their interests (Kriesberg, 1998). Policymaking is especially relevant at two points in the conflict cycle, preconflict and postsettlement. Before conflicts become severe and destructive, effective policy may meet people's basic needs and thereby limit future escalation while promoting the use of political institutions to settle disputes. In the middle of a conflict, policy is less likely to be effective in changing the course of events, as governments and other agencies often lack the will, capacity, and credibility to act decisively on substantive problems. Following intense conflicts, policy can make significant contributions to the development of constructive outcomes both by addressing real needs and by communicating inclusiveness and empowerment to all groups in a society.

This chapter has three sections. The first discusses what constitutes policy and particular issues surrounding policymaking in areas that have experienced intense conflict. At the core of policy is the delivery of services to citizens and issues of voice and empowerment. Policy focuses on the actions of public authorities, namely state institutions. In addition to state actors, however, it is crucial to consider the role of organized groups within the society, such as NGOs, that often include at least some outside actors, international organizations, neighboring states, protest groups, paramilitary organizations and/or their political representatives, and diaspora communities. All of these can be involved in the definition of political issues needing consideration, the adoption of specific policies, and efforts to implement them. Politics and policymaking are intimately intertwined in conflict zones, focusing attention on particular social problems and responding to policy cycles that ebb and flow, enabling actors to take advantage of political windows that can open and close fairly quickly (Downs, 1972; Jones, 1994).

The second section considers four stages in the policy process—agenda setting, decision making, implementation, and evaluation—describing key aspects of each stage and suggesting the kinds of resources and skills needed to be successful at each point in the policy cycle. It is important to recognize that the objective evidence that a problem exists is not sufficient to mobilize action to address it. There is also a need for advocates to demand collective action, to formulate policy, and to implement it successfully so that the lives of people in the society are changed.

The third section asks what constitutes good policy and utilizes the criteria of justice and efficiency to consider whether policy moves a society toward a more peaceful way of dealing with differences. Good policy, it is suggested, must do two things: address the real needs of people in the society, and develop and sustain politics that are inclusive on both the substantive and symbolic levels in conflict-torn societies.

Policymaking in Conflict Zones

Conflicts differ greatly from one society to the next in ways that policymakers must consider as they conceptualize and implement specific proposals. In addition to scope, intensity, and duration, conflicts vary in the specific interests and identities that are involved and the past history of the society in which they occur. There is also significant variation in the extent to which the conflict involves outside actors, regional powers, and international organizations.

Policy in conflict zones can be difficult, and often controversial, for at least three different reasons. In the first place, in most divided societies there is often a sense that previous regimes have pursued policies that unfairly benefited some groups and discriminated against others. As a result, any new policy must emphasize how it is more inclusive than previous actions so that group-based alienation and distrust of state authorities are addressed. Second, many regimes in conflict zones lack the capacity to formulate and implement policy effectively. As a result, nonstate or extra-state actors often become involved at all stages of the policy process in ways that produce problems of cross-cultural communication and coordination among the different actors in the policy community. Finally, in conflict zones, the building of institutions and practices that offer empowerment and long-term effectiveness is needed to overcome historical memories from past conflicts. Often this means that attention to the inclusive symbolic aspects of policymaking and implementation is especially important in the peacebuilding process. This chapter recognizes that long-term conflicts are about identities as well as interests and that the underlying emotions of threat or fear that characterize high conflict need to be addressed as part of peacebuilding (Ross, 1993). One step to inclusiveness is building wider identification with the community in general, and the state in particular, so that redistribution of resources and policy innovation are experienced as widely beneficial and not merely as the provision of selective benefits to certain groups. Of course, this is hardly achievable overnight and often involves a race between rising expectations and the capacity of local institutions.

Politics and Policymaking

In all settings, politics affects policy dynamics in a number of ways. In conflict zones, the linkage is often exacerbated as shortened time frames, deep fears and threats to groups, and an atmosphere of long-term distrust create pressures on policymakers. A skeptical public creates a heightened need to demonstrate immediate results and effectiveness even though the resources needed for success are often scarce or unavailable. As a result those involved in policy need to be especially attentive, as they design programs and begin to implement them, to how the intense need for goods and services following conflict and local political dynamics interact. Of course, NGOs in conflict situations may do all they can about these questions and still be overwhelmed by needs on the ground. Sometimes, however, a better understanding of the complex political landscape and the options available can increase the chances of success. Anderson (1999), for example, emphasizes the importance of using program resources to build capacities and what she calls local connectors among political, social, and religious groups in divided societies.

The interaction of policy and politics can also seriously limit interorganizational cooperation. Problems arise between state agencies, or between state agencies and other actors, when each has different priorities and when they include competition over resources and personnel. In such settings, policy decisions are often made not on the basis of technical merits, nor in a way that will bridge interagency, community, and political differences, but as a result of self-protective political maneuvers, including interdepartmental bargaining and trade-offs. Such maneuvering also applies to relationships between state agencies and NGOs, and at times there is competition, as well as differences of opinion, between NGOs and state agencies about how best to implement programs. At the same time, there are good examples of successful inter-NGO and NGO-state agency coordination, such as the Community Development Centre's efforts to assist displaced families in North Belfast, where differences between NGOs and state agencies over program implementation were transformed into a cooperative relationship through the establishment of interagency working groups (see chapter 5).

Political considerations are often significant in conflicts among state agencies, nonstate actors, and external actors in conflict zones, since each has a very different constituency and support base. Humanitarian organizations, as Anderson (1999) reminds us, who arrive in strife-torn regions with millions of dollars of aid to distribute become players in the local political scene and their actions can affect the direction of the conflict. Especially in rapidly changing situations, there is no doubt that the relationship among internal and external actors, as well as within each group, can be complicated and tense. Rather than think this can be avoided, it is far better to consider anticipating ways to cope with these differences when they arise and to transform the problems into manageable ones.

Policy and politics are also linked through what Kingdon (1994) calls "iron triangles." In his analysis of linkages among congressional staffs, career civil servants in administrative agencies, and interest groups, he uses this term to describe connections among somewhat like-minded persons working on common policy issues in different locations in the American political system. Because of their common concerns and interests, these actors coordinate their efforts and contribute different skills to steering a policy through the rough waters of decision making and subsequent implementation. Interest groups articulate their particular concerns and mobilize public support, congressional staffs focus on designing the appropriate policy and seeing that it is funded, while the administrators emphasize issues of implementation and the policy's viability on the ground. The like-minded people coordinating policy in specific areas are, at the same time, excluding outside voices and interests. In conflict zones, similar patterns of exclusion occur when political groups and NGOs articulate perspectives that are not welcomed by those in power. While the specific linkages Kingdon finds in the United States are not necessarily visible elsewhere, specific cross-institutional coalitions that operate in a similar fashion are widespread.

Policy Actors

Many people and groups, both within and outside a society, play a role in the policy process. Often, participation itself is contested when some actors seek privileged positions, while others aim to be included in, or to exclude others from, the process. In short, involvement in policymaking can be as contested as the policies themselves.

The "policy community" refers to those groups and people making and implementing policy in any particular domain. This term is often used to refer to specialists in the legislative, executive, academic, and civil society domains (for example, Kingdon, 1994). However, when considering conflict-torn societies, it is useful to extend the notion of the policy community to include others such as civil society and NGOs, as well as international organizations, which are also involved in developing and implementing policy in many conflict-torn societies.[2] Probably the most widespread example of this is the involvement of the World Bank and other international economic agencies in establishing and implementing economic recovery policies in countries coming out of conflict. Bank staff, in consultation with political leaders, frequently develop detailed policy recommendations for countries and hold out the promise of funding these programs if the bank's preconditions are met. In addition, in the formulation of peacebuilding policies, states often solicit expertise not only from large organizations like the World Bank, but also from NGOs, to address problems in specific areas such as health care, resettlement of refugees, and education. In order to do this well, NGOs need to understand the crucial political and social relationships in a society, key change makers, and various access points in the country's policy community.

In many normative and empirical models of policymaking, there is often little concern with the participation of those who will be directly affected by the policy. In contrast, conflict resolution theory argues that good agreements arise when all stakeholders in a conflict are involved. This becomes difficult in settings where not all the parties are willing to talk with each other and an issue arises of whether talks should move forward with those who are willing, or whether additional effort should be made to bring all stakeholders together either indirectly or directly.

There are also differences of opinion among theorists about how widespread participation should be at each stage of policymaking. A basic source of tension is between those who suggest that policy is best made by those with technical expertise in specific substantive areas and those who seek a wider inclusion of local communities, NGOs, civic organizations, and the mass public at different stages of the policy process. At the core of this question are important issues of voice, inclusion, and the value of participation as a basis for building support during implementation.[3] Not surprisingly, this issue can be complicated in societies where only some of the policy actors are from within the society and where governments fear infringements on their sovereignty if outside voices are too loud or too powerful. In addition, in high-conflict societies, while there will be some who seek to limit outside voices, there are often others who see themselves as weak and vulnerable and who seek to involve outsiders as potential allies.

There are multiple actors who can be involved in the policy process. Understanding who is involved, what positions they hold, and who holds critical influence on issues can be essential in the art of influencing policy. It is particularly important to recognize that in a setting with a history of distrust, and often in the absence of a strong institutional framework for conducting discussions and making decisions, certain actors or groups will quickly feel excluded or manipulated. The challenge for policymakers is therefore to develop inclusiveness where there has been a lack of such inclusion, so that substantive problems are addressed in the formulation of policy and the policy, once developed, is framed in such as way that it elicits broad support.

The following seven groups are the possible major actors involved in the policymaking process in conflict zones:

- *State officials* will normally be involved in all phases of the policy process. This can of course be problematic, particularly when they are, or have been, associated with specific groups who are visible players in a conflict. Nonetheless, except for situations such as Somalia, Sierra Leone, or Afghanistan, where there is, or has been, no effective state, policymaking and implementation is a primary state function. Among state officials, it is sometimes useful to distinguish between those who are politicians (and perhaps elected) and those who are administrators. Each has different skills and resources and will behave differently in many policy conflicts (Cobb and

Ross, 1997). Politicians, whether elected or appointed, are usually attentive to public opinion and tend to frame issues in general, symbolic terms. As a result, they can be highly averse to risk and thus tend to avoid bringing attention to issues that may weaken support or stir up trouble. Administrators focus more on technical matters, and their effectiveness is generally tied to their mastery of the complexities of an issue. Administrators, even more than politicians, move into new areas cautiously. Their first reaction when a new policy is proposed is often to emphasize potential problems it might raise and to assert that they are too busy to give it the attention it needs (Cobb and Ross, 1997: 17). Yet administrators and politicians need each other. Politicians can help build support for a policy, while administrators are needed for its implementation in specific contexts. Recognizing these distinctive functions can be useful for NGOs seeking to influence policy, as is seen in the case of the Belfast-based Community Development Centre, which used these differences to make progress in gaining support for their policy issue of achieving a coordinated response by the statutory agencies and the community to issues of displacement caused by violence (see chapter 5).

- *Intergovernmental organizations* (IGOs), such as United Nations agencies or the European Community, are often actors in the policy processes of conflict zones. IGOs frequently become involved in a conflict to address substantive problems such as public health, humanitarian relief, or peacekeeping operations. As a result, there are often IGO representatives and experts on the ground and with knowledge of the local conflict, who are drawn into policy questions. Of course, they often have their own policy perspective, reflecting power arrangements and ideologies in their member states, which affects their motives for action, what they are willing to do, and how they are willing to do it. This can complicate their relationship with local actors and can involve these outsiders in internal political battles, after which they become seen as partisans of one side and their credibility is weakened.

- *Neighboring or states in the same region* are attentive when there is long-term conflict close by. In some instances, they may have particular, partisan interests in the conflict, as is the case when there is a common ethnic or cultural linkage between them and one of the groups in the conflict zone. In Hungary, for example, people pay particular attention to policies and government attitudes toward Hungarians in Slovakia and Romania. In other cases, there may be regional coalitions and interests that are defined in strategic terms and link groups in a conflict zone to outside allies. In either case, other states often try to shape internal policy outcomes and are at times drawn into the conflicts, sometimes reluctantly and sometimes willingly. In the case of the latter, when a conflict-torn society has valuable resources, such as oil or diamonds, neighbors can become active through military and financial involvement, as occurred in Liberia and Sierra Leone.

- *Organized groups*, such as trade unions, political parties, and business associations, are often involved in the policy process because they are likely to benefit or suffer from a particular policy. In addition to those likely to be directly affected, there are groups that become involved in policy debates not because of the direct impact on their own members but because of ideological or other concerns, such as human rights or humanitarian relief organizations (Nagel, 1987: 129-38). NGOs of this sort may consist of members from within the society, of outsiders, or some combination of the two. Internal organizations often have better political connections within the society, while external ones can often mobilize greater resources and technical expertise. Owing to these different skills and support bases, coalitions between the two can be very effective. TOSAM (see chapter 9) illustrates how effective coalitions between internal and external organized groups were in helping both the Turkish and Kurdish communities to reframe and readdress their historic problems and develop a strategy to increase democracy and good governance in Turkey as part of that process.

- *Community groups* are geographically defined local actors who have common interests by virtue of their shared locations. In fact, community groups often consist of previously unorganized people whose grievances were not necessarily a significant part of policy discussions. When these groups are organized, they are often able to articulate concerns such as environmental degradation, inadequate schools, or the need for police protection. For South Africa's community-based policing efforts are one example of defining a policy community in a new way as part of an innovative approach to a serious societal problem (see chapter 7).
- In conflict zones, *protest groups* and *paramilitaries* often become major voices in politics both before and after a conflict is formally settled. Sometimes these groups operate within the political sector and represent the political positions of former, or even present, opponents of the regime. In addition, some members of these groups become vocal in interest groups, community organizations and NGOs as they make a transition from focusing on the conflict itself to a more diverse and peaceful political role (McShane, 1998).[4]
- *Diaspora communities* are people who live outside a society but who retain ties to specific communities in the conflict zone. They can provide insiders with resources and moral support for continuing a conflict, as some American Jewish groups have done in the Israel-Palestine conflict, or as Tamils in Great Britain and Canada have done in Sri Lanka. Often, members of these groups have very clear ideas about what is the appropriate policy for a society even if they live thousands of miles away, and their politics are often hard-line in ways that exacerbate the conflict. At times, however, diaspora or exile communities become part of peace processes and dialogue that leads to conflict settlements, as was the case with South African exiles in the 1980s (Lieberfeld, Sparks, 1995; forthcoming).

Stages of the Policy Process

The policy process can be understood as a series of stages that show how policy unfolds over time. However, it is important to recognize that the neat distinctions between these stages are conceptual rather than empirical. Making and implementing policy, especially in conflict zones, is rarely as linear a process as stage-based discussions imply. Nonetheless, there is real value in identifying distinct stages of the policy process for the simple reason that the problems that arise at each one are distinct and the skills and resources that actors need to be effective differ at each stage.[5]

Agenda Setting

Agenda setting is the process of identifying a problem as being one that needs serious attention from government and/or other institutions that possess sufficient resources to do something significant about it (Cobb and Elder, 1983; Cobb and Ross, 1997). "Agenda" is used here to refer to both the concerns that the public perceives as needing governmental action and the policy options actively under consideration by state or other agencies. The former, called the *public agenda*, consists of issues that the public (or vocal groups within it) think are worthy of serious attention. Every agency, whether it is a legislative, judicial, or administrative body, has a docket, the *formal agenda,* which consists of items that receive serious consideration at any point in time (Cobb and Elder, 1983: 85-87; Kingdon 1994: 4). Invariably there are more contenders for serious attention than just those that receive it at any one time. As a result, agenda setting is the political process whereby choices are made about which problems become the focus of attention. In periods of crisis, such as the aftermath of natural disasters or intense conflicts that displace thousands of people and create humanitarian disasters, it is easy to understand why an issue moves to the top of an agency's agenda. However, the answer to what is prioritized seems to be best understood in terms of political dynamics rather than objective indicators such as the severity of the problem or the number of people affected. The Community Development Centre's focus on the issue of displaced families in North Belfast clearly illustrates how it is often politics rather than severity of crisis that propels an issue onto the formal agenda (see chapter 5).

Problems or issues that make it onto the formal agenda have three characteristics (Cobb and Ross, 1997: 7). In the first place, there must be some objective evidence that a problem exists. Often this can be demonstrated through dramatic stories in the media or through statistical evidence such as survey results, public health reports, government studies, crime statistics, or census data. Although such statistical evidence can be, and often is, contested, it can nevertheless help in showing that the problem has an objective element and is not just emanating from the voices of a disaffected minority. As Stone notes, "the most common way to define a policy problem is to measure it" (1988: 127).[6] The second characteristic is that the public is generally already convinced that action needs to be taken on the problem. Most commonly, evidence for this is found in press and media accounts, public opinion polls that rank serious problems, or studies of specialized population groups focusing on certain issue domains.[7] The third consideration is whether the issue is already on the formal agendas of other countries with similar social systems. If the answer is yes, then there is a case for asking why the issue has not yet reached the formal agenda of the country in question.[8] Concern can be rapidly diffused across societies when states are highly attentive to what others are doing about particular problems. This was evident, for example, in addressing the environmental degradation in Central and Eastern Europe after the fall of the Soviet Union.

The relationship between the public and formal agendas can tell us something about policymaking in any society. When the two are closely aligned, policymakers are responsive to citizens' demands. However, there is also the possibility that decision makers will effectively persuade the public to view a specific problem as especially important and in need of immediate action. Where there is a large gap between the public and formal agendas, it can be a sign of unresponsiveness as decision makers resist considering problems the public wants them to address. This resistance, however, might arise from other sources, such as an ideological unwillingness to consider an issue or a serious lack of resources, including money and skilled personnel. It might also occur when innovative leaders identify problems as significant that do not yet resonate with the public. This last situation may be especially relevant in societies coming out of conflict where leaders are willing to make changes faster than the public.

Cobb, Ross, and Ross (1976) propose three general processes of agenda setting that capture different ways in which the public and formal agendas can be related. The *outside initiative model* emphasizes nongovernmental sources of policy initiation focusing on the efforts of single persons or groups to transform their concerns into those of a larger citizen-based movement (Cobb and Elder, 1983; Cobb, Ross, and Ross, 1976). An obvious example is Gandhi's independence movement in India. A second is TOSAM's initiatives to galvanize public debate and support for a societal review of the historical problems between the Turkish and Kurdish communities (see chapter 9). Issue initiation can, however, come about in two additional ways. *Mobilization* occurs when public officials launch a campaign to gain public attention and support for an issue as a way to gain entry to the formal agenda, and then to mobilize support once the issue is actively considered. Examples include many education, health, and development programs that originate in government, either from political leaders or administrators. A third model, called *inside access*, describes how an issue originates with a very narrow group of actors and is placed on a formal agenda with very little attention from the public. Fearful that public opinion will hamper their chances for success, proponents limit knowledge to the societal elites, namely to bureaucrats, legislators, and affected groups (Cobb, Ross, and Ross, 1976). This strategy is especially visible in the Track One and a Half diplomacy efforts to work among elites to further the Georgia-South Ossetia peace process (see chapter 4).

The politics of agenda setting invariably mobilize supporters who favor the consideration of a new issue as well as opponents who want the matter ignored. In this political battle, proponents and opponents mobilize material and symbolic resources to persuade actors in the relevant institutions to take action on an issue or to ignore it. In conflict zones, agenda battles can sometimes escalate quickly when groups respond to policy proposals on the basis of who is supporting and who is opposing their consideration as much as their actual substance (Cobb and Ross, 1997). In addition, competition among issues such as questions of prisoners and decommissioning of weapons can push more bread-and-butter considerations such as education or community development off either the public or formal agenda.

Decision Making

Just because an issue gets on the formal agenda does not mean that the issue will get the kind of consideration that the proponents hoped for. In areas of conflict in particular, political leaders will often give the impression of inclusion of critical issues on the formal agenda, but will not be willing to give those same issues serious attention in terms of actually progressing a policy option.[9] To be successful at the decision-making stage, proponents of issues need to master the art of identifying legislative, administrative, or executive allies, or learn how to make the appeals themselves to relevant judicial bodies in the appropriate legal framework of their society. Where agenda setting is often successful with highly symbolic appeals, success at the decision-making stages requires more technical knowledge of legal and administrative politics. It is important to recognize that the legal and political frameworks for decision making vary across societies. In some states power is diffused among legislative and administrative units, while in others it is more centralized. In certain cases, political officials take the lead in policymaking, while in others, administrative agencies and career specialists play a major role. Under these different conditions, the dynamics of policymaking will take on different forms.[10]

The question of how comprehensive a policy should be often arises during decision-making debates. Often this plays out over design and implementation issues. Some policymakers want to front-load planning and design efforts, and see social problems through a medical model in which a team of technicians works to eradicate a disease through intensive inoculation and/or treatment. However, many critics argue that social problems are not amenable to such analyses and solutions. Instead, they argue, policy should be made more incrementally, as policymakers and communities learn what does and does not work in specific communities (Campbell, 1969; 1998 and Scott, 1998; Wildavsky, 1979). Differences in the two approaches can become bitter as the more comprehensive-minded see the incrementalists as foot-dragging, while the incrementalists see the comprehensive planners as arrogant, wasting valuable resources, and uninterested in learning from local experiences (Lindbloom, 1977).

A related question is that of how the voices of communities and experts are integrated into policymaking. This issue is at the heart of the debate between those who emphasize technical expertise in the design of policy and those who stress the importance of local context and community voices. Although there is some overlap of this distinction and the one just made between comprehensive planners and incrementalists, it is not exactly the same. For example, comprehensive planners can, at least in theory, listen attentively to community voices. The issue of diverse voices revolves around two main considerations: how much does context matter, and what does the complexity of local involvement add to the quality of a program? When a problem is seen as essentially technical and amenable to a universal solution, as is often the case for many health-related NGOs, there is little effort to include local voices. However, a weakening of local voices can also mean that there is little of the local buy-in that is needed to achieve long-term goals.

Implementation

The simple fact that a policy exists is no guarantee that it will be implemented successfully, as illustrated by the UMAC case study on policing in South Africa (chapter 7). Here we see a policy that, although written into law, was not carried out on the ground until UMAC eventually addressed it as an issue of implementation. There are a number of potential barriers to effective implementation, four of which are considered here. First, implementation requires resources including local skills and knowledge that may be absent. In areas of conflict, implementation is often the stage where outsiders are called in to fill in gaps in knowledge and expertise. Examples of this include the outside agencies training judges in Rwanda and police in Kosovo. Second, once policies are adopted, the public attention surrounding them often diminishes rapidly, and administrators who opposed the policies in the first place simply make them a low priority when it comes to implementation. Third, new issues often come along that replace older ones as urgent policy concerns. Finally, many new policies require public support, or at least compliance, that is not always forthcoming. One need only look at policies on HIV/AIDS programs in both industrialized nations and on the African continent to see a clear illustration of these four barriers to implementation. As a result, legislative mandates can be unfunded, administrative rulings ignored, or judicial decisions rendered meaningless.[11]

At the implementation stage, proponents and opponents tangle once again. Here, the skills and resources each side can call upon differ, and the fate of the policies that may have successfully passed political tests at the agenda-setting and decision-making stages can produce an entirely different outcome than proponents expected. Implementation of new or changed policies is the point at which old patterns need to shift and new ones need to be put in place. Clearly, this can trigger significant problems, some of the most obvious of which are:

- *Prioritization and choice making*: What should be done, in what order, and who is to decide? Complex programs often have many parts and there are frequently differences in opinion about the order in which they should be addressed between the center and the field or even between different regional teams.
- *Resource issues*: Rarely does a program have all the resources that are needed at the outset. Choices need to be made about where to work, how limited resources can be extended to achieve maximum effects, and whether new resources can be raised to expand a program's reach.
- *Technical issues on the ground*: Implementers make decisions on the ground every day. An obvious cross-cultural example involves policing. Thousands and thousands of police departments need to consider on a daily, weekly, monthly, and yearly basis, implicitly or explicitly, such mundane matters as: Where do local officers spend their time? When do they patrol? What kinds of links do they develop with local communities? What crimes receive the most attention? These factors can have widespread consequences for citizens and are particularly important in areas coming out of conflict where police behavior is invariably a source of past grievance and conflict (Skolnick, 1994).
- *Reaching people to be served*: While program makers have mandates to act, there can be real uncertainty about who is to receive the services they have to offer, how these recipients are to be identified, and how much resources they ought to receive. These matters are often contested on the ground as local units interact with communities and mediate between the higher levels and local service providers, and they are particularly problematic in conflict societies when significant groups in the population are skeptical of public authorities (Pressman and Wildavsky, 1973).

Evaluation and Revision of Programs

It is indeed rare that a program works exactly as intended, and this means that evaluation is integral to an effective policy process. If a policy is adopted, what is expected to happen and what actually takes place? In some cases, there is a good fit and policy achieves what is intended. In other cases, the gap is large and the challenge is to figure out why this is the case and make appropriate revisions. Of course, the answers may not be easy to come by, since failures may be attributed to a range of different factors; there may be claims that the policy was inappropriate, or that it was under-resourced, or that the will to implement it was lacking. All actors need to consider what works and why it works in general, and in specific settings (Campbell, 1969; 1998; Wildavsky, 1979). The commitment to working on the problem is not the same as the belief that a specific policy is the only way to achieve the intended goals. Good programs evolve in a variety of ways as policymakers and practitioners learn what is effective, as they encounter new difficulties, and as policies begin to serve larger numbers of people and new communities.

Good evaluation is not simple, for policies can be evaluated on a number of different levels. Often, results show that a policy is effective in some ways and not others, so a society needs to decide what is "good enough." Shively offers two frequently used, but quite different, standards to evaluate policy; these are further discussed below. They are *justice* and *efficiency* (Shively, 2001). Each draws attention to very different aspects of any policy and these differences are often the source of deep disagreement in conflict zones. Justice criteria are about fairness and inclusion, questions that are often at the heart of prior conflicts. Efficiency standards ask whether the proposed or current policy is the most effective way to reach a particular goal. In conflict situations where contrasting, group-based interpretations of previous government policy are prevalent, new policy must be presented in ways that build support while also achieving specific goals that can justify the policy in terms of efficiency.

Formulating and Implementing Good Policy: Fairness and Efficiency as Goals

Good policy must accomplish two goals: it must do something substantive about a problem, and it must not make one part of society feel excluded or believe that the policy seriously disadvantages them. Achieving both these goals is not always easy, and to achieve both there is a need for context-specific presentation and implementation of policy. In short, policymakers and implementers need to be attentive to Shively's twin criteria of success: justice and efficiency (Shively, 2001: 118-36). Whereas efficiency is about getting the greatest direct return for expenditure, justice is about communicating a sense of fairness about the policy throughout society. Administrators need to be attuned to the political context in which they operate and to recognize that the policy requires more than just technical competence to be successful.

Questions of efficiency are important in societies where resources are scarce and citizens' demands are high, but sometimes they must be balanced by considerations of fairness. For example, if schools or roads are built in territory primarily associated with one ethnic community, it is often important to undertake commensurate (although not necessarily the same) steps in the home areas or neighborhoods of other groups. At each stage of the policy process, the goals of efficiency and justice play out a little differently, and it is worth considering this dynamic.

In the agenda-setting phase, efficiency raises concerns about the extent to which a proposed policy is likely to be effective in meeting its goals.[12] In contrast, justice at this phase emphasizes the extent to which groups in society feel they have a voice; in particular, to what extent do groups perceive that others in their society, and perhaps external actors as well, acknowledge their significant grievances?

During decision making, considerations of efficiency and justice are often merged in complicated ways. When prominent members of one group suggest a policy that a different group deems either inappropriate or unneeded, it is easy to hear that as a devaluation of the group itself. When there is a long history of animosity between the groups, even sincere disagreements about policy are easily transformed into group antagonism. In such situations, it is probably important that policy be framed in broad terms so that a significant proportion of the population—not just a narrow majority—see it in positive terms. For example, during the negotiations in Northern Ireland, the chair of the sessions, United States senator George Mitchell, proposed that significant consensus would be required on major elements of the agreement. This meant that these elements would need majority support from both the majority Protestant and minority Catholic communities.

During implementation, efficiency is likely to be invoked around matters of cost and potential corruption, while justice concerns arise when groups become jealous of how others seem to be benefiting from programs. To a great extent, such competition cannot be completely absent in policy conflicts in societies where resources are scarce and where intergroup antagonism has been a persistent feature of political life for some time. That said, there are times when such antagonism can be tempered and disagreements kept within bounds.

Symbolic Inclusiveness

Policy can hardly be understood solely in terms of the substantive issues under consideration. All significant policy has symbolic as well as substantive meaning. This symbolism is likely to be especially salient in societies with recent experiences of intense conflict. To be successful in terms of peacebuilding, those involved in the policy process, therefore, have to take specific steps to address the symbolic dimensions and underlying emotional aspects of the policies they advocate or implement in ways that emphasize those policies' inclusive, broadbased nature. In settings where there are still unresolved resentments from the past and changes in political arrangements that leave many uneasy, this is a particularly difficult challenge.

Cobb and Ross (1997), in their discussion of conflicts in agenda setting, focus attention on symbolic strategies. Although their emphasis is on those who oppose the consideration of new issues, the analysis they offer is helpful in thinking about ways that policy in conflict zones can help heal past differences. They argue that in policy debates, parties make many choices about how to present their positions and characterize those of the other side. These choices and actions can, on occasion, have a significant effect on peacebuilding efforts.

A fundamental choice that policy proponents and opponents make is between substantive discussions focusing on aspects of a policy or parts of it, and a focus on the group supporting or opposing it. Associating group labels with one or another policy position is polarizing, while emphasizing substantive problems can draw attention to interests that cross-cut identities. When group labels become dominant in the way policies are identified, group loyalties are readily mobilized and questions about the policy's substantive content are pushed to the sidelines.

Both majority and minority groups who feel abused resort to such mobilization, and when the press and third parties also see policies through this group perspective, the likelihood of polarization increases. An example of such polarizing activities was seen in Bosnia, where the first reconstruction initiatives focused on the rebuilding of mosques and churches, which then became viewed as symbols of the continued antagonism between the surviving Muslims and the dominant Serbs in the Serb-controlled Republic of Serbska.[13] In such contexts, policy advocates need to work hard to emphasize alternative, more inclusive frames if their favored policies are to gain widespread support.

A second choice for policy actors is how they publicize new policies that have peacebuilding potential. In making and implementing policy, state agencies can take small but significant symbolic steps to emphasize a policy's fairness and potentially broad appeal. Publicizing and *showcasing* redistributive programs that communicate an agency's intention to provide resources or services to a previously aggrieved group can be useful. In South Africa, for example, after years of exclusion, the Mandela regime made great efforts to publicize its early efforts in the provision of housing and education to demonstrate its intention to behave differently in these areas, to the way in which the previous regime had acted.

Another option is the establishment of state or quasi-public *commissions* that can undertake serious examinations of a problem and produce far-reaching reports suggesting significant changes in policy. While Cobb and Ross acknowledge that such commissions are sometimes used to delay consideration of new issues or are viewed as paying lip service to an issue, they also have a potential to legitimize grievances and suggest new approaches to them. In Northern Ireland, for example, a special body was appointed to examine the issue of contentious parades.[14] It recommended a new procedure for dealing with the parades, taking crucial decisions out of the hands of the local police, who were widely seen as pro-Protestant, and putting them in the hands of a more neutral Parades Commission. In South Africa, the Truth and Reconciliation Commission (TRC) was charged with holding hearings on the crimes of the apartheid era and making recommendations about how the new government should deal with them. The TRC held thousands of hours of hearings throughout the country that led to extensive revelations of misdeeds by the apartheid government, the African National Congress (ANC), and others. Whether or not the broad goals underlying the commission have been achieved still remains to be seen, but there can be little doubt that the TRC was part of a broad strategy to create a new symbolic understanding of South Africa as a pluralist and nonracist nation.

A different strategy is to build symbolic inclusiveness through the incorporation of major figures from all groups in society in the policy process and in state positions. The constitutional arrangements for Northern Ireland spelled out in the 1998 Belfast Agreement offer an excellent example of how cross-community decision-making structures can provide strong incentives for previously opposing groups to cooperate. The agreement contains provisions so that on significant issues, such as the election of the two top officials, and on important issues of policymaking, there must be majority support from both the Protestant and Catholic communities. Similarly in South Africa, the two leaders of the TRC were Desmond Tutu, a black South African, and Alex Borraine, a white South African. While this principle of inclusion and representation in state agencies and government can sometimes be perceived merely as a form of co-optation, this is not always the case, and in conflict zones it can be a crucial step toward securing support for policy developments.

Associating new policies with symbols or metaphors that frame present policy in a way that will have a broad appeal in all communities is another useful strategy. This can of course be especially difficult in divided societies where there is little shared symbolic content. A dramatic example of such a symbolic gesture was Nelson's Mandela's donning a Springboks rugby jersey, a shirt previously associated with Afrikaner culture and racial supremacy, to demonstrate his commitment to building a new, nonracial society. By doing so, he was communicating that symbols of the past did not have to be abandoned but could take on a new, more inclusive meaning. Sometimes symbols link a policy to groups outside the society such as regional communities, or groups positively associated with morality and progress. For instance, the decision of the newly independent East Timorese to send a national team to the Summer Olympics in 2000 was a symbolic assertion of their upcoming formal declaration of statehood as the newest member of the world community. Of course, such actions are sometimes part of a cynical effort by which symbols are co-opted for manipulative purposes.[15]

Conversely, an example from the Bosnia and Herzegovina case illustrates an attempt at symbolic inclusion that failed. Article 5 of the Dayton Agreement called for shared symbols of cultural heritage to be included in the new government of the Federal Republic of Bosnia.[16] This policy, imposed by the international community and applied selectively, had little local support and ultimately did not succeed. It is important to remember that symbolic inclusiveness cannot just be visual and external, to be effective, it needs to be matched by programs addressing substantive issues and must be perceived as just by the local population.

Finally, it should be noted that specific language associated with a policy can be important in its presentation to the public, and characterizing policies in certain ways can make them more appealing and inclusive. When the symbols associated with a policy draw attention to its long-term positive benefits, its potential widespread impact, and its linkage to previously successful policies (perhaps in other societies), and when the policy is characterized in clear terms that are easy to understand, the support for it is likely to increase.[17]

Conclusion

This chapter has focused on general features of the policy process with particular attention to conflict zones. In conclusion, I emphasize three specific challenges that policymaking must face in conflict zones if it is to serve as an instrument of peacemaking and peacebuilding.

First, in most divided societies, there is a sense that previous regimes have pursued policies that have unfairly benefited some groups and discriminated against others. New policies must emphasize that they are palpably more inclusive than previous ones so that group-based alienation and distrust of the state diminishes. *Inclusion* needs to be an explicit part of the policy process. Building wider identification with the community in general, and the state in particular, so that redistribution of resources and innovation are experienced as widely beneficial and not merely the provision of selective benefits, is critical. Visible involvement of significant actors from previously excluded communities and greater provision of services to needy groups is crucial, but what really matters is how people come to evaluate both the motives and results of state action. Although success may not be achievable overnight, and the work is often challenged by a race between rising expectations and the capacity of local institutions, it is critical to exemplify fairness and inclusion as integral to successful policy.

Second, *effective and indigenous delivery* of goods and services is also critical. Many regimes in conflict zones lack a capacity to formulate and implement policy effectively, and as a result, nonstate or extra-state actors often become involved at all stages of the policy process. Such involvement can produce problems of cross-cultural communication and coordination among the different actors in the policy community. This situation is complicated when the goal of efficiency is the primary one for outside agencies and is at odds with a local emphasis on fairness and empowerment. Outsiders coming in to do a job can be important, but effective and long-term action requires training local personnel to take over the implementation of programs that remain on the ground after the outsiders have finished their tours of duty and have returned home, in order for programs to have a lasting effect.

Finally, in conflict zones, the building of institutions and practices that offer empowerment and long-term effectiveness is needed to overcome historical memories from past conflicts. Often, this means that paying attention to both the *substantive* and the *symbolic* aspects of policymaking and implementation is especially important. There is often a temptation to focus policy on meeting the immediate material needs of people who have suffered in the midst of long-term bitter conflicts. These needs are real, but so too are the emotional wounds and the deep fears and memories of past experiences. Policymaking offers an excellent opportunity not only to help people better their position in a society, but also to change their feelings about the possibilities for the future and that of their children. Symbolic steps are needed to build connections and recast policy and alter an atmosphere of distrust and envy. Crucial to this is building wider identification with the community in general, and the state in particular, so that redistribution of resources and new policies are experienced as widely beneficial and not merely the provision of selective benefits. At first glance it seems paradoxical that government agencies, bureaucrats, and technical experts can communicate such messages. Yet their capacity to provide resources and solutions to the daily problems people face in divided societies, such as clean water, health care, education, and employment, can offer an opportunity for empowerment and institution-building that can help to put their society on a new path toward a more cooperative and peaceful future.

Notes

1. Edelman (1964), for example, describes in detail one important pattern in which government regulatory policies can provide symbolic reassurance of the unorganized and tangible benefits for a relatively small number of organized groups. Creating regulatory agencies to oversee areas such as environmental protection or financial transactions can persuade the public that a problem is being addressed while, at the same time, permitting those who have been involved in these areas to continue to benefit tangibly.

2. This expansion of relevant policy actors is probably appropriate in all societies in certain areas such as trade or the environment, and it is particularly relevant in considering policy in many less affluent societies, irrespective of the amount of conflict they have recently experienced.

3. Sidney Verba explores the evidence for the participation hypothesis, namely the notion that involvement in group decision making increases commitment to group decisions and facilitates implementation of decisions once they are taken (Verba, 1961: chapters 9-10).

4. A frequent source of tension concerns whether paramilitary groups, or their political representatives, can join in a political process before they have formally renounced violence or have disarmed.

5. For an excellent overview of the policy process and a discussion of major approaches to it, see Jones (1994).

6. Of course, the numbers can always be debated, as "the choice of measures is part of strategic problem definition, and the results of measures take on their political character only with the costume of interpretive language" (Stone, 1988: 146).

7. It is not obvious what this number needs to be other than "a significant portion of the populace." For one thing the political significance of the number is always weighted by the intensity of feelings on the issue in real conflicts, and its distribution across groups in a society.

8. An obvious example for such comparative analysis is the social welfare legislation which was passed in most Western European countries by the turn of the nineteenth century, but that did not occur in the United States until the 1930s. Health insurance in America has lagged behind other countries as well. This gap suggests that opposition strategies were being pursued aggressively, and effectively, in the United States.

9. The term "serious attention" is used to make it clear that there are some issues that are on the agenda of a state agency only to please a particular constituency or political figure. These issues will not be acted upon, nor will significant resources be devoted to them by the agencies involved.

10. It seems plausible to hypothesize that, in conflict societies, decisions are more likely to be politicized in terms of the merger of substance with the personalities and ethnic or political identities of their proponents, sometimes diverting attention away from the proposals themselves.

11. For excellent classic discussions of implementation issues, see Bardash (1979) and Pressman and Wildavsky (1973).

12. This question is raised at other times as well, but here I emphasize that it can be important in agenda decisions.

13. According to an OSCE report:www.ihhr/reports/osce01/ Religious%20Intolerance/ReligiousFreedom%ReportJune01.pdf.

14. There are over three thousand parades each year in Northern Ireland, and most of these are Unionist/Loyalist parades. Due primarily to changing demographics, many of these are contentious and some result in violence.

15. In the United States, the term "greenscamming" refers to the way in which some developers cynically argue that their projects will be good for the environment even when there is a good argument that the opposite is actually the case. Orwell, of course, was the master, in teaching us about the dynamics of this process.

16. Article 5: 1.6 says: "Bosnia and Herzegovina shall have such symbols as are decided by its Parliamentary Assembly and approved by the Presidency." See www.nato.int/ifor/gfa/gfa-an4.htm for full text.

17. The same characteristics, of course, can be used to polarize opposition and to build fear. Policymakers need to be aware of how they present programs and of possible ways in which opponents can characterize policies in damaging, negative ways (Cobb and Ross, 1997: chapter 2).

References

Anderson, Mary. 1999. *Do No Harm: How Aid Can Support Peace—or War*. Boulder, CO. Lynne Rienner.

Bardash, Eugene. 1979. *The Implementation Game: What Happens after a Bill Becomes a Law*. Cambridge: MIT Press.

Campbell, Donald T. 1969. "Reforms as Experiments." *American Psychologist* 24: 409-29.

———. 1998. "The Experimenting Society." *Methodology and Epistemology for Social Science: Selected Papers of Donald T. Campbell*, edited by E. Samuel Overman. Chicago: University of Chicago Press, 290-314

Cobb, Roger, and Charles D. Elder. 1983. *The Politics of Agenda Building: Participation in American Politics*. Baltimore: Johns Hopkins University Press.

Cobb, Roger, and Marc Howard Ross, eds. 1997. *Cultural Strategies of Agenda Denial: Avoidance, Attack and Redefinition*. Lawrence: University Press of Kansas.

Cobb, Roger, Jennie–Keith Ross, and Marc Howard Ross. 1976. "Agenda Building as a Comparative Political Process." *American Political Science Review* 71: 126-38.

Downs, Anthony. 1972. "Up and Down with Ecology: The Issue Attention Cycle." *Public Interest* 28: 38-50.

Edelman, Murray. 1964. *The Symbolic Uses of Politics*. Urbana: University of Illinois Press.

Felsteiner, William, R. I. Abel, and Austin Sarat. 1980-1981. "The Emergence and Transformation of Disputes: Naming, Blaming, and Claiming." *Law and Society Review* 15: 631-53.

Jones, Bryan D. 1994. *Reconceiving Decision-Making in Democratic Politics: Attention, Choice and Public Policy*. Chicago: University of Chicago Press.

Kingdon, John. 1994. *Agendas, Alternatives and Public Policies.* New York: Harper-Collins.

Kriesberg, Louis. 1998. *Constructive Conflicts: From Escalation to Resolution.* Lanham, MD: Rowman & Littlefield.

Lieberfeld, Daniel. Forthcoming. "Evaluating the Contributions of Track-Two Diplomacy to Conflict Termination in South Africa, 1984-90." *Political Psychology.*

Lindbloom, Charles E. 1977. *Politics and Markets: The World's Political-Economic Systems.* New York: Basic Books.

McShane, Liz. 1988. *Politically Motivated Ex-Prisoners' Self-Help Projects.* Northern Ireland Voluntary Trust.

Nagel, Jack. *Participation.* 1987. Englewood Cliffs: Prentice-Hall.

Pressman, Jeffrey L., and Aaron B. Wildavsky. 1973. *Implementation.* Berkeley and Los Angeles: University of California Press.

Rochefort, David, W. and Roger Cobb, eds. 1998. *The Politics of Problem Definition: Shaping the Political Agenda.* Lawrence: University Press of Kansas.

Ross, Marc Howard. 1993. *The Management of Conflict: Interpretations and Interests in Comparative Perspective.* New Haven, CT and London: Yale University Press.

Scott, James. 1998. *Seeing Like a State: How Certain Schemes to Improve the Human Condition Have Failed.* New Haven, CT and London: Yale University Press.

Shively, W. Phillips. 2001. *Power and Choice: An Introduction to Political Science.* Seventh Edition. Boston, MA: McGraw Hill.

Skolnick, Jerome. 1994. *Justice without Trial: Law Enforcement in Democratic Society.* New York: Macmillan.

Sparks, Allister. 1995. *Tomorrow is Another Country: The Inside Story of South Africa's Road to Change.* Chicago, IL: University of Chicago Press.

Stone, Deborah. 1988. *Policy Paradox and Political Reason.* Glenview, IL. Scott Foresman.

Verba, Sidney. 1961. *Small Groups and Political Behavior: A Study of Leadership.* Princeton, NJ: Princeton University Press.

Wildavsky, Aaron B. 1979. *Speaking Truth to Power: The Art and Science of Policy Analysis.* Boston, MA: Little, Brown.

Chapter 3
The Challenges of Influencing Policy in Conflict Situations

Hizkias Assefa

This chapter raises some fundamental questions about the challenges faced by conflict management and coexistence NGOs in trying to influence policy in conflict situations. It begins with an analysis of various understandings of policy and the policy process, and then examines the challenges to NGOs in influencing policy, particularly in relation to the kinds of activities they undertake, their various roles in relation to the conflict, their local or international identities, and the stage of the conflict at the time of intervention. It also addresses problems, such as mandate, that can be thorny issues for NGOs when they undertake political advocacy work, as well as particular challenges faced by NGOs, especially international NGOs, who may be engaged as mediators in local conflict situations. It concludes by urging NGOs to scrutinize not only the processes they use to achieve their aims, but also the aims themselves, in order to enhance their conflict management and coexistence work.

Policy Processes in Conflict Situations

Governments, and their counterparts in organized opposition movements, play an integral role in perpetuating and alleviating large-scale social conflicts, hence influencing their decisions is an important aspect of NGO policy work. When discussing NGO impact on policy, there are various questions that need to be addressed, such as how policy is influenced by outside actors, and whether or not it is possible to know if specific actions have triggered the policy change.

The most common understanding of how policy is influenced presupposes a direct connection between action and result. This suggests that an input, in the form of information or policy recommendation, is provided by NGOs to policymakers and the engagement that follows between the two actors leads to the adoption of a new or adjusted policy. Engagement in the policy process might, for example, take the form of education, advocacy for a particular cause, or lobbying public officials in order to influence them. In this simplified version of the process, the policymakers become persuaded by the merits of a proposal and adopt the recommended course of action. The direct impact of the input can be observed in the level of correlation between recommendation and the actual policy adopted. While the process described appears to be fairly rational and linear, this is rarely how it works in the policy world. Democratic decision making, which often involves a multitude of actors, must serve to accommodate diverse inputs and interests. When actors with divergent interests participate, it is inevitable that the debate will take many unexpected twists and turns, producing an outcome that is often quite different from that envisaged by the initial input. While one can ascertain the role played by the NGO in the process, it is often difficult to pinpoint the precise impact they have had in affecting policy. Few and far between are the cases so clear-cut as to indicate where plan leads to action and the action produces the planned result in that order.

In large-scale social conflict situations, where issues are very complex, the challenges of a chaotic policy process are multiplied manyfold. In such cases, there are many diverse perspectives on the issues and strongly held views on how they should be handled. There are also groups who benefit either from the existing policies or from an absence of policy. Therefore, even if an NGO can make a clear case that a certain policy change would lead to the containment, mitigation, or resolution of a conflict, the proposal's adoption or rejection might ultimately be determined by which powerful group's interests are served or hampered, rather than merely by the rationality of the proposal. In such instances, policy decision making is not a rational and linear process, but rather an outcome of all sorts of bargaining, horse trading, and at times, power plays between various powerful stakeholders. An assortment of changes, amendments, new concerns and interests become injected into the original proposal before the outcome is announced. At times, it may be difficult to recognize the connection between the initial recommendation and the final policy adopted. The saying "a camel is a horse put together by a committee" captures the essence of this understanding of making and influencing policy.

Conceptual and Practical Challenges in Policy Activities

Some of the activities that conflict management and coexistence NGOs commonly perform in the process of influencing policy pose fundamental conceptual and practical challenges. This chapter specifically examines those that arise when NGOs assume roles in political advocacy as well as third-party functions such as mediation and facilitation.

Political Advocacy

Advocacy is increasingly becoming a common activity of NGOs in conflict situations. More and more humanitarian and development NGOs operating in conflict areas are including it in their organizational mandate. A typical characteristic of most advocacy work is adopting a position regarding the conflict (which may often coincide with the position of one of the conflict parties) and representing it in a judicial process or before courts of public opinion in order to get support for that position and, if need be, to get a policy adopted in its favor.[1]

NGO use of political advocacy to affect policy raises a multitude of questions, such as: Whose views do the NGOs represent, and whose agenda are they promoting? Where do they get the mandate to speak on behalf of the groups they claim to speak for? What is the impact of their political advocacy on the conflict itself, and what are the ethical implications of these activities? The importance of these questions and the seriousness of their implications for conflict management and coexistence work depend on the particular roles being undertaken by the NGOs—that is, whether they are undertaking their advocacy function in the context of performing primary or secondary party roles, or as third-party mediating roles. It also depends on their identity—in particular, whether they are national or foreign NGOs.

In a number of conflict situations, the representative nature of NGOs has often been called into question. Frequently, NGOs have been engaged in advocacy activities in the name of one of the conflict parties, civil society, or the public at large. In many cases, however, there is little evidence that the NGO has been asked to speak or act by the groups on whose behalf it claims to do so. There may even be situations where NGOs disguise their own organizational interests (building their political and social stature, ensuring their own financial survival, and so on) under the guise of advocating for conflict issues or parties. Advocating for "child victims of war," for example, might be included in a humanitarian NGO's relief program simply because the issue might be in currency and there are ample donor funds available for it. Unfortunately, there are few mechanisms by which the people who are supposedly benefiting from this advocacy can control the activities of the NGOs that claim to speak on their behalf. The group spoken for, be it "civil society," "the general public," or "the women of Bosnia," is often so amorphous that it may not have designated spokespeople to check or control an NGO's claims and activities. Undertaking such representative roles inappropriately can raise serious ethical and credibility problems.

Of particular difficulty within this context of advocacy is the phenomenon of government-sponsored nongovernmental organizations (GONGOs).[2] Civil society and NGOs are typically expected to play watchdog functions vis-à-vis governments on issues of public governance. Although GONGOs may engage in worthwhile work, their claim to advocate citizens' concerns and interests in policy processes, especially when those concerns go contrary to prevailing public policy, is questionable. Instead of genuinely voicing civil society concerns, a number of GONGOs have acted as fronts for governments to manipulate the civil society agenda so that the latter end up rubber-stamping already formulated government policies.

Another problem with some NGO advocacy work has been the tendency to move the forum of discussion out of the country and into some foreign venue, without recognizing the impact that this might have on the conflict itself. Thus, advocacy can, at times, exacerbate rather than ease conflict. For example, in certain deep-rooted, protracted conflicts, some NGOs believe that powerful foreign governments should be involved in exerting pressure on the party against whom they are advocating. In the Sudan conflict, for example, some NGOs want the United States or the EU to put sanctions either on the Sudan government or the Southern factions in order to make them behave in a manner conducive to managing the conflict. Therefore, such NGOs have been lobbying and advocating in the corridors of power in the United States and Europe in order to influence the policies of these governments. However, the Sudan government and the other parties thus targeted by these advocacy groups have reacted by seeking other NGOs to advocate for them in those countries as well. The consequence has been increased competition among the protagonists to recruit international NGO advocates to their sides and an intensification of their mutual animosity. Another unfortunate outcome of this kind of advocacy has been the removal of serious discussions of war and peace away from the country itself and into Washington, London, and Brussels.[3] Ultimately, it is only those who can mobilize advocacy NGOs that can participate in these discussions and influence decisions being made by outsiders about Sudan. In most instances, the citizens who have no access to advocacy NGOs become spectators in their own affairs, while decisions are being made abroad.

This sort of advocacy has managed to create the impression that what matters is not how well the protagonists are able to communicate with their adversaries at home, but how much they can persuade powerful foreign actors to take their side. It seems that the more the protagonists refine their skills to garner the support of outside advocates, the more they ignore the need to communicate constructively with their adversaries. The ultimate tragedy is that one day, when the war is over, the protagonists will have to live with each other without the advocates. By that time, without both their respective advocates and powerful outsiders exerting pressure, an unhealthy habit will have been formed, making it difficult for the protagonists to collaborate directly with each other.

Another example of this can be found in the case of post-Mengistu Hailemariam Ethiopia.[4] The highly sophisticated and protracted advocacy and public relations campaign that was aimed at foreign governments helped overthrow the Mengistu regime in 1991. However, it eventually led to a distortion of communication inside the country. A decade after the war, there remains a deep mistrust and alienation on the side of those within Ethiopia who had lost out in this public relations war. To this day, communication between internal political adversaries is externally focused.[5] Those that dominated the advocacy competition against the Mengistu regime do not pay much attention to the frustrated voices of their domestic protagonists. Instead of working problems out between themselves through honest discussion and give and take, they tend to rely on the proven strategy of international public relations and advocacy in order to build foreign alliances. As a result, there is a great discrepancy between how things look politically from abroad and how they look from the point of view of insiders. Given that the domestic opposition receives little hearing at home, they often attempt desperately to garner support from advocacy groups in the United States and Europe, in order to be taken seriously at home.

This way of operating fosters the mentality that one has to persuade foreign governments to put pressure on the political adversary, or resort to violence in order to be heard. In short, NGO advocacy in conflict situations, particularly when aimed at foreign and powerful governments, can lead to a distortion of communication among the protagonists at home. This in turn can trigger more alienation, instability, and violence, even after the conflict is ostensibly over.

Another important challenge in this regard is how advocacy aimed at influencing foreign governments, regardless of whether it is done by local or international NGOs, can, by internationalizing a conflict, make it less amenable for resolution. Although intervention by outside governments can help, it is not always in the interests of the conflict parties or the victims caught in the conflict. The invitation to intervene could provide an opportunity for the intervener to inject its own agenda, which could further complicate the conflict. The reason for the United States' intervention in Sudan is not merely to stop the war, but is also driven by a desire to halt Islamic expansion in the region.[6] Here, the issue of mandate becomes even more critical, and questions may rightly be asked about who granted these NGOs the right to invite foreign actors into the conflict without asking permission from the population. Sometimes the best way to manage and resolve conflict is to insulate it from foreign agendas. In fact, some of the most successful peacebuilding and reconciliation work has been in areas where the conflicts have not been overly politicized by intervention on the part of outsiders such as powerful governments, international NGOs, and the media.

The identity of the NGOs doing advocacy work can also compound the problem. When NGOs are foreign rather than local, additional questions emerge not only about representation and mandate, but also about motivation. To what extent can advocacy by international NGOs disguise the interests and preferences of their own governments and donors, although the advocacy is allegedly done in the name of local actors in the conflict? Given that funding for international NGOs often comes from their governments or societies, there can be major concerns about how free they are to advocate for issues that might be contrary to the interests of those funders. In some cases, the question even arises as to how their advocacy might serve as an entry point for their governments to interfere in the conflict.

For their part, international NGOs may not be aware of how they are being used by their own governments, or, if they are, they may view it as their national, if not financial, duty to do so. Therefore, serious moral and ethical questions can be raised regarding the legitimacy of foreign NGOs involved in advocacy, particularly in situations where such advocacy may end up increasing alienation between protagonists in the name of such abstract concepts as "justice," "democracy," or "liberation."

At least with local NGOs, there is some ultimate accountability for their behavior. A miscalculation of strategy or a misuse of power and resources on their part will not only negatively affect their society, but also affect themselves as citizens. Local NGOs may reap the consequences of their mistakes, and are therefore likely to be very careful about how their actions might produce societal damage. Such constraint may not exist for foreign NGOs, whose ultimate sacrifice might be simply to withdraw from the country when things do not work. They will not be there to suffer the consequences of any escalating alienation in the societies concerned as a result of their work. So the possibility of doing damage without much accountability for the consequences is higher when advocacy is handled by international rather than local NGOs.

Another challenge in advocacy work, particularly for international NGOs, arises when NGOs become enamored with the cause or the party they have adopted and become more vociferous in representing the party's views than the party itself. Sometimes such NGOs are so invested in the crusade of "winning" for their favored issue or party that their pursuit of "victory" becomes an obstacle to the exploration of common ground or compromise among the protagonists. They tend to take purist positions and view anything less than "victory" as a betrayal of "the cause." Therefore, they can discourage the parties from exploring options that may help resolve the conflict. Since international NGOs are not as closely affected as the protagonists or the citizens themselves, they can afford to stick to uncompromising positions that are untempered by the reality of the conflict. There have been times in my mediation work in Sudan, Rwanda, Kenya, and Sierra Leone when I have found NGO advocacy groups much more difficult to deal with than the protagonists themselves.

While the preceding observations have been in regard to political advocacy, there are similar concerns about human rights advocacy in situations of conflict. Just as in political advocacy, there are many instances where human rights advocacy has been aggressively pursued to the detriment of future harmonious coexistence. There is no question that respect of human rights is a minimum requirement for coexistence. However, advocacy for human rights should not be seen just as an end in itself, but rather as a stepping-stone to working toward a more harmonious society. Local and international NGOs involved in human rights or conflict resolution work must be cognizant of that fact and try to work collaboratively with each other where possible.[7]

While these are some of the conceptual challenges involved, there are also the everyday problems of doing advocacy work. Ensuring the quality and credibility of advocacy work can prove challenging, particularly for local NGOs. Domestic NGOs, in poor countries rife with conflict, are not set up only to do advocacy work. They have some other primary function but add on policy advocacy as a secondary activity because they believe it enhances their primary function. However, doing advocacy work on top of other activities can be quite demanding. It typically requires gathering, sifting, analyzing, verifying, and succinctly presenting large amounts of information to appropriate organizations and individuals on an ongoing and timely basis. This requires research capacity, specialized staff, and financial resources. Such skills may not be easily available and the required funds may not be readily mobilized from domestic sources. If the organization's staff or funding comes from abroad, its legitimacy and credibility could suffer, leading to accusations that the organization is an agent of foreign interests. An important challenge for local NGOs is, therefore, that of how to be both grounded in the local reality and viewed as a legitimate voice, even if some of their resources come from outside.

A related question is that of how to be taken seriously by those that are lobbied—that is, how to ensure that the information presented by the NGO gains the policymakers' attention. Often, small NGOs find it difficult to pull enough weight on their own to have the desired impact. Therefore, coalitions and partnerships may be necessary to capture the attention of power brokers. Unfortunately, relationships between conflict management and coexistence NGOs are more typically characterized by unhealthy competition than by collaboration. Much work needs to be done in the peacebuilding field to ensure coordination, coherence, and mutuality among practitioners. Collaboration is, of course, more meaningful and effective if it emerges organically from a shared philosophical vision and strategic framework, but this is unfortunately rare. What is more common are short-term tactical alliances around a specific policy issue. Such alliances can suffer from differences in long-term goals and operating styles which can cause much friction and frustration, thereby decreasing the effectiveness of the work.

Another challenge relates to the need to be aware of the effectiveness of advocacy work at each stage of the conflict cycle. As indicated by Marc Howard Ross in chapter 2, advocacy is most effective in pre- and postconflict situations. When disaster is first looming, preemptive interventions could be effective. However, in the precrisis stage, parties can be caught up in the passion of the conflict and resist any advocacy for peace, believing that they can coerce their adversary into acquiescing to their will. Unfortunately, by the time the "stalemate" or "impasse" phase is reached and the parties become more amenable to considering other alternatives, much bloodshed and destruction have already been wrought. Coexistence and peacebuilding NGOs can get frustrated by the feeling that they are heard only after the damage is done.

Mediation and Facilitation

Mediation and facilitation are two types of activity that conflict resolution and coexistence NGOs can use to influence policy. If one of the conflict parties is a governmental actor, then these third-party roles, if handled properly, provide avenues for influencing governmental policy orientation and action. Many of the activities often referred to as Track Two activities can be seen as strategies not only for resolving conflicts, but also for influencing the policy of the conflict parties.[8]

Unlike advocacy, where the aim is to make a case directly for alternative policies or outcomes in a conflict situation, the influence in mediation and facilitation comes from the NGO's capacity to effectively guide a process of negotiation which both conflict parties perceive as acceptable and satisfactory. The essential qualities that enable the third parties to play their roles effectively—that is, their perceived integrity, trust, respect, impartiality, and expertise—can give them the capacity to influence the behavior of the parties in many ways without necessarily pushing for a certain outcome to the conflict. They can influence the parties in numerous ways: to consider dialogue and negotiations to address the issues of their dispute rather than relying on violence and mutual coercion; to mitigate their attitudes of mutual hostility and mistrust; to accept certain principles of fairness, justice, and sustainability in the search for solutions; to reexamine their positions and become more reasonable and flexible; and to explore options and solutions not considered before. Guiding a process which is characterized by equity, justice, give and take, and a focus on the mutual interests and needs of the parties can have a tremendous influence on the outcome of a conflict. However, since the influence exercised in mediation and facilitation is subtle and indirect, it must be handled with tremendous sensitivity and caution.

Challenges can arise when local NGOs play third-party roles in a national dispute. As citizens of the society involved, NGOs are likely to be affected negatively or positively by the conflict and are likely to favor one solution over another. Therefore, when they are involved in mediation and facilitation roles, a certain amount of confusion of roles is likely. The major protagonists might view NGOs as primary or secondary parties, even though the NGOs are presenting themselves as third-party mediators. This brings its own challenges and problems. Conflict parties' perceptions that a third party may have a vested interest in a particular solution can raise serious transparency and ethical problems, and the parties may lose faith in the mediation process itself. An NGO's capacity to influence the protagonists' behavior could therefore be diminished markedly. This is not to say that local NGOs cannot play third-party roles. Their knowledge of the conflict and understanding of the development of the protagonists' thinking over time is a very useful asset. However, for local NGOs to play the role well, it is vital that they show a high level of integrity, discipline, and restraint, and that they do not interject their own preferences in their role as third party. This is obviously quite difficult, and local NGOs have to work hard to earn the protagonists' trust and perception of even-handedness.

Comparatively speaking, the problem of perceived impartiality may be mitigated if the mediating NGO is international. Because such NGOs are supposedly outside the sphere of the conflict, the protagonists may perceive them as not having taken sides, and may believe that they can therefore be trusted to be impartial and objective. There are, however, several problems that can arise with international NGOs. The first is that, because they are outsiders, they may not fully understand the nuances of the conflict and may therefore not be able to guide the mediation process effectively. The second is that, depending on the scope of the disputed issue, even international NGOs could have vested interests in specific solutions. In cases where the mediators are international NGOs from powerful countries with economic, political, or security interests in the conflict societies, the mediator's independence and impartiality may be questioned. Since many NGOs receive their funding from powerful countries, questions may linger in the minds of the conflict parties regarding the third party's ability to be independent of the agendas, concerns, and policy interests of those upon whom their survival depends.

Great harm can be done to the image of mediation as an effective mechanism for handling conflict, especially in the eyes of those who do not fully understand it, if negative impact results from processes undertaken by supposedly neutral parties who are subsequently perceived to have a vested interest in a particular solution. Conflict parties begin to see mediation as political maneuvering and manipulation and therefore become cynical about it. Consequently, protagonists who could be helped by genuine mediation become resistant to offers of intervention, thereby allowing the suffering and destruction of war to drag on. As a mediator, I believe that mediation has an immense potential for not only dealing with conflict effectively but also building meaningful long-term relationships between former protagonists. However, the fallout from improperly handled mediation can destroy its credibility, and with that, its great potential.

The challenges associated with NGO third-party activities are exacerbated when mediation is combined with advocacy activities to influence policy. NGOs need to consider to what extent they should be mediators and at the same time be involved in advocacy work, since advocacy could compromise the even-handedness necessary for the facilitation process. In most instances, effective mediation requires the mediator to keep a very low profile and resist conducting negotiations via the media. Mediation is about providing a safe space for the parties to explore issues and solutions without being embarrassed about adjusting their positions or accommodating their adversaries. Advocacy, however, often relies on publicity. Involving media coverage in one's advocacy strategy could compromise any ongoing mediation efforts. It is therefore very important for NGOs to be aware of how various publicity tactics could serve to hinder or help their overall strategy.

Interestingly, one observes a number of third-party efforts by NGOs that claim to facilitate mediation while at the same time being engaged in public activities to demonstrate to the world that one of the parties is at fault and therefore must give in to the demands of the other. While often it is actors operating from a position of power who behave like this, such as global or regional powers, the same confusion of roles can also be observed by the bigger, well-connected, and resource-endowed NGOs associated with such governments. Such examples can be observed in the Intergovernmental Authority on Development-sponsored mediation of the Sudan conflict, the United States-sponsored mediation between the Mengistu regime, and the anti-Mengistu insurgency movements in Ethiopia and their affiliated local and international NGOs, and the mediation of the Dayton Accord in the former Yugoslavia. In such instances, although some of the conflict parties do not trust the mediator's impartiality, they cannot reject the mediation offer for fear of facing sanctions or of being branded as "warmongers" or "obstacles to peace." At times, the third parties may fail to recognize the implicit contradictions between their advocacy activity on the one hand and their mediation activity on the other. The unfortunate consequence of this combination of activities is that the party being coerced to submit to this process will not have a long-lasting commitment to its outcome, because the outcome is a product of coercion rather than a genuine quest to meet its interests. Therefore, the conflict is likely to remain unresolved.

A related issue is the extent to which NGOs should partner with governmental actors in their mediation activities. Although collaboration toward shared goals is desirable, such partnership can generate its own set of practical challenges. Governmental actors are more likely than NGOs to have secondary party roles in conflicts within their country. They may also have an underlying political agenda that could influence their mediation approach, and they are likely to favor processes and outcomes that are consistent with their existing policies. At the same time, the NGO's power base vis-à-vis the governmental partner is not equal, and this can relegate the NGO partner to playing second fiddle in the process. If there is deep philosophical, strategic, and tactical compatibility between the two actors, this power inequality may not matter. However, if there is divergence in their philosophies and strategies, the NGO may end up being co-opted and forced to toe the government line, restrained from taking certain initiatives, or simply ignored. The NGO might find it difficult to withdraw from the process, as doing so could embarrass the government, which could result in undesirable consequences. So the NGO could be stuck in a process where basic mediation values are compromised, and be unable to correct the situation.[9] The implications of such partnerships must be carefully examined by NGOs before they engage with more powerful actors who might only be interested in demonstrating for the sake of appearances that they are working with civil society actors.

In undertaking both advocacy and mediation work, NGOs need to recognize that their identity, motivations, and tendency to internationalize a conflict without due regard to the internal necessities of dealing with the conflict all need to be carefully examined. If not addressed, these factors can affect the credibility and capacity of conflict management and coexistence NGOs to influence policy successfully in order to ameliorate and resolve conflicts. It is also important to recognize that advocacy can at times work at cross purposes with mediation and facilitation, and NGOs must be aware of the challenges of formulating a coordinated strategy of conflict resolution and policy influence in their work.

Conclusion

The purpose of this chapter has been to raise some fundamental questions about what NGOs do in the name of conflict management and coexistence, the challenges that emerge from their work, and how these challenges become exacerbated in the process of trying to influence policy. Conflict management and coexistence NGOs are urged to scrutinize not only the process they use to achieve their aims but also the aims themselves, and the consequences of their actions on the public they claim to serve, in order to enhance their conflict management and coexistence work.

Unfortunately, there has been a tendency to believe that everything that goes under the name of peace, conflict management, or coexistence is good and should be fostered. But, as this chapter suggests, this is not always the case. Many things done in the name of peacebuilding can be harmful. Unfortunately, peace work is not like development work, where mistakes can be more easily rectified. Inappropriate handling in conflict situations can have irreversible consequences to human life, emotions, and future relationships in societies. Some of the suffering arising from conflict is not only a result of the complexity or difficulty of the issues at hand, but also of improper handling by those attempting to manage or resolve them. The handling of conflict is not a mere technical response to a human problem. Rather, it is a deep intellectual, psychological, and even spiritual engagement. Aside from the requisite technical skills, conflict management and coexistence work is highly value-driven, with its own ethical and behavioral disciplines. The work is not merely about undertaking activities, but engaging in them with genuine intent and motivation. The risk of doing harm to people, to the process at hand, and to the field of conflict resolution and peacebuilding itself, is immense. Sometimes the negative consequences of such mishandling only become evident over the long term.

A lot of care is taken in handling a person's physical and emotional wounds. Those entrusted with their treatment, such as physicians, psychiatrists, and psychologists, are usually highly qualified people who are held accountable for their actions. But we tend to be more cavalier when handling the even more complicated emotional wounds of human collectivities. We often do not exercise the caution and care that this kind of healing calls for. This chapter is a reminder of that necessity.

Notes

I would like to express my deep gratitude to Gretchen Van Evera for her editorial assistance in the preparation of this chapter.

1. This is not to say that all advocacy work is partisan. It is possible for NGOs to advocate for a dialogue process which benefits both sides of the conflict. In such instances, some of the challenges discussed in this section may not arise.

2. In the post-Cold War international order, civil society and NGOs in many Third World countries have become competitors of governments as channels of international aid and vehicles for democratic governance. Donor agencies have accused those governments of corruption, authoritarianism, and being obstacles to reform, and have been willing to deal more with NGOs than with the governments. Therefore, a number of governments had been motivated to create their own NGOs to front for them in order to have access to international donor funds and democratic legitimacy.

3. Examples are the Sudan Peace Act passed in the United States House of Representatives, 13 June 2001; the European Parliament Resolution on Sudan, 17 December 1998, condemning the Sudanese government for its repeated violations of human rights and international humanitarian law; and the debate on Sudan in the UK Parliament at Westminster, 26 October 2001.

4. The revolutionary regime of Colonel Mengistu took power from Emperor Haile Selassie in 1974. In turn, Mengistu's regime was overthrown in 1991 by an alliance of armed insurgency groups who remain in power.

5. For example, the U.S.-Rwanda Peace Plan. See http://secretary.state.gov/www/briefings/statements/1998/ps980603.html.

6. For the enactment of the Sudan Peace Act, the United States Congress took evidence from a Christian organization, the Family Research Council, which claimed that militant forces considered Sudan the gateway for Islamic expansion into the rest of Africa, the Middle East, and the rest of the world. www.rim.org/muslim/Sudan2.htm.

7. For a more detailed treatment of this subject, see Hizkias Assefa, *Justice and*

Reconciliation—A Misunderstood Relationship (2003, forthcoming).

8. The case studies in this volume from TOSAM and CMG provide examples of NGO strategies that incorporate these approaches.

9. Some argue this point from a philosophical ground, saying that NGO and governmental mediation should be separate but complementary processes since their objectives, motivations, and styles may not be the same. The less powerful actor, the NGO, is likely to rely on the development of trust and confidence with the protagonists as its main instrument to lead the mediation, while the more powerful third party is likely to resort to pressure and leverage as strategies to bring the parties to agreement. If these styles and approaches are combined in one actor, they might lead to confusion and failure in the mediation process rather than success.

Reference

Steinberg, Natalie. 2001. Background Paper on GONGOs and QUANGOs and Wild NGOs. www.worldfederalist.org/ACTION/ngorpt1201.html

Chapter 4
Track One and a Half Diplomacy: Searching for Political Agreement in the Caucasus

Susan Allen Nan

This case study presents lessons learned from the experience of Conflict Management Group (CMG) and the Norwegian Refugee Council (NRC) in a series of conflict resolution workshops that influenced peacebuilding policy on both sides of the Georgia-South Ossetia conflict. CMG and the NRC intended their series of conflict resolution workshops to encourage productive peacebuilding policies and augment the officially mediated peace talks. By teaching policy analysis skills, allowing exchange of views, and encouraging joint consideration of many policy options, CMG and the NRC[1] helped shape more effective peacebuilding policies in Georgia and South Ossetia. Since the beginning of the workshops, changes in policy by Georgia and South Ossetia have led to decreased tensions and increased stability and cross-conflict cooperation in the region. Key to the success of the efforts of CMG and the NRC were their unique collaboration between two different NGOs, their trust building with both parties, the long-term nature of their work, and their skillful facilitation of unofficial interactions among official leadership on both sides of the conflict. This unofficial work with high-level officials is a form of Track One and a Half diplomacy.[2] It defies categorization within either the official negotiations of Track One diplomacy or the unofficial activities of Track Two diplomacy. Track One and a Half diplomacy combines the official influence of Track One with the unofficial approaches of Track Two.

Organizational Background

CMG and NRC formed a unique partnership that brought together very different strengths to facilitate a conflict resolution workshop series and encourage productive peacebuilding policies for the Georgia-South Ossetia conflict.

Founded in 1984, CMG is a nonprofit organization of less than twenty full-time staff, based in Cambridge, Massachusetts. It was founded to provide for the practical application of negotiations and innovations developed at the Program on Negotiation at Harvard Law School. Its mission is to spread peace-promoting skills and help people manage their differences. CMG has a strong expertise in negotiations, skills training, and dialogue facilitation. CMG's expertise in facilitating joint brainstorming in conflict resolution workshops was instrumental in shaping the CMG-NRC workshop series.

Founded in 1946, the NRC is a large humanitarian organization with approximately seventy employees in its head office in Norway, and many more worldwide. The NRC assists refugees and internally displaced persons with repatriation and other humanitarian assistance. The NRC's local offices in Tbilisi, Georgia, and in Tskhinvali, South Ossetia, were in close contact with Georgian and South Ossetian leaders and were core contributors to the effective facilitation of the CMG-NRC workshop series.

CMG and the NRC partnered to implement the conflict resolution workshop series. For the most active years of the program, until funding became elusive, NRC provided a project coordinator on the ground in the region, with strong in-depth knowledge of the conflict. CMG provided the process expertise to prepare for and facilitate the workshop series.

Conflict and Peace Process Background

CMG and the NRC faced a difficult task in seeking to augment the official negotiations after a complex and bloody conflict that displaced thousands.

Under the Soviet Union, South Ossetia was an autonomous *oblast* of the Georgian Soviet Socialist Republic. In 1989, some South Ossetians supported the Abkhaz complaints against Georgian oppression and spoke of unification with North Ossetia in Russia, and tensions worsened between the more pro–Soviet South Ossetia and the Georgian republic, which increasingly turned away from the Soviet Union. In December 1990, amidst Georgian abolition of South Ossetia's autonomy and a South Ossetian declaration of itself as an independent Soviet Republic separate from Georgia, a full-scale armed conflict broke out, killing over a thousand people.[3] Georgians in South Ossetia, and Ossetians in other parts of Georgia, fled. Both sides spread stories of atrocities committed by the other during the war. The fighting ended with the introduction of forces from the Soviet Ministry of Internal Affairs in January 1991, but tens of thousands of people remained displaced.

The peace process gradually attracted more international attention. After the

Georgian declaration of independence from the Soviet Union in 1991, and international recognition of Georgia's independence in 1992, the Soviet peacekeeping forces were replaced in the summer 1992 by a tripartite Russian-Georgian-Ossetian peacekeeping force. In 1994, a quadripartite team consisting of Russian, Georgian, North Ossetian, and South Ossetian leaders met to negotiate outstanding issues and seek a comprehensive political settlement in South Ossetia. In this settlement, Russian peacekeepers would maintain a ceasefire pending peace negotiations while South Ossetia would continue to seek recognition of its independence and Georgia to preserve its territorial integrity. The ceasefire has held, with peacekeeping troops separating the two sides since 1992.

Negotiations mediated by Russia and the Organization for Security and Cooperation in Europe (OSCE)[4] began in 1995, and are still continuing at the time of this writing (2002). The OSCE, as in intergovernmental body, has represented many countries interested in a peaceful solution to the conflict, and has facilitated political negotiations as well as technical-level cooperation between the parties. These multifaceted negotiations have led to reduced tensions, significant agreements, and even a reduction in peacekeeping forces. However, in spite of cooperation on many practical matters, such as economic links, and ongoing negotiations, a final political settlement has yet to be reached.

The peace process surrounding the Georgia-South Ossetia conflict includes both official and unofficial activities. The unofficial work that had the most direct impact on official negotiations was arguably the CMG-NRC work, although Caucasus Links (and its predecessor, Vertic) were also helpful. The CMG-NRC conflict resolution workshop series began with a workshop in Norway in January 1996; at the time, official negotiations were under way but had made little progress since the 1991 ceasefire and introduction of peacekeeping forces. The tone of the official negotiations was often hostile, and tensions remained high. The CMG-NRC conflict resolution workshop series sought to introduce more productive approaches into the peacebuilding policies being created by teaching skills to, and facilitating joint brainstormings with, high-level leadership from both sides of the conflict. This was a unique and influential role within the overall peace process.

This chapter focuses on the ways in which the unofficial CMG-NRC workshop series helped shape official policy toward the peace process within the South Ossetian and Georgian leadership. Explaining this transfer effect from unofficial workshops to official policy requires some explanation of the official parts of the peace process. These involve both official negotiations and confidence building supported by the official mediators.

Official Negotiations

The OSCE has worked closely with Russia to mediate the official negotiations between Georgia and South Ossetia from 1995 to the present day. The official negotiation process brings the leaders of South Ossetia and Georgia together to discuss a final political settlement and ways to build toward such a settlement.

As the OSCE mediators have structured the process, it includes high-level (even presidential) summits, regular meetings of the Joint Control Commission (JCC) (an internationally facilitated Georgian-South Ossetian body that focuses on monitoring developing needs and technical implementation of agreements), and related working groups addressing practical issues of joint interest such as economic development.

The OSCE was not always embraced by the South Ossetians in its role as mediator, according to two South Ossetian officials I interviewed in 1998. When the first OSCE mission arrived in South Ossetia in December 1992, South Ossetians were wary of the official OSCE position supporting the territorial integrity of Georgia. While Georgia is a member state of the OSCE and South Ossetia lacks such status, the OSCE has, through time, become more accepted as a bridge builder and process facilitator for official negotiations, particularly as the military observation it conducts is seen as an important aspect of its overall role.

The official negotiation process has led to some tangible results. Georgia and South Ossetia signed an encouraging official agreement on 16 May 1996 with Russian, North Ossetian, and OSCE mediation. The memorandum of understanding called for greater economic ties, return of refugees, and a search for a mutually acceptable South Ossetian political status.

Confidence Building Supported by Official Mediators

In addition to official discussions related to a political settlement, the mediators seek to build confidence between the parties by facilitating cooperation on practical matters. The JCC addresses some practical areas of cooperation through related working group meetings—these are events, held almost every week, at which Georgians and South Ossetians meet to address practical problems. According to both a Georgian and a South Ossetian member of the JCC, the working groups decided that, at their level, they cannot settle the political status question, so they generally avoid arguing about it, instead focusing on relevant practical questions. The security authorities from both sides and the relevant ministry departments attend JCC meetings. One participant explained that many practical problems are not easily understood on both sides, because each side sees the whole conflict differently. Thus, the participant argued, it is important that both sides explain their perspectives through frequent, practice-oriented meetings.

In addition to supporting practical cooperation through the official JCC structure, the OSCE supports many of the various NGO-based confidence-building measures. The OSCE's role may be simply to encourage the parties to participate in some of the peacebuilding activities sponsored by NGOs, or the OSCE may occasionally participate in NGO-organized activities, too. For example, the OSCE participated and assisted logistically with a migration conference that the NRC sponsored in 1997. This conference brought Georgians and South Ossetians together around issues of migration. An OSCE official also participated in the October 1997 Helsinki Citizens' Assembly meeting in Armenia with journalists from the southern Caucasus, including South Ossetian and Georgian journalists.

The OSCE itself occasionally seeks to build confidence by bringing together scholars and journalists, a role more usually played by Track Two (NGO-based) conflict resolvers. The OSCE held two meetings of scholars in 1997, one on the themes of economy and rehabilitation, in Tbilisi in April, and the other on democratization, held in Tskhinvali in September. An OSCE meeting of journalists in Warsaw in the late spring of 1997 included Abkhaz, South Ossetian, and Georgian attendees. Following this, the OSCE helped start the Georgian-Ossetian joint information center in September 1997. All interviewees involved in joint journalists' initiatives noted that such work with journalists helps increase the amount of objective information available on both sides of the conflict.

Unofficial Parts of the Peace Process

In addition to the official negotiations and other roles played by official mediators in the Georgia-South Ossetia conflict, there are many roles played by unofficial interveners. These roles, and the specific events and initiatives some NGOs have undertaken to assist peacebuilding in the Georgia-South Ossetia peace process, have been documented elsewhere.[5] As described by interveners and participants, the immediate goals of these unofficial interventions include:

* building conflict resolution skills, knowledge, and local capacities for peace;
* confidence-building measures;
* strengthening cross-conflict linkages via NGOs' special interests;
* building regional identity and addressing regional issues;
* psychosocial rehabilitation;
* humanitarian assistance;
* democracy and civil society building; and
* unofficial facilitated dialogues amongst negotiators.

Each of these interventions is aimed at one of three levels of social actors: high-level leadership, mid-range leadership, and grassroots. High-level leadership includes the political leadership linked to official negotiations. Mid-level leadership includes those political leaders with links to the high-level leaders, as well as journalists and the leadership of active NGOs. Grassroots efforts include cultural events, large-scale public events, work with youth, and local community development.

Of particular interest to the present focus on the transfer of results from unofficial conflict resolution initiatives to official policy are those interventions that focus on high-level participants.[6] These Track One and a Half diplomacy interventions show the most direct effect on official negotiations.

Strategies and Tactics: Track One and a Half Diplomacy

This chapter examines how high-level unofficial conflict resolution efforts, in particular the CMG-NRC workshop series,[7] directly impacted the peace policies involved in the Georgia-South Ossetian peace process. These high-level unofficial interventions form a specific type of conflict resolution approach. The interveners are unofficial NGOs, yet many of the participants are themselves official negotiators or highly placed officials setting relevant policy for one or the other side of the conflict. This type of initiative falls between the traditional definitions of Track One diplomacy (official diplomacy) and Track Two diplomacy (unofficial diplomacy), and is here referred to as Track One and a Half diplomacy. Track One and a Half diplomacy allows direct transfer from unofficial meetings and workshops to official policy and the official negotiations process.

The CMG-NRC workshop series sought to augment the official negotiation process. This was done by involving official leaders and policymakers from the two sides of the conflict in unofficial training and dialogue sessions. As it had unofficial status, the CMG-NRC workshop series could introduce elements that the official process lacked. Yet, because of their access at the highest levels, CMG and the NRC were able to make their contributions directly relevant to the leadership. The workshop series sought to improve understanding, relationships, and peacebuilding policies amongst influentials on both sides of the conflict. The policies impacted included policies on negotiation and the various issues considered in the negotiations, such as economic development in South Ossetia, return of refugees and displaced people, and so on.

CMG and the NRC worked together from 1995 to 2000 to facilitate a successful series of unofficial dialogues between high-level Georgians and South Ossetians, referred to here as "the CMG-NRC workshop series." As described below in some detail, the CMG-NRC workshops were highly effective in building relationships and changing the tone of communication between influential Georgians and South Ossetians. The workshop series was a long-term project, continuing over five years. The workshops made significant impacts on official peacebuilding policies.

The following discussion includes an examination of the development and structure of the workshops, including specific tactics employed by CMG and the NRC, participants' reflections on their experiences, effects attributed to these workshops during the research interviews, and challenges faced by CMG and the NRC in facilitating the workshop series. The focus of this presentation is on the direct effects of these workshops on the official negotiations through relevant peacebuilding policy impact.[8] The CMG-NRC workshop series involved negotiators from the official negotiations process over a period of five years. This strong link between unofficial conflict resolution work with high-level representatives and official peace policies makes the process highly significant to the overall peace process.

Development of the CMG-NRC Workshop Series

CMG was invited to work on the conflict over South Ossetia by President Shevardnadze, after an international diplomat and former visiting fellow at Harvard University (where CMG is based) spoke highly of the work of Roger Fisher[9] to the Georgian leadership. Upon receiving the invitation, CMG considered South Ossetia a promising area for intervention because, as a relatively less intense postwar conflict where the parties had been close before the war, it seemed an area where their negotiation assistance could have the most productive impact.

Thus, in 1995, a delegation from CMG traveled to Tbilisi and Tskhinvali with the assistance of the Tbilisi and Tskhinvali offices of the NRC. The NRC acted as a local coordinator to the United States-based CMG. In this first trip, CMG sought to assess the conflict situation and the parties' choices relating to negotiations. The group went directly to Tskhinvali on arrival in the Caucasus. It is significant that the group immediately traveled to Tskhinvali, and proceeded to spend the night there after their long trip. This itinerary was highly symbolic because most Westerners stayed only in the relative comfort and security of Tbilisi and spent significant time in Tbilisi before going on to Tskhinvali for a day trip. The direct approach to Tskhinvali and the association with the respected NRC were reported by a South Ossetian workshop participant to have increased the South Ossetians' level of confidence about the group. As arranged prior to their arrival, the delegation met with the leader of South Ossetia, Ludwig Chibirov, and later the President of Georgia, Eduard Shevardnadze, and discussed the conflict and CMG's approaches to conflict resolution. These visits cemented the project's relevance to the ultimate policymakers on each side. In addition, the delegation made public presentations about conflict resolution in each city, thus increasing their legitimacy in the eyes of the public on both sides. On the basis of this Tskhinvali and Tbilisi visit, and after consideration of many options for intervention, the CMG team suggested an unofficial workshop of influential South Ossetians and Georgians to explore joint interests in Oslo in January 1996. Such a workshop would not duplicate other work, but could fill a gap in the peace process while utilizing CMG and the NRC's strengths appropriately. At the presidential level, both sides agreed to participate, and formally requested that CMG organize the first workshop.

Even beginning with this first visit, CMG and the NRC had good relationships with the official mediators. They met regularly with the OSCE to exchange views on the peace process, including basic information and peace process strategy. By keeping an open channel of communication with the OSCE, CMG and the NRC sought to minimize any discomfort on the part of the official mediators and ensure that the official mediators did not feel threatened or excluded by the unofficial process.

Structure of the CMG-NRC Workshop Series

The first stage of the project involved three facilitated brainstorming sessions and negotiations training for joint groups of influential Georgians and South Ossetians, and a fourth more substance-focused meeting. The first two brainstorming sessions occurred near Oslo, Norway, in January and May 1996, and the third in Norwood, Massachusetts, in June 1997. The fourth meeting occurred in Barcelona, Spain. Each of the meetings took place well outside of the conflict context, so that participants would be able to focus on dialogue across the conflict divide. The meetings included a participant mix of senior government officials and influential unofficial individuals.

CMG identified participants for the first workshop very carefully. CMG benefited from strong local knowledge of Georgian politics through a staff member's close personal contacts in Tbilisi. Even so, a CMG team made a second trip to the region specifically to identify appropriate participants for the first workshop. The team focused on identifying who was who in terms of peace policy development on each side, and particularly in South Ossetia, where CMG did not have such close personal contacts to provide good background information. The OSCE and NRC also provided important insight into the local policy development process and key players on each side. As there were no operating hotels South Ossetia, the CMG teams stayed with local families on each trip, and evening conversations invariably included not only good food, but also valuable insights into the local peace process policy scene.

With these sources of information, CMG considered a framework for participant selection that had been developed through previous CMG work on facilitated joint brainstorming addressing the conflict between Ecuador and Peru. This framework guided CMG to select participants who were influential enough to push for good ideas that came out of the workshops, but who were not themselves the final decision makers for the largest conflict issues. In addition, the framework guided the CMG team to look for participants who were open to learning new approaches, who would experiment with new ideas without needing to make commitments, and who would be creative. The CMG team interviewed potential participants, discussing possibilities for workshops and learning their reactions to the idea of talking with the other side and of exploring new ways of entering into dialogue together. Invitations were not issued during these meetings, as the team wished to complete the full series of meetings prior to constructing a carefully balanced group. The CMG team devoted an entire mission to the region to identifying appropriate participants because they felt good participant selection would be essential to starting the workshop series off productively.

During the selection mission, the CMG team added three more criteria to the framework for participant selection. These three criteria were issue expertise, variety of party affiliations, and interpersonal compatibility.

In terms of issue expertise, the CMG team realized that some issues of common concern to both sides would be appropriate areas of discussion in the first workshop. Some of these areas included issues of security, crime, local contact, and local needs. Thus, CMG sought to include experts from each side who would be able to focus on substantive questions related to these issues. They included people who could speak knowledgeably about the security situation surrounding the peacekeeping structures, the law enforcement challenges presented by organized crime exploiting the de facto border and lack of cooperation between Georgians and South Ossetians, and the needs of local citizens in the Georgian areas surrounding South Ossetia. In particular, local needs were represented in the first workshop by the inclusion of an MP from Gori, the largest Georgian city near South Ossetia.

The second additional criterion, variety of party affiliations, became important because elections in Georgia had been held not long before, and it was not yet clear who would have what influence on Georgian peace process policy. The CMG team decided to include opposition politicians in order to have representatives from across the political spectrum, and thus to ensure that the dialogue process would not be sabotaged by disgruntled factions who were not included, or by future shifts in political power. By including politicians from many factions, the CMG team sought to build an alliance or coalition on each side that would support improved peacebuilding policy development.

The CMG team considered interpersonal compatibility in selecting participants by considering what individual participants would find to talk about with their counterparts on the other side in the initial workshop sessions. The CMG team decided, for example, to bring expertise on security issues to the first workshop by including a South Ossetian and a Georgian who had fought together in Afghanistan but now represented their opposing sides, and who had influence on security policy on both sides. The team surmised, correctly, that these two would immediately find something to talk about.

Finally, a contextual assessment of the conflict dynamics involved led the CMG team to recommend that North Ossetian perspectives be included in the workshops as a stabilizing voice.

Although the first workshop was supported by the official leadership on both sides, CMG issued invitations to selected individuals to participate in the workshop specifically in their personal capacities. Participation in their personal capacities meant that they did not represent their place of employment and could make only personal commitments while at the workshop. Prior to arriving, participants understood that the meeting agenda would include exercises and skills building in negotiation, brainstorming ideas related to the Georgia-South Ossetia negotiation process, and both formal and informal talks with each other. The project goals centered around building relationships, teaching constructive negotiating processes, and developing substantive ideas that might contribute to the official negotiation process.

At the time of the first workshop, very early in the peace process, there were only two other international unofficial conflict resolution interveners addressing the conflict. Vertic's work served to open up dialogue through young politicians. The University of Maryland Center for International Development and Conflict Management (CIDCM) partners project included a Georgian and a South Ossetian in its mid-level regional peacebuilding activities. In this context, the CMG-NRC workshops introduced a new dynamic into the overall peace process by directly affecting official peacebuilding policies at the highest levels.

The first workshop, in January 1996, brought six senior participants from Tskhinvali and six senior participants from Tbilisi to Norway for a week of discussions facilitated by a CMG team. The participants ranged from presidential advisers to unofficial but respected opinion leaders on each side. The issue of status was off-limits; cultural and economic ties, refugees, and joint interests formed the focus of discussions. CMG presented frameworks for analysis of underlying interests related to these issues. Participants learned to understand each other's perspectives better by considering issues, their causes, possible approaches, and the range of constructive strategies available. As this was the first such postwar meeting of groups from the two societies, time was also spent on perceptions of each other. A South Ossetian participant reported that the press statement the groups decided on at the end of the workshop reflected simply that the groups had met and talked and thanked the sponsors.

After the workshop, the NRC maintained a local presence in Tbilisi and Tskhinvali, and then CMG came to do another assessment of appropriate next steps. The leadership on both sides remained supportive of the idea of continuing with a second workshop, and of introducing consideration of the very sensitive issue of the status of South Ossetia. This led to another one-week Oslo meeting in May 1996, with a few additional participants (more official negotiators) and consideration of the status question included on the agenda. It resulted, according to one participant, in a variety of interesting ideas relating to the status question. One participant reported that at this stage CMG was an informal substitute for the formal process, which was not working.

Additional CMG activity was delayed due to regional political changes such as elections and the restructuring of the South Ossetian government, but in June 1997 CMG held another one-week workshop in Massachusetts. Again, a few new participants joined the workshop. Participants in this workshop were all involved in some way in the official conflict management process as negotiators. The participants ranged from ministers (of industry, security, and refugees and migration) to presidential representatives and parliamentarians.

After three meetings that had built relationships and taught constructive negotiation processes, CMG and the NRC determined that negotiators on both sides of the conflict were ready to examine some of the substantive issues of the conflict more directly in an informal and unofficial way. CMG and the NRC provided that opportunity with a July 1998 meeting in Barcelona, Spain. The focus of this meeting was on learning from the experiences of autonomy relations between the center and periphery in Spain. Speakers presented on the aspirations of the Basques and the formation of the Catalonian Constitution. While some joint brainstorming was facilitated, and informal time for relationship building remained, these previously central goals were overshadowed by the focus on joint learning. The Barcelona meeting came at a time of political uncertainty in Russia, and geopolitical shifts indicated that the conflict would not be settled in the current context. But additional information about constitutional arrangements of autonomy could better inform the individuals who would negotiate similar issues in the future.

After the Barcelona meeting, CMG and the NRC discussed with participants the need for a Steering Committee. This group could hold meetings closer to home, facilitate more frequent meetings, and decrease the cost of international travel. The Steering Committee meetings ushered in a new phase of the CMG-NRC workshop series, in which the Steering Committee, made up of high-level officials involved in negotiations from both sides of the conflict, informally and unofficially shared perspectives on issues relevant to the official negotiations. CMG and the NRC attempted to transfer more of the leadership of the project to the new Steering Committee.

Outcomes: Transfer from Unofficial
Workshops to Official Policies

Participants in the CMG-NRC workshops discussed their experiences with enthusiasm for the positive impacts of the workshops, and many saw the workshops as an integral complement to the official process. Across the board, participants reported that these informal meetings allowed a real exchange of views. Participants said that the workshops helped them clarify the approaches of both sides to the conflict, which helped them know how to avoid particularly problematic or sensitive questions on the official level. The meetings gave participants time to relax together and even to play pool in the evenings. Participation in personal capacities allowed expression of new ideas, and dialogue without Russians present was also significant to some participants. In addition, many found Roger Fisher's lectures on his methodology very helpful. Several related the importance of understanding the interests on which negotiating positions are based; this understanding helped participants shape more effective policies. Others discussed the importance of using a structured process to examine issues, their causes, various possible approaches, and constructive strategies.

Each participant interviewed described his/her own profound realization connected with the workshops. One South Ossetian related an epiphany during the first CMG workshop. He was asked what it was he wanted from the conflict resolution process; through answering the question, he realized in a way that he hadn't before, that the Georgians also genuinely wanted to get something out of the conflict resolution process. This deep realization allowed him to really listen to Georgian perspectives for the first time since the war began. His new understanding of Georgian perspectives made his influence on relevant South Ossetian policies more informed and effective. Another participant related her initial discomfort at meeting the other side for the first time since the war, and her enjoyment of an introductory activity the first evening. The groups were divided into pairs, each comprising one South Ossetian and one Georgian; the two members of each pair got to know each other, then introduced each other to the group. They learned who had children, who liked chocolate, and other such humanizing details. As a result in part of this sort of personal connection, many participants have remained in contact across the conflict lines even outside of the official negotiations.

In addition to this personal and informal factor, the substantive brainstorming was an important aspect of the workshops for many participants. One participant described the growth of "living ties" and understanding. Another noted that the absence of formal suits and a formal table allowed both mutual trust and a deeper understanding to develop. Still other participants were impressed by the sheer number of concrete ideas generated by the sessions (many of which have found their way into official policy and agreements) and the depth of understanding participants gained for other perspectives.

CMG workshop participants attribute many positive conflict resolution effects to their workshop experiences. These range from intangible changes in the atmosphere of the negotiations to specific documents and projects that were initially developed during workshops and later adopted as official policy in the official negotiations. Considering the range of these results, the CMG-NRC workshop series and some of Caucasus Links/Vertic's work can be said to have had three basic effects that transferred to the official negotiations:

1. improved *relationships* between official negotiators for each side;
2. improved negotiation *processes*; and
3. *concrete ideas* for effective peacebuilding policies.

1. Transfer of Improved Relationships

Interviewees placed a very strong emphasis on the importance of the relationships built between highly placed official negotiators on both sides of the conflict as a result of the workshops, and the meals and informal interactions that surrounded the workshops. Participants in the CMG-NRC workshop series emphasized the rehumanization of individuals on the other side of the conflict that they experienced through participating in workshop exercises and informal discussions in environments such as late night pool games. Participants were convinced that improved relationships, which brought with them the ability to talk informally on breaks from intense official negotiating sessions and to call each other by phone for personal consultation when hot issues erupted, significantly improved the official negotiations.

Time and again, participants spoke of the informality of the CMG-NRC workshops and the effect this had on the official process. They saw the personal connections and trust developed at CMG workshops affecting the official meetings of the Joint Control Commission. Official mediators noted these shifts in relationships and rapport, and also attributed the improved tone of official negotiations to the relationship-building nature of the unofficial workshops.

2. Transfer of Improved Processes

In addition to improved relationships, the unofficial interventions transferred improved negotiations processes to the official negotiations in the form of direct communication and new processes for examining difficult issues. Negotiators and official mediators alike reported that the CMG-NRC workshops contributed to an improved tone in many official meetings.

In addition, the unofficial interventions led to more direct communication between official representatives of each side. The CMG workshop in Norway was the first unofficial long-term meeting of such highly placed officials from each side since the war. Participants in the Norway workshop and subsequent workshops reported that they call each other, and even visit each other, as a result of the communication opened up by the unofficial interventions. Official mediators reported that this direct contact improved the process of official negotiations, because the official negotiators were able to address some questions directly before issues grew into larger problems.

Participants in the CMG-NRC workshops also reported improved processes for the discussion of difficult issues that were presented in the Norway and Norwood meetings. Two participants (one from each side of the conflict) described in detail the way they gained an understanding of the other side's crucial issues, their causes, possible approaches, and the range of constructive strategies available. These two participants, at least, found this methodology helpful in allowing more productive policies. An official mediator observed the shift in conversation to a tone that allowed for the possibility on some issues, such as economic reconstruction, there might be win-win outcomes in which policies could be made which would benefit both sides.

3. Transfer of Concrete Ideas

The CMG-NRC workshop series also made some very direct inputs into the negotiations process through concrete policy ideas for steps forward or projects that would support the official negotiations.

Substantive ideas were generated during the exercises conducted at the workshops. Many of these were then adopted as official policy and approved in the official negotiations process, although some took months or even a year to be adopted through the official process. Three of the five participants interviewed mentioned economic development progress as related to specific economic development projects discussed in the Oslo meetings. The 16 May 1996 Memorandum, mentioned above, was discussed at the first Oslo meeting. The 4-5 March 1997 Moscow document on economic development in South Ossetia was also developed in part at a Norway meeting.

In at least one clear case, ideas from the workshops worked preventively to counteract emerging tensions in the official negotiation process. In the summer of 1997, tensions were mounting over issues of refugee return. If many refugees had rushed across the border that summer, there would have been practical difficulties in hosting them. One task in the June 1997 Boston workshop was to produce a draft common statement on reasons for the conflict and the conflict's consequences. By the end of the exercise, at least one participant was convinced that an official public statement incorporating most of the language of the draft statement would help improve the climate and prospects of the official negotiations. In July 1997, a Georgian participant went to a UNHCR-CIS[10] conference that provided an opportunity for an official public policy statement on Georgian attitudes toward Ossetians. The participant made a statement based on the draft from Boston, and later even joked with his South Ossetian colleagues that he had plagiarized their common work in Boston. The UNHCR, International Organization on Migration (IOM), and the OSCE's Office for Democratic Institutions and Human Rights (ODIHR) organized conferences that gave exposure to the statement, and the NRC distributed the statement widely at the local level in South Ossetia. The statement was thus noticed by many people involved in the official negotiation process, and was appreciated by the South Ossetian leadership as a Georgian policy statement. The well-worded statement played an important role, as it averted a possible new increase of tension and allowed common efforts to encourage controlled refugee return.

Participants credited the substantive contributions of the unofficial process to the official negotiations to the structure of the CMG-NRC workshops. The workshops allowed exploratory analysis in an unofficial environment. Participation in personal capacities meant that no one would be seen to be making commitments in their official capacity. New ideas could be presented without any worry of commitments being inferred when, in fact, ideas were simply being explored. Thus, new ideas could be tested much more openly than in the official negotiation process. Brainstorming sessions let participants see a range of possibilities, some of which were new ideas that had not been considered in the official process. The joint problem-solving assignments (such as that of Georgians and South Ossetians working together on a joint statement that might be made by their leadership) led to improved understanding of each other's perspectives and developed products useful to the official negotiations (such as the official Georgian policy statement that "plagiarized" the common work in Norwood). Official mediators confirmed that new ideas had emerged after the CMG-NRC workshops, and also credited the unofficial processes with contributing to the official process through improved policies.

Challenges

There were three main challenges that CMG and the NRC faced in implementing the workshop series to improve peacebuilding policies and negotiation. These challenges centered on maintaining the partnership, obtaining funding, and incorporating new participants into the workshop series as the leadership in the conflict zone shifted.

Partnership

CMG and the NRC are very different organizations, and brought very different strengths to the partnership. As detailed above, CMG brought a process expertise, and the NRC brought a local presence. Both of these strengths were essential to the workshops' impacts on policy, as the effective processes brought by CMG could only be properly implemented with the strong local knowledge and presence offered by the NRC. In addition to these strengths, each organization also brought its own organizational culture, ways of decision making, time frames for planning initiatives, and so on. The partnership took some work to maintain. Extra time was spent on people from one organization briefing people from the other, reporting back and forth, and developing future plans together. While the strengths of the partnership were worth the investment in building the working relationship, that investment should not be underestimated by others contemplating similar partnerships. Such arrangements require face-to-face time, phone calls, e-mails, and an awareness of the needs of a healthy partnership.

Funding

The CMG-NRC workshop series initially received funding for its early workshops from the Norwegian government. However, when that source was no longer able to sponsor the bulk of the workshop costs, funding became more difficult to obtain. After several short-term grants, the project concluded due to a lack of funding. While the project did make a significant impact on peacebuilding policy in the conflict zone, it might have made even more impact had it been able to continue. The funding of *long-term* conflict resolution initiatives is a challenge that the conflict resolution field needs to overcome together.

Incorporating New Participants

Another challenge for this long-term initiative was that of how to respond to changes in leadership in the conflict zone and how to reach a wider audience of influentials on each side of the conflict. Should new negotiators or others who have influence on peacebuilding policy be invited to join the group, and if so, how? CMG and the NRC elected to build the workshop series on a core of participants from the first workshop. This core came to the second workshop and set a productive tone for it. Then, a core from the second workshop came to set a productive tone for the next one. While each workshop added some new faces to the group, each workshop also kept some of the same people from previous workshops. This allowed both an important development in the tone and depth of conversation from one workshop to the next, and also an incorporation of new participants as needed. In most long-term policy-focused work, individual policymakers will change over time, and new policymakers must be embraced without restarting the whole process from the beginning. For the workshop series, a set of core participants from previous workshops helped incorporate new participants effectively. In addition, meetings with the presidents on each side helped ensure that the CMG-NRC team was working with influential and trusted policymakers and that there would be no backlash against individuals involved in the workshops or the policy options explored therein. While working with individual participants, the workshop series created a structure and movement for policy change that was larger than the individuals involved.

Conclusion

The unofficial contributions to the Georgia-South Ossetia peace process brought improvements in the relationships, process, and substance of the official negotiations. These were largely introduced by the high-level Track One and a Half CMG-NRC workshops. These workshops involved people officially engaged in the negotiations process or setting relevant policies, and thus had a direct mode of transfer to the official negotiations. The official negotiators and policymakers were themselves the direct carriers of new relationships, processes, and substantive ideas to the official policy and negotiation process after their participation in unofficial workshops and meetings. Participants noted the cumulative effects over time of the CMG-NRC workshop series, citing relationships that grew stronger over time, dialogue processes that participants became more and more comfortable with, and substantive ideas that were developed over a series of meetings. Many interviewees referred to a cumulative effect of multiple unofficial interventions all contributing as a whole to the peace process, but these transfer effects were indirect and difficult to trace.

The successes achieved by and the challenges faced in this work can be summarized as a series of lessons learned:

- *Policies are developed in long-term processes.* One key to the success of the CMG-NRC workshop series is that it took place over several years and built relationships, insights, and process skills slowly over a period of time. The peacebuilding policies in Georgia and South Ossetia were shaped through long-term involvement.
- *Skills building and exchange of views impacts policy.* The workshop series led to improved peacebuilding policies in South Ossetia and Georgia by focusing on skills building and exchange of views, in addition to considering concrete policy options. Policymakers reported using new skills (such as frameworks for analysis of options) and improved understanding of each other's views in drafting revised policies. This impact on policy development may have been as important as the concrete substantive policies explored at the workshops.
- *Unofficial approaches with officials allow direct impact.* The workshops had a very direct impact on peacebuilding policy by involving those individuals who shape the policies on both side of the conflict as direct participants in the workshops. While many conflict resolution initiatives hope for

indirect transfer to the policy process, this workshop series had a direct connection to the policy process.

- *Partnerships can bring needed strengths.* Neither CMG nor the NRC could have accomplished this particular set of workshops, nor this direct impact on policy, without the assistance of a partner that brought the strengths necessary for this undertaking: local presence in the case of the NRC and process expertise in the case of CMG. In addition, each organization brought a particular legitimacy that strengthened the role the partnership could play.
- *Long-term funding is important.* Despite the successes of the project, interviewees were unanimous in the view that more could be accomplished by a continuation of the series. Unfortunately, such long-term funding has not been available.

Note on Methodology

Although some limited information is available in public news sources, the bulk of the information for this case study was gathered through interviews with participants in the many unofficial and official conflict resolution initiatives addressing the conflict over South Ossetia. These informants were asked about their experience of the effects of conflict resolution efforts, the complementarity of multiple efforts, and suggestions for improving the peace process. In 1998 and 1999, I conducted twenty-seven interviews; the initial results have been reported elsewhere, where this case study was one of three in a larger focused comparison study.[11]

This case study of policy impact by unofficial intervention was possible only because key individuals shared their experiences and insights with me in 1998 and 1999. Highly placed official negotiators on both sides of the conflict agreed to give interviews about their experiences in the unofficial and official parts of the Georgia-South Ossetia peace process, as did official and unofficial mediators. The official policymakers and negotiators interviewed gave self-reports of the transfer that they personally experienced in working both in unofficial workshops and the official policy and negotiation process. These self-reports were triangulated with the observations of official and unofficial mediators working on the peace process. Thus, individuals themselves reported what they had experienced, and mediators reported what changes they had observed in the same individuals.

Additional interviews were conducted in 2000, some with the same individuals, to update the study and prepare a case study for the Reflecting on Peace Practices Project.[12] That case study remains confidential, as do the results of those interviews, but no information in those recent interviews contradicted previous findings. Frequently, confidentiality concerns severely constrain the possibilities for research into sensitive and ongoing peace processes; in this case, however, confidentiality concerns simply dictate that no additional details gleaned in the more recent interviews are incorporated into this case study.

Notes

I would like to thank Lara Olson, the NRC's former project coordinator for the CMG-NRC conflict resolution workshop series, and currently project director for the Reflecting on Peace Practices Project for the Collaborative for Development Action. Lara not only provided detailed interviews for my research while she lived in Tbilisi and Tskhinvali, but also engaged in very helpful exchanges about the case over several years since then. In addition, I wish to thank Arthur Martirosyan of Conflict Management Group, who also participated in many interviews with me over several years, as well as all the people who gave so generously of their time and insight as I conducted this research, but to whom I promised anonymity.

1. For more information on these organizations, see their websites at www.cmgroup.org and www.nrc.no/engindex.htm.
2. Susan Allen Nan. 2002. "Complementarity and Coordination of Conflict Resolution Efforts in the Conflicts Over Abkhazia, South Ossetia, and Transdniestria" (Doctoral dissertation, George Mason University, Fairfax, VA, 1999).
3. Vladimir Mukomel, "Voruzhonie Mezhnatsional'nie I regional'nie konflikti: ludskie poteri, ekonomicheskii usherb, I sotsial'nie posledstviia," in *Identichnosts i Konflikt v Postsovietskih Gosudasrtvah.* (Moscow: Carnegie Endowment for International Peace, 1997). Mukomel lists eleven hundred dead in South Ossetia.
4. The Organization for Security and Cooperation in Europe promotes negotiations toward the peaceful settlement of conflicts in Georgia. For more information, see www.osce.org/georgia.
5. Nan, "Complementarity and Coordination."
6. Systematic documentation of the many initiatives that have been undertaken to address the Georgia-South Ossetia conflict can be found elsewhere (Nan, "Complementarity and Coordination"). This chapter focuses on the CMG-NRC initiative.
7. It should be noted that, in addition to the CMG-NRC workshop series, Caucasus Links also engaged in some Track One and a Half diplomacy. Caucasus Links picked up the work of its predecessor organization, the British-based NGO Vertic. Vertic and Caucasus Links focused largely on parliamentary-based aspects of the larger peace process, as well as the potential contributions of younger politicians. Vertic played a significant role in jump-starting stalling negotiations after a fall 1996 decline in the intensity of negotiations. Several interviewees recounted Vertic's bringing the Speaker of the South Ossetian Parliament to Tbilisi to meet with the Speaker of the Georgian Parliament in a surprise move that thawed relationships and broke a long postelection lull in negotiating activity.
8. While this chapter focuses on transfer of results from unofficial workshops to official policies, the CMG workshop series is more extensively documented in two confidential and unpublished case studies written for the Reflecting on Peace Practices Project (RPP), a joint project of the Collaborative for Development Action in Cambridge, Massachusetts, and the Life and Peace Institute in Uppsala, Sweden. It is possible that RPP will get clearance to release these case studies in the future. Susan Allen Nan, "Partnering for Peace: Conflict Management Group and the Norwegian Refugee Council Collaborating on the Georgian-South Ossetian Dialogue Project" (October 2000). Lara Olson, "The Georgia–South Ossetia Dialogue Project: A View from the Inside" (March 2001). Because of confidentiality promised to interviewees for these RPP case studies, no information exclusive to the case studies appears in this chapter.

9. Roger Fisher is Professor Emeritus at Harvard Law School and cofounder of CMG. He coauthored, with William Ury, the best-selling win-win negotiation book, *Getting to Yes* (Boston, MA: Houghton Mifflin, 1981).

10. United Nations High Commissioner for Refugees, Commonwealth of Independent States.

11. Nan, "Complementarity and Coordination." Please note that I also conducted a second series of twenty-four interviews in 2000 for the Reflecting on Peace Practices Project, which focused more on the recent developments and the partnership between CMG and the NRC. The results of this second series of interviews remain confidential due to agreements with interviewees, and are not in any way incorporated into this case study. The results of the second series of interviews do not contradict any of the general conclusions reported here.

12. Nan, "Partnering for Peace."

throughout Northern Ireland who began to object to Orange Order parades passing through their area, demanding that these parades be rerouted. Parading was catapulted into the political spotlight, becoming increasingly divisive and passionately contested.

Such parading is particularly problematic in interface areas, such as North Belfast, which has a history of sectarian violence and mutual distrust. The intermingled demography of the area, where Catholics and Protestants live in adjacent streets, with attendant hostility and unrest, means that in times of political tension, mutual suspicion and distrust can rapidly turn political disagreement into civil violence. Within the one square mile of North Belfast, six hundred people have been killed during the conflict, and the resultant feelings of fear and hatred between the communities make it a particularly volatile neighborhood (Fay et al., 1997). North Belfast is an area of acute socioeconomic deprivation. A 1994 University of Ulster study found that the population in this area had "over twice the Northern Ireland average level of unemployment, while [households in the area] received twice the average level of both Income Support and Family Credit. Sixty-nine percent earned less than £5,000 per annum compared with a Northern Irish average of forty-five percent. . . [This area] also suffered from considerably lower levels of educational attainment and poorer standards of health" (Brendan Murtaugh, in Jarman and O'Halloran, 2000: 10).

This volatility came to a head between June and September of 1996, when civil disturbances occurred sporadically in North Belfast. Trouble initially flared when the Tour of the North parade was forced through a Catholic neighborhood on 22 June. However, it was a parade on 7 July at Portadown,[5] a small town about thirty miles from Belfast, which initially sparked off the worst of the violence in North Belfast. In Portadown, at the Drumcree church, the Security Forces and the Orange Order became locked in a four-day standoff over the decision by the authorities to refuse to allow the order to undertake its traditional parade through what was now a Catholic area. This decision was hugely symbolic for many Protestants throughout the country, who subsequently engaged in sympathetic demonstrations and roadblocks in support of the order. For the Protestants in North Belfast, the protests were particularly meaningful. Roadblocks presented an opportunity to express their growing resentments and frustrations. They feared that their culture and position, which had been secure when they felt themselves to be a confident majority within Northern Ireland, was under threat, and these sentiments were compounded with growing unease at the increasing numbers of Catholic families being moved into "Protestant" neighborhoods. They also perceived that their community was incrementally being marginalized and excluded from the decision-making process. However, many Catholics in the area felt that the presence of large groups of Protestant roadblockers was intentionally belligerent and intimidatory. Intercommunal relationships in these flashpoint interfaces, which are fragile at best, descended to new levels of distrust and suspicion. Neighbors began hurling verbal abuse at each other, and the situation descended into violent disorder on 8 July. Cars were hijacked and set alight, businesses and schools were burned, and families were threatened. Many homes were visited by masked men claiming to be from either loyalist or republican paramilitary groups, and families were told they had to leave their homes. People had to move out quickly, in some cases taking only what belongings they could carry, and individuals who refused to leave were physically assaulted. One hundred and ten families were forced to leave their homes as a result of sectarian intimidation in the short space of a few weeks.[6] The ideal of advancing residential integration, which had been a hoped-for objective of the developing peace process, suffered a serious setback, as the expulsions were intended to define religious and political "territories" and boundaries for each community.

The consequences of this spontaneous explosion of street disturbances and sectarian intimidation took the state authorities and governmental statutory agencies by surprise. Not since the height of the Troubles in 1971-1975 had such a displacement of the population occurred. Under normal circumstances, the Housing Executive[7] is responsible for rehousing families who wish to relocate because of sectarian harassment or intimidation, but in this instance the organization was overwhelmed by the size of the problem it encountered. Since the vast majority of displaced families were dependent on state welfare, statutory agencies such as the Housing Executive, Health and Social Services, and the Social Security Agency (SSA) were faced with difficult and overlapping problems. Families had to be immediately rehoused in temporary accommodation. Storage facilities were required for their belongings, and this was combined with administrative alterations to welfare entitlements. Such activities require funding and coordination, but the statutory agencies were lacking in both. This disorganized approach by the statutory agencies was recognized by the Community Development Centre (CDC), a local cross-community Belfast-based NGO. From the outset, the CDC realized that the communities needed to be involved with the policymakers in order not only to address the symptoms of the problem—that is, displaced and distressed families—but also to resolve the deep-rooted causes, such as a lack of dialogue and understanding between the communities, coupled with feelings of uncertainty and exclusion in the changing political arena.

Based upon this clear need for conflict resolution mechanisms to redress the grievances of the displaced and traumatized families of North Belfast, this case study presents an analysis of a community-based NGO effectively intervening in the public policy sphere of Northern Ireland. It examines how the CDC became a popular, credible advocate for the displaced families of North Belfast, and how the organization implemented a strategy of bridging the gap between governmental statutory agencies and the community through the establishment of the Interagency Working Group for Displaced Families (IAWGDF). This chapter will evaluate and assess the tactics utilized by the CDC as it attempted to overcome obstacles and challenges, and will conclude with "lessons learned" from the experiences of the CDC as it impacted policy development and implementation in Belfast.

The Community Development Centre

The Community Development Centre was established in 1974 as an umbrella organization comprising a network of grassroots bodies that were located in twelve municipal wards of Belfast. Comprising a staff of twenty, the CDC is a nonpolitical and explicitly antisectarian organization. It operates in areas of socioeconomic deprivation and is committed to "promoting, supporting and developing a range of community responses to tackle social and economic disadvantage" (Jarman, 1997: 5). It is involved in coordinating local community projects dealing with a wide range of problems, including alcohol abuse, street crime, welfare dependency, high unemployment, low job skills and literacy rates, poverty, and the persistence of long-term illness. The CDC also runs outreach centers in areas where there is little local community development activity. As part of its mission, the CDC is dedicated to "actively pursuing an antisectarian policy and . . . providing opportunities for increased dialogue and communication across the community" (Jarman, 1997: 5). This policy is illustrated by the CDC's commitment to facilitating joint projects with groups from both traditions in order to improve understanding, tolerance, and respect. One such project was the North Belfast Interface Project,[8] created in the early 1990s, which dealt with issues relating to residential segregation and a lack of resources for young people. It organized a series of "single identity"[9] workshops to promote self-confidence, awareness, and security; these were linked to cross-community workshops to cultivate communication and understanding of the "other." Years of pursuing an intercommunal approach to the running of socioeconomic community projects involving delicate collaboration and coordination with a diverse range of groups from across the political spectrum, has given credibility to the CDC as an impartial organization. This reputation for transparency and perceived neutrality of the organization by both communities in Northern Ireland should not be underestimated. The CDC's experience in fostering dialogue, coordinating local community groups, and articulating the human needs of the underprivileged in North Belfast placed it in an ideal position to take proactive steps toward impacting policy in the aftermath of the 1996 disturbances.

During the 1996 crisis, CDC staff took immediate action in the areas worst hit by the violence. They provided assistance to families who had been intimidated out of their homes by finding immediate temporary shelter for them (often in the CDC offices) and trying to organize storage space for belongings. They liaised with government statutory agencies on behalf of the traumatized families. Although this work was conducted in an ad hoc fashion, it demonstrated the CDC's ability to react quickly to fill the void left by overstretched and poorly coordinated statutory agencies. Previous crisis circumstances had led the CDC to develop working relationships with officials from a number of statutory agencies. The 1996 crisis dramatically raised the CDC's public profile, as it established the organization as a credible advocate for the displaced families. It sparked the beginning of a working relationship with the statutory agencies of Belfast on the ground level (local welfare offices, local housing offices, and the social service agencies, for example). The CDC thus became the de facto link between local communities and government statutory agencies.

Policy Issue and Stakeholders

The CDC assumed a crisis management role during, and in the immediate aftermath of the disturbances. This included arrangements surrounding homelessness assessment, emergency payments, furniture removal and storage, temporary rehousing, child care arrangements, and other support services. The Northern Ireland political establishment was deficient in its policies and procedures for effectively dealing with interface violence and the displacements it caused. Thus the CDC entered the policy arena to assist statutory agencies in reconstructing procedures and policies to address the needs of such large numbers of displaced families.

These displaced families were reportedly frustrated and dismayed at the inconsistent and at times sluggish response of the statutory agencies to their plight. CDC activists documented their concerns. Some of the key complaints were in regard to the absence of an efficient communication structure through which information about statutory agency services could be relayed to the community. A social security system ill-equipped to deal with additional claims; the Housing Executive's inability to safely secure families' belongings; the provision of temporary accommodation in hotels and guest houses located in areas not serviced by public transportation; inadequate availability of housing stock to rehouse families in the communities of their choice where they would feel safe; and a lack of community-based counseling support. As the crisis faded from the media spotlight, CDC representatives reported that many families felt abandoned and that their needs, fears, and problems had been quickly forgotten by the public and government. Faced with, on the one hand, traumatized and disillusioned victims of intimidation, and on the other, statutory agencies whose response to the crisis was less than coordinated, the initial objective of the CDC's policy engagement was to institute improved crisis management procedures amongst the statutory agencies of North Belfast. These objectives expanded, however, as the CDC realized that a policy vacuum existed and the organization needed to take the initiative in moving the multitude of groups involved in this political issue not only toward an effective resolution of the summer 1996 crisis but also toward measures that would prevent such violence from recurring in the future.

The CDC quickly realized that there were three key groups with a stake in the permanent resolution of the crisis: members of the local communities; the statutory agencies whose job it was to provide services to the community; and the Northern Ireland political leaders, who needed to display a concerned response to the events. The displaced families required immediate assistance in terms of temporary accommodation, replacement housing, and financial support. The statutory agencies, specifically the North and West Belfast Health and Social Services Trust (NWHSST), the Northern Ireland Housing Executive (NIHE), the Social Security Agency, and the Royal Ulster Constabulary (RUC), came under heavy criticism for not providing an adequate and timely response to the needs of the community during the crisis. And, under the spotlight of a highly sensationalized world media event, Northern Ireland's political leaders were also under pressure to be seen to be taking appropriate action to redress the situation. The CDC therefore began to develop a strategic plan which would involve all of the above groups in addressing the problem.

Strategic Response

The CDC adopted a strategy with the overarching objective of coordinating a collaborative partnership between governmental statutory agencies and community representatives. A major component of this strategy was to enact "bottom-up"[10] tactics. This would be combined with innovative "top-down" initiatives to apply pressure at the elite governmental level to overcome political blockages. The tactics employed by the CDC to implement its strategy involved:

- convening a meeting between representatives from the local communities, statutory agencies, Northern Ireland government officials, and the police, to discuss the existing organizational structures for handling the consequences of interface violence;
- launching an inquiry into the events of 1996, which took into account the perspectives of both the Protestant and Catholic communities in the North Belfast interface area;
- documenting and publicizing the findings of this inquiry;
- identifying and developing a mechanism—that is, the IAWGDF—through which the needs of the community could be met by the statutory agencies;
- formulating workable options and procedures for the implementation of joint community and statutory agency initiatives following the setting up of the IAWGDF; and
- utilizing key political contacts for the CDC to influence policy change at the elite political level.

The points above outline the framework of how the CDC approached the issue of displaced families, but the detail of how these tactics were carried out to gain influence in the state's operations is where the real lessons can be drawn.

The first order of business was to identify the current practices employed by the statutory agencies responsible for dealing with the displacement of families as a result of sectarian intimidation. Was there any existing overarching coordinating body to cope with displacement on such a massive scale? What were the gaps in public policy that needed to be filled? The CDC wanted to play an active role in addressing this policy vacuum. With this purpose in mind, the director of the CDC[11] approached a senior civil servant within the NWHSST with whom she had an established relationship. It was decided that a meeting would be called between representatives of the CDC and representatives of the relevant statutory bodies, including the NWHSST, NIHE, SSA, and RUC. During this meeting, the question of overall coordination of emergency response was the main topic of discussion. It became apparent that it had been mistakenly assumed by the government and statutory agencies that the Belfast Action Teams (BAT),[12] which had been established by the government in 1987 to combat poverty and civil tension, had responsibility for coordinating services in an emergency. This mistake had come about because of a restructuring in 1994 that had resulted in a merging of the BAT programs into a new urban regeneration initiative. During the course of this restructuring, the emergency response resources of the BAT had been lost and not replaced elsewhere. To overcome this shortfall, it was recognized that a new mechanism needed to be established which would assume responsibility for overall emergency coordination during periods of civil unrest and population displacement.

The CDC recognized that this gap in the organizational structure was ultimately the responsibility of the Northern Ireland Office (NIO).[13] They therefore adopted a twofold strategy. Their first step was to identify an influential individual in the NIO who was sympathetic to the CDC mission and who would be willing to provide assistance in achieving the CDC's strategic objectives. This individual was identified with the help of a leading academic in the field who had experience in researching the organizational structure of the governance of Northern Ireland. The individual identified had a personal interest in the plight of displaced families and an intimate knowledge of the inner workings of the NIO. She provided the CDC with important information about governmental structure and perceptions of the CDC, and helped the CDC to gauge reaction to its efforts to push the issue of displaced families up the government agenda.

The next step of the strategy was to exert external pressure on the NIO using lobbying tactics and a media campaign. The CDC recognized that Northern Ireland political parties are the most effective medium for lobbying and pressuring the British government to action. The CDC therefore contacted the leaders of all the political parties in Northern Ireland and requested that they dispatch a fax to the NIO demanding coordinated policy initiatives for dealing with the issue of displaced families. The CDC prepared a suggested text so that the message to the NIO would be consistent. In combination with this, the CDC informed the leading Northern Irish political parties that they had prepared press statements to direct the media spotlight onto the plight of displaced families. This proved to be an invaluable incentive to the political parties because they realized that they had an opportunity to assume a leadership position on the crisis before an embarrassing pubic outcry erupted. It had the desired effect, as all but one of the political leaders faxed the NIO as requested. Subsequently, the press statement about the crisis was delayed until the politicians could claim that they were engaged in positive community action.

Alongside this political maneuvering, the CDC sought to enhance their credibility as advocates for the North Belfast communities by commissioning an independent inquiry into the events of the summer of 1996. Four panelists, predominantly from academic backgrounds, were asked to interview a range of families, individuals, political leaders, church leaders, and community activists about the disturbances and their aftermath. The inquiry had the following objectives:

- to provide people with an opportunity to give their version of events so that these could be shared with others;
- to identify ways in which the community sector felt that dialogue within the area, and between the communities, could be improved;
- to consider the appropriateness of the responses to the crisis among statutory bodies and other key players; and
- to make recommendations for future actions by the statutory sector and other key sectors in order to minimize hardship during periods of civil unrest (Jarman, 1997).

The output of this inquiry was a publication entitled *On the Edge: Community Perspectives on the Civil Disturbances in North Belfast, June-September 1996*. It took approximately a year to produce, during which time the CDC applied pressure via the use of lobbying devices on the statutory agencies, campaigning for the inclusion of community representatives in their decision-making processes on issues related to displaced families. The inquiry kept the issue of displaced families on the public agenda, enabling the media to report on a progressing story and inhibiting the statutory agencies from ignoring or simply archiving the repercussions of the crisis under a mountain of internal memos and reports.

On the Edge was officially launched at a public forum in May 1997. Representatives of the statutory agencies were invited to the event as panelists to field questions concerning their role during the crisis. Simultaneously, the CDC distributed five hundred copies of *On the Edge* to politicians and senior civil servants responsible for the issues relating to displaced families, and key individuals with relevant responsibilities were invited to privately discuss the findings of the report. *On the Edge* illustrated the hardship experienced by the communities during the summer of 1996 and alluded to difficulties experienced by the statutory agencies in dealing with the crisis. The publication, however, was not designed to criticize the statutory agencies, and the CDC did not seek to publicly humiliate or alienate the statutory agencies, who were a vital component of future policy improvements. For this reason it had been decided that the report would be written in two parts, allegedly "due to the complexity of some of the issues raised" (Jarman, 1997: 8), and that part II, which concentrated on the response of statutory agencies and other key actors in the crisis, would not be published until 1999. In pursuing this tactic, the CDC enhanced its stature and reputation as a competent community advocate. It sent a firm message to the statutory agencies and the government that it would not allow the issue to disappear off the public agenda, and by delaying the publication of part II, it created a "breathing space" for collaborative action to be taken.

During this period, internal meetings were ongoing amongst the statutory agencies concerning the issue of displaced families, but these meetings lacked community representation. The CDC believed that it needed to be included in these internal discussions if they were to have any impact on the future policy.

In light of the strategic pressure tactics and public success of *On the Edge*, the CDC was able to negotiate for its inclusion in planning meetings. As a result of this interaction between the statutory agencies and the CDC, part II of the inquiry report, entitled *Drawing Back from the Edge,* released in 1999, was not as critical of the statutory agencies as had previously been intimated in 1997.

Policy Outcomes: The Interagency Working Group for Displaced Families

The displaced families from 1996 were handled in an ad hoc fashion over several months, leaving many families feeling disgruntled and abandoned by the statutory agencies. They were vulnerable not only to the spontaneous explosion of sectarian intimidation in the interface area but also to the policy vacuum created as a result of the unpreparedness for civil violence displayed by the government, statutory agencies, and security forces. The CDC wanted to assist in formulating policy initiatives which would address the situation and the needs of people in the interface areas and develop contingency plans to cope with the potential consequences of future violence. Following the publication of *On the Edge*, the IAWGDF was established as the mechanism through which the community's voice could be heard on issues of displaced families. It consisted of statutory agency, governmental, and community representatives. One of the main objectives of the IAWGDF was to debate the key recommendations of *On the Edge* and translate these lessons into a basis for policy change.

The IAWGDF subsequently produced a document, entitled *Operational Procedures for Displaced Families*, which defined the roles and responsibilities of statutory agencies in assisting displaced families in the event of civil disturbance. The report envisaged the establishment of a central coordinating body, to include community representatives. It outlined clear operational procedures for dealing with the provision of temporary rehousing, furniture removal/storage, child care arrangements, and homelessness assessment, all of which were identified by the CDC as key issues from its community inquiry. In addition, the document specified a framework for exchanges of information, informal contacts, and augmenting community liaisons. *Operational Procedures for Displaced Families* was intended as a "living document" to be developed and updated jointly between the statutory agencies and community representatives.

However, some policy implementation issues were beyond the power of even the most senior civil servants. One such issue, for example, concerned the need for the provision of financial assistance to displaced families living in temporary accommodation, who were incurring high financial costs as a result of their predicament. Under the legislation existing in 1996 and 1997, this financial assistance could only be provided to the families in the form of loans, yet many displaced families were on welfare support and were therefore unable to cope with the financial effects of such loans. The civil service recognized the inappropriateness of the situation, but they could not alter the legislation to remedy the problem. Faced with this dilemma, the civil service availed itself of assistance provided by the CDC to exert political pressure on the NIO. The director of the CDC had an existing working relationship with the Secretary of State's wife[14] which she used as leverage to gain direct access to Westminster.[15] Given the high-profile nature of the relatively recent events of 1996, the CDC was able to make a direct representation to the Secretary of State on this issue. The legislation was subsequently reinterpreted to allow for extra emergency payments instead of loans. As a result of this change, the statutory agencies were able to enact policies to operationalize the distribution of payments to displaced families through the Social Security Agency. This was a policy which had been advocated in *Operational Procedures for Displaced Families*.

The CDC achieved this policy outcome via collaboration with the statutory agencies, assisting these agencies by learning about and understanding their problems, and using this knowledge to generate a solution by influencing its elite political contacts. This dual strategic approach was more effective than simply pressurizing the statutory agencies or the government without any realization of the impediments each actor confronts in attempting change. Knowledge of the policy process and an understanding of relationship dynamics are crucial for an NGO to effect legislative change. The CDC realized that it had to become politically astute in devising strategies that would keep the issue on the public agenda and utilizing the media spotlight to persuade local politicians to publicly support its cause.

From 1997 to 1999, the IAWGDF was the mechanism for the coordination of policy and procedures in addressing intercommunal violence in the North Belfast interface. The summers of 1997 and 1998 saw a significant reduction in the violence accompanying the issue of contentious parades. This was attributed by many to the major community initiatives that were implemented by the IAWGDF. There were many issues that required action. There was a need to manage the "rumor mill" which contributed to a heightening of tension and suspicion between Protestants and Catholics, leading to an escalation of violence. More cooperative working relationships were also required on the ground between community activists and the security forces to assist in calming interface areas and alerting each other of potentially explosive incidents. The solution to both these problems, spearheaded by the CDC, was the creation of a "mobile phone network." This was a system whereby Protestant and Catholic community leaders maintained constant channels of communication with each other and with key representatives of statutory agencies during the 1997 and 1998 summer crises. The ability of the CDC to operationalize and secure funding for the mobile phone network was a result of its participation in the IAWGDF. The necessary coordinating aspects of the network, such as out-of-hours contact phone numbers for statutory agency representatives, were documented in *Operational Procedures for Displaced Families*. This initiative was important in helping community activists dispel potentially volatile rumors before they snowballed into violently destabilizing events. The network helped the cooperative relationship between the CDC and the statutory agencies as they worked successfully together for the common good. Such a community-government partnership was welcomed by the statutory representatives, and its workings were incorporated into their policy and operations.

The chairman of the IAWGDF (himself a civil servant and policymaker) recognized that the unusual circumstances of the 1996 displacements had unearthed "clear gaps in policy." He regarded the inclusion of community representatives into the working group as a positive experience[16] and claimed there was significant improvement in the relationship between community representatives and public bodies.

Political and Institutional Challenges to Impacting Policy

There were two overarching and interrelated challenges facing the CDC in its advocacy for displaced families. The first was a changing political landscape which heralded peace for Northern Ireland; the second was a diminishing will on the part of the statutory agencies to continue to effectively implement policies developed through the IAWGDF, given this new political context.

The signing of the Good Friday Agreement in 1998[17] meant that the issue of displaced families began to fall from the political agenda. A more peaceful climate in Northern Ireland presented its own challenges to community NGOs attempting to impact policy. Summer interface violence was decreasing, and while this was assisted by procedures implemented by the IAWGDF, it was also helped by the decreasing tension associated with the development of peace. One of those involved with the initiatives on displaced families commented that "the euphoria of the peace process may have led to some false sense of achievement . . . amongst community representatives who felt headway had been made in their coordination with statutory bodies."[18]

As the crisis atmosphere decreased after the relatively "successful"[19] summers of 1997 and 1998, the IAWGDF community representatives were becoming increasingly anxious at their growing perception that community organizations were the real drivers behind the continued operation of the working group. Meetings of the group became less frequent and the CDC felt that summer preparations increasingly consisted only of perfunctory working sessions with only half-hearted participation by the statutory agencies. In addition, there were disturbances happening in regions outside of Belfast during this period which were obviously in need of the policies and procedures developed in the Belfast working group, thus raising the need for coherent policy transfer. The statutory agencies in Belfast were, however, not effectively communicating developments and procedures with other regions in Northern Ireland. There was a definite sense amongst community representatives that the momentum and senior support from the government agencies for the IAWGDF was deteriorating.

Interviews conducted with policymakers and community representatives concerning the interactions between their sectors revealed frustrations on both sides. The differing perspectives and agendas highlighted some general challenges in incorporating civil society into government decision making, and the issues raised included topics of mandate/mission, time horizons, and a disagreement about the exact scope of the issues to be addressed as part of the discussions of the IAWGDF.

The mandates of the community relations sector and government agencies are often incongruent. Local community networks such as the CDC can focus specifically on single issues such as violently displaced families. However, government agencies are generally unable to operate on such narrow remits. Statutory agencies responsible for public health, social security, or housing may have overlapping responsibilities necessitating their input into the complex topic of interface violence. Thus an NGO is faced with the challenge of dealing with multiple agencies simultaneously.

This dilemma was highlighted in the minutes of the IAWGDF. After a presentation made by community representatives on interface communities and the peace process, the point was made that "the issues around interface communities do not fit neatly with core responsibilities of any one public agency, and therefore the complexities of interface violence do not get 'unravelled.'"[20] Hence the community representatives felt it was important that policy mechanisms such as the IAWGDF should analyze the factors which contribute to the violence; should debate and recommend procedures for mitigating the possibility for future violence; and should establish a framework for the definition of roles and responsibilities of various actors should the violence recur. This would enable effective coordination amongst statutory agencies and enable them to avail of the expertise and knowledge of the local community network.

However, differing time perspectives about the need for long- or short-term commitment to developing solutions hindered agreement between the community representatives and the government agencies on the above suggestions. While CDC representatives were speaking the language of long-term sustainable development for the interface communities, government agencies were more strictly concerned about particular episodes of violence. Community representatives felt that the scope and agenda of the IAWGDF should be developmental—that is, that it should address the issues of families in interface areas who were not only displaced during particular episodes of violence, but also dispersed and distressed.[21] This led community representatives to use the IAWGDF as a forum to raise policy issues such as the need for the provision of counseling services in the interface areas, preventative measures for averting violence, and the economic regeneration of the neighborhoods themselves. However, the statutory agency representatives felt that these long-term issues would be more appropriately addressed in other forums for community development, and they were reluctant to expand on the issue of displaced families to encompass wider community development issues. These different perspectives created misunderstandings between the two sectors as to the objectives of the working group.

One factor which contributed to these contradictory interpretations was the lack of a clearly defined mandate for the responsibilities and scope of the IAWGDF. From its beginnings, the IAWGDF's agenda was left open to interpretation. Statutory agency representatives narrowly viewed the purpose of the working group as being limited to the public sector response to displaced persons, whereas community representatives adopted a broader outlook, wanting to utilize public sector involvement in the working group to tackle all the issues which contribute to interface violence in general. Multiple government agency representatives described the IAWGDF as a working group that became unwieldy and unfocused. The chairman also said that by 1998, the IAWGDF had begun to outlive its usefulness as an emergency coordinating unit when the working group began to move beyond displaced family issues and became instead a catchall forum for the remonstrations of community representatives on a broad range of socioeconomic issues in North Belfast.[22] This drift in focus may, in part, explain the statutory agencies' reluctance to engage with the IAWGDF after 1998, but other more complex political reasons also bear examination.

In retrospect, policymakers and community representatives both agree that these particular difficulties were in large part due to a lack of clarity as to the scope of issues on the agenda of the IAWGDF. In 2002, a third-party team was commissioned to evaluate the functioning of the working group. As a result, an initiative is under way to draw up agreed terms of reference for the working group to focus its operations and get the IAWGDF once again working efficiently as a collaborative mechanism for policy formulation.

Conclusion

This case study on the Interagency Working Group for Displaced Families demonstrates the opportunities for community-based NGOs to move beyond simple lobbying tactics and embark upon a multifaceted strategy to gain access and collaborate with government agencies. During an instance of sudden civil crisis, when there is an absence of effective governmental measures for dealing with victims, a local community organization with a reputation for trustworthiness, neutrality, and community advocacy can influence policy. The CDC took deliberate steps to elevate its credibility in the policymaking arena in order to ensure that governmental statutory agencies would consider it to be competent, professional, and important enough to be included in the advisory working group. Some of the CDC's tactics included exploiting governmental contacts, persuading the leadership of the political parties to lobby actively for its cause, establishing a public inquiry which gave the community a voice, and maintaining media interest in the issues with which the organization was concerned. All this combined to give the CDC access to the policymaking process.

Below are some of the recommendations that have been gleaned from interviews with both community relations representatives and policymakers involved in the IAWGDF.

Community NGO Recommendations

- Identify influential individuals within the governmental structure: Try to locate sympathizers to your agenda and, if possible, utilize a preexisting relationship.

- Acquire knowledge in the policy area, especially in the legislative and implementation process.
- Network with the leadership of local political parties: They may be interested in elevating their reputations with their constituents by lobbying for a popular cause. They have a high profile and excellent access to the media.
- Identify implementation gaps within existing legislation: Devising realistic and practical tactics to fill a policy vacuum is easier than trying to create new legislation.
- Deconstruct the overarching policy strategy: Create coherent objectives accompanied by clear achievable goals. Even minor initiatives can yield positive repercussions in the wider conflict context.
- Devise common understandings based upon genuine communication: When engaging with policymakers in a partnership arena, work toward building trust and a common understanding about the role and mandate of any working group. If possible, define terms of reference and scope for investigating solutions. Consensus and compromise are crucial.
- Adopt a professional approach: Recognize that passionate and emotional advocacy, while a key component of community work, is not considered acceptable behavior in the policymaking arena. An overtly emotional attitude may be misinterpreted as aggression by policymakers, leading to a deteriorating partnership.
- Be flexible: Be prepared to switch tactics in the shifting political and policy landscapes. Understand the wider political circumstances and constraints on policymakers. Become an astute political opportunist, recognizing and exploiting favorable circumstances to your advantage.

Policymaker Recommendations to NGOs

- Pressure tactics: Do not condemn the state structure that you are attempting to impact. Constructive criticism of a statutory agency's provision of services is acceptable, but do not blame them for societal ills.
- Use facts and statistics to support your argument: Reports relying on anecdotal evidence are generally dismissed by governmental agencies. To impact policy, you must adopt a professional approach.
- Recognize the constraints of civil servants: If possible, be prepared to advocate for their needs at the upper echelons of political power.
- Avoid creeping expansions of the policy agenda: A loss of clear, simple, and coherent mandate can lead to impracticality of goals and a loss of effectiveness. This will impair group dynamics and may lead to the gradual disengagement of policymakers from the cooperative process.
- Consistency of representatives: Use the same personnel consistently, where possible, in order to build on working relationships with policymakers.
- Organize the policy objectives into short- and long-term goals: Be prepared to adapt these goals according to the internal dynamics of the bureaucratic structure.

Methodology

The evidence for this chapter was gathered via a series of interviews from April–June 2002. The primary method was face-to-face formal interviews with key individuals from The Community Development Centre, The Interagency Working Group on Displaced Families, civil servants, and relevant policymakers from the Northern Ireland Office. Empirical research was conducted concerning the delivery of statutory services in the interface. Also the author had access to the minutes of IAWGDP meetings, in conjunction with draft and formal Position Papers in order to evaluate the operation and focus of the Working Group.

Notes

The author wishes to express his deep gratitude to Fiona Barr for her special editorial assistance in the writing of this chapter.

1. "The Troubles" is a colloquial name referring to a period of political violence in Northern Ireland from 1969 to 1998. Decades of discrimination, socioeconomic tension, and political division over the constitutional position of Northern Ireland contributed to the outbreak of violence. Paramilitaries from sections of the Catholic and Protestant communities engaged in a guerrilla-type conflict which also involved members of the British security forces. This cycle of killings, bombings, and property destruction claimed over three thousand five hundred lives. The period began to come to a close with the beginning of an inclusive peace process in 1994 which resulted in voluntary paramilitary ceasefires, and which subsequently resulted in the signing of the Belfast Agreement in 1998 by all political parties.

2. Refers to the Catholic community and the Protestant community in Northern Ireland. Symbolically, the conflicting parties are referred to by their religious designation. Therefore, conflict resolution or peacebuilding activities are denoted as "community relations"; this is "the spectrum of activities, programmes and projects in Northern Ireland that seek to overcome the divisions within society and promote reconciliation among the two major communities" (Church and Visser, 2001: 3).

3. The Orange Order is a religious order for men, drawn exclusively from the Unionist/Protestant community.

4. Refers to local residential organizations whose primary purpose is to vociferate community objections to the Orange Order parading through "their" neighborhood.

5. Portadown, a town outside of Belfast, was the location of a bitter confrontation between Catholic residents and a Protestant Orange Order march. The absence of dialogue and compromise between the two groups has resulted in a stand-off situation at a church at Drumcree each July since 1995. This "local" conflict has resulted in violent repercussions throughout the rest of Northern Ireland. As yet, no lasting compromise has been reached.

6. See Office of the First Minister and Deputy First Minister, Managing Disorder—Responding to Interface Violence, www.research.ofmdfmni.gov.uk/managingdisorder/violence.htm.

7. A government-funded public body. Established under the 1971 Housing Ex-

ecutive Act, as a regional statutory agency responsible for allocating public housing throughout Northern Ireland.

8. "An 'Interface' is a term used to describe the common boundary between a predominantly Protestant/unionist residential area and a predominantly Catholic/nationalist residential area; while an interface community is the community which lives alongside an interface" (Brendan Murtaugh, in Jarman and O'Halloran, 2000: 7). Often these interface areas are physically divided by brick walls, steel fences, or major road networks. "They provide some psychological security and help to create a stronger feeling of communal identity and solidarity . . . reaffirming a physical claim to possession of specific territory" (Jarman and O'Halloran, 2000: 10).

9. Single identity work is aimed at increasing the confidence of a community so that it can subsequently reach out and involve itself in networking and in joint program development at either a cross-community or cross-border level (Church and Visser, 2001: 13).

10. Refers to a strategy whereby an organization engages in activities at the community level which are designed to create support for a particular issue, which is then harnessed and translated into pressure for change at the elite governmental/political level.

11. Vivienne Anderson, director of the CDC.

12. BAT was a government initiative to combat inner city deprivation and foster economic and urban regeneration. It consisted of nine Belfast Action Teams, through which civil servants had a mandate to provide government funding to local capacity building projects such as youth training or cross-cultural dialogue.

13. Since 1972, when power was taken away from the unionist government in Northern Ireland, the NIO has been the source of UK governmental responsibility in Northern Ireland, and is directly accountable to the UK government at Westminster, London. There is a Secretary of State in charge of the NIO, along with four or five ministers, all of whom are appointed by the Prime Minister of Britain. Since the Belfast agreement, most of the powers of the NIO have moved to the Assembly, which is run by Northern Ireland politicians.

14. In 1996, the Secretary of State for Northern Ireland, the highest British governmental position in this region, was Sir Patrick Mayhew. His wife was Lady Mayhew.

15. "Westminster" refers to the legislative branch of the British government.

16. Interview with the chairman by the author.

17. The Good Friday Agreement was the result of negotiations between the main political parties in Northern Ireland and the British and Irish governments. It created power-sharing political institutions and its provisions were ratified via a referendum by 71 percent of the population of Northern Ireland.

18. Interview by the author.

19. As defined by the decrease in the numbers of families displaced from their homes as a result of sectarian intimidation.

20. IAWGDF Minutes of Meeting held on 9 December 1998 at 3:30 p.m. in Glendinning House, Murray Street, Belfast.

21. "Displaced, dispersed, distressed" came to be the phrase used to describe those families that were forced to leave their homes (displaced), forced to move in temporarily with family or friends in another location during periods of intense conflict (dispersed), and were affected psychologically by events of interface violence (distressed).

22. Interview by the author.

References

Belfast Interface Project. 1999. "Inner East, Outer West: Addressing Conflict in Two Interface Areas." Belfast, Ireland: Belfast Interface Project.

Church, Cheyanne, and Anna Visser. 2001. *Single Identity Work: An Approach to Conflict Resolution in Northern Ireland.* Derry/Londonderry, Ireland: UNU/INCORE.

Community Development Centre. 1998. "Annual Review, 1997-1998." Belfast, Ireland: Community Development Centre.

Fay, M., M. Morrissey, M. Smyth, and T. Wong. 1997. *The Cost of the Troubles Study: Report on the Northern Ireland Survey.* Derry/Londonderry: UNU/INCORE.

Gillespie, Norman. 2001. "Evaluation Report: Outer Interface Working Group." Belfast, Ireland: Belfast Regeneration Office.

Hamilton, Michael. 2001. "Working Relationships: An Evaluation of Community Mobile Phone Networks in Northern Ireland." Belfast, Ireland: Community Relations Council.

Jarman, Neil, ed. 1997. *On the Edge: Community Perspectives on the Civil Disturbances in North Belfast.* Belfast, Ireland: Community Development Centre.

Jarman, Neil. 1999. *Drawing Back from the Edge: Community-Based Response in North Belfast.* Belfast, Ireland: Community Development Centre.

Jarman, Neil, and Chris O'Halloran eds. 2000. *Peacelines or Battlefields: Responding to Violence in Interface Areas.* Belfast, Ireland: Community Development Centre.

Persic, Callie, and Stephen Bloomer. 2001. *The Feud and the Fury: The Response of the Community Sector to the Shankill Feud, August 2000.* Belfast, Ireland: Springfield Intercommunity Development Project.

Smyth, Marie, Mike Morrissey, and Jennifer Hamilton (of the Institute for Conflict Research). 2001. *Caring through the Troubles: Health and Social Services in North and West Belfast.* Belfast, Ireland: North and West Belfast Health and Social Services Trust.

Chapter 6
Legitimizing the Role of Women in Peacebuilding at the United Nations: A Campaign Approach

International Alert[1]—Ancil Adrian-Paul, Kevin Clements, Eugenia Piza Lopez, and Nicola Johnston

Women's perspectives on peace and security have traditionally been a marginal concern on the global security agenda. Their experiences in armed conflict often go unacknowledged, and their role in peacebuilding efforts is normally dismissed. Although women around the world may be found engaging in informal grassroots diplomacy in conflict zones, they have generally been excluded from the formal reconciliation and reconstruction processes in postwar transformations. In recent years, however, some women have sought to overcome this obstacle of exclusion, insisting that their distinctive experiences in war are worthy of focused attention by global policymakers.

This chapter tells the story of the Women Building Peace campaign, which was developed with support from over two hundred organizations around the world and coordinated by International Alert (IA).[2] By creating a widespread international awareness of the particular horrors of war that are suffered by women, including rape, sexual torture, prostitution, and slavery, the campaign aimed to catalyze the United Nations Security Council and the European Parliament into a reaffirmation of the positive role that women could play in conflict resolution and peacemaking. The campaign[3] secured widespread support from local, national, and international agencies, and eventually succeeded in securing resolutions from both the United Nations Security Council and the European Parliament.[4]

In order to assess the strategy and success of the campaign, this case study first looks at IA's expertise on the gender dimensions of conflict and the context that instigated the campaign, namely the neglect of women in the global security agenda and their exclusion at the negotiating table. The chapter then articulates International Alert's strategic vision and identifies the tactics utilized to impact policymakers in the intergovernmental arena. It goes on to analyze the challenges confronted by IA, along with the lessons learned from the campaign.

Setting the Stage: IA and the International Community

One of the first organizations to work specifically on the gender dimensions of peace and conflict was IA. In 1995 it initiated a program on women and peacebuilding in the Great Lakes of Africa (Burundi and Rwanda), and it has since expanded this work to other countries in the Great Lakes region, as well as to the Caucasus and West Africa. Under the auspices of its Global Issues Department,[5] IA established its Civil Society and Peacebuilding Program in 1997, a forerunner to the Women Building Peace campaign. This program serves a vital role in the organization, ensuring that IA's work is informed by a gender perspective and highlighting the importance of the inclusion of women in all aspects of peacebuilding.

As IA's expertise grew in the area of gender awareness and conflict, it became increasingly apparent that the policies being developed by the international community to empower and advance women's status, particularly those of the United Nations and the European Union (EU), were failing to move beyond rhetoric. Security policies related to women at local, national, regional, and international levels, such as the 1979 United Nations Convention on the Elimination of All Forms of Discrimination against Women (CEDAW)[6] and the 1995 United Nations Beijing Platform for Action (PFA),[7] which was aimed at advancing and empowering women and women's participation in all developmental and peace processes, were failing to be implemented and mainstreamed. Women continued to be left out of the political process at all levels, including those associated with peacebuilding (Anderlini, Manchanda, and Karmali, 2000). It was within this policy vacuum that IA developed the Women Building Peace campaign in 1999.

Women's Experience of Conflict

In explaining why IA recognized the need to get involved in this type of campaign, it is important to outline the experiences of women in situations of armed conflict. One of the serious consequences of a society's descent into violence and disorder is that women and girls become easy targets of gendered and systematic sexual aggression by the warring factions, with perpetrators ranging from regular armed forces to peacekeepers.[8] Sexual torture, rape, sexual slavery, forced pregnancy, forced abortion, forced prostitution, forced eviction, and other such measures are often used to attack women individually and their culture as a whole. As a result, women have been exploring legal strategies in national and international courts to demand accountability, justice, and reparations.[9]

The economic impact of conflict on women is also extremely injurious. This includes a marked increase in poverty, a drastic deterioration in nutrition, and numerous other cultural, political, and social disadvantages.[10] Furthermore, due in large part to insufficient understanding of the impact of armed conflict on women, a clear gap exists in their protection, specifically in the delivery of humanitarian assistance (UNICEF and UNIFEM, 2000).

Women are frequently put at risk by a lack of appropriate facilities for refugees and the internally displaced. Often the camps constructed for these groups of people, the majority of whom are women, are poorly designed and insecure, thus putting women and girls at continued risk of sexual and other types of harassment.[11]

Finally, women are often marginalized in peacebuilding processes. Although normally less visible than men, women have long been integrally involved in seeking solutions to issues intrinsic to peacebuilding. These include ecological balance, demobilization, and the reintegration of former child soldiers, along with demilitarization and disarmament. Women are highly visible in the building of street-level peace accords, peace villages, and bicameral citizens' committees, and in the promotion of a culture of tolerance at the local community level. Women are resource managers, advocates for others in emergency and crisis situations, and leaders in community organizations (Manchanda, 2001). Whereas the role of older women as informal influencers and advisers to community leaders is traditionally respected, women are rarely found at the negotiating table, particularly at the national and international levels. This exclusion from elite-level decision making has confined women's political participation to marginal civil society groups, with a resultant lack of recognition for their generally innovative and dedicated peacebuilding endeavors.

Traditional peacekeeping deployments have revealed that conflict situations can be further exacerbated because peace support operations fail to include women and their perspectives. Peacekeeping, a traditionally male-dominated field, has gradually begun to change; United Nations peacekeeping operations are no longer simply one-dimensional interstate military deployments, but now include such varied tasks as civilian policing, election and human rights monitoring, repatriation of refugees, demobilization of soldiers, de-mining, and humanitarian relief. With these changes, a new set of work opportunities has emerged. There is a need to ensure that women take up these opportunities, particularly given that modern armed conflicts affect civilians on an unprecedented level and the majority of those needing assistance are women and their dependents. It is also increasingly recognized that women employed in both the military and civilian components of peacekeeping forces can help to improve the behavior of male peacekeepers toward local women and therefore assist in minimizing friction between the United Nations and the host country's population (Karame and Bertinussen, 2000).

First Stage of the Campaign: Mobilization of Women from Different Conflict Areas

In early May 1999, an international conference entitled "Women, Violent Conflict and Peacebuilding: A Global Perspective"[12] brought together fifty women from forty conflict areas including Palestine, Mexico, Bosnia, Burundi, Afghanistan, and Lebanon. Organized by IA, the Centre for Defence Studies (Kings College) and the Council for the Advancement of Arab/British Understanding (CAABU), participants were chosen from organizations with a focus on women and peacebuilding who had been involved in advocacy on this issue for at least three years and were representative of local women. The conference, funded by the United Kingdom Department for International Development (DFID) and the National Lottery Board, provided a space for women to share their experiences of armed conflict, and their positive role in peacebuilding. It provided an opportunity to discuss and assess existing international mechanisms to promote women's advancement and empowerment and to reflect on the degree to which these mechanisms have been interpreted and entrenched into national laws. Women also explored peace and security strategies and the mechanisms by which their concerns could be highlighted internationally.

The conference participants unanimously agreed on the need for a global campaign which could become a rallying point for women's issues. Based upon preexisting commitments made by the international community regarding women and peacebuilding, they devised five concise demands[13] and decided to embark upon a global campaign to advocate for their recognition and implementation. The five demands were that the international community:

1. include women in peace negotiations as decision makers;
2. put women at the heart of reconstruction and reconciliation;
3. strengthen the protection and participation of refugee, internally displaced, and other war-affected women;
4. end impunity and ensure redress for crimes committed against women; and
5. provide women's peacebuilding organizations with sufficient and sustainable resources.

The Women Building Peace Campaign

In May 1999, IA launched a global campaign entitled "Women Building Peace: From the Village Council to the Negotiating Table." The campaign sought to provide a coherent platform for women's demands, to redress their exclusion and increase the visibility of their positive contribution to peace and development processes, and to encourage the international community to adhere to the commitments made at Beijing. The five demands formed the cornerstone of the campaign, which aimed to achieve the following objectives:

• Policy impact: integrating women's perspectives on peace and security issues into the policies of the United Nations (specifically the Security Council and Department of Peacekeeping Operations), along with the EU and member states of both organizations.

- Participation and partnership: the creation of a loose coalition of women's organizations from all regions working collaboratively to highlight the campaign's five demands.
- Promoting and highlighting women's role in peacebuilding through the launch and delivery of a collaborative Millennium Peace Prize with UNIFEM.
- Promoting the release of funds: raising awareness of the need for an increase in resources allocated to women and women's organizations involved in peacebuilding, conflict reconstruction, and reconciliation.

The campaign was launched at the Hague Appeal for Peace Centennial Celebration Conference in May 1999. According to the organizers, this was the "largest international peace conference in history"[14] with representatives from NGOs, policymakers, heads of state, and even royalty from the Middle East in attendance. It therefore presented an ideal forum at which to launch the campaign. Queen Noor of Jordan, with her affiliation to the Hague Appeal, agreed to IA's request to officially and publicly endorse the Women Building Peace campaign. IA took advantage of this high-profile opportunity to disseminate an interactive CD-ROM on women, conflict, and peace, and to facilitate workshops on cross-cutting issues such as the protection of women's human rights in conflict and postconflict situations.[15]

The Strategy to Secure the United Nations Resolution

The primary aim of the campaign was to highlight the five demands regarding women in peacebuilding, by convincing members of the Security Council to adopt a resolution detailing a specific policy which could be implemented by governments, the United Nations system in general, and other IGOS. It was hoped that such a policy device would encourage and enable participating stakeholders to examine and incorporate the needs of women into their own national policies. The United Nations Security Council was identified as the key target of the campaign because its primary function is the maintenance of peace and security and its resolutions are binding on member states. The beginning of the campaign coincided with an evolutionary mood in the United Nations Security Council, which was embarking upon the incremental expansion of its remit, as evidenced by thematic debates on issues such as the protection of civilians and the HIV/AIDS epidemic. It was therefore an opportune time to push the issue of women, peace, and security onto the Security Council's agenda.

Given that the Security Council meeting was in October 2000, the task of achieving an agreed resolution by that date was daunting.[16] The IA was acutely aware that momentous policy initiatives such as the adoption of a Security Council resolution are not achievable by any one organization working unilaterally. Rather, successful global advocacy initiatives require tight multi-level collaboration among a number of actors. It thus became apparent that in order to secure a resolution, the IA-led campaign would need to work closely with a number of key stakeholders, particularly in New York, in order to ensure widespread and representative support for the initiative and to shape and impact policy at the global level. The campaign staff therefore decided to create an International Advisory Committee to guide the campaign and to engage with crucial stakeholders such as local and international women's groups, NGOs, United Nations member states, the EU, and United Nations agencies.

The International Advisory Committee

A nineteen-member committee comprised of representatives from countries in pre-, open, and post-conflict situations from across the world, as well as women's organizations working in nonconflict countries, was created to act in an advisory capacity to the campaign. Participants included the U.S. headquarters of UNIFEM; the Center for Women's Global Leadership at Rutgers University, New York; Bineta Diop, of Femmes Africa Solidarite; Bisi Adeyele Fayemi, of Akina Mama wa Afrika; and other organizations selected for their geographical location and their expertise in one or more of the themes underpinning the campaign. Essential in the selection of each organization was their advocacy capacity and profile in the United States, and thus their ability to support and promote the campaign's objectives and articulate women's demands at the global level. IA's ability to influence and shape policy was enhanced as a result of its collaboration with these organizations, as various members of the International Advisory Committee had access to policymakers and institutions which IA, as a London-based organization, did not. This was a vital measure, as it developed key strategic linkages, added to campaign knowledge, and built on distinctive competencies.

Engaging the Stakeholders

Local and International Women's Groups

In order to engender a widespread and supportive foundation, the campaign organized a series of systematic consultations with women's organizations from around the world. These meetings, held in the South Caucasus, South East Asia, London, West Africa, and South Africa, with participants from the Great Lakes, French West Africa, South Asia, the EU, and US-based NGOs, helped to further define the aims, objectives, and focus of the campaign. These meetings proved extremely useful, with the consultations in the regions providing a country- and local issue-based focus, and the New York and European meetings contributing to the refinement of the cross-cutting themes, adding the global perspective that would appeal to the international community.[17] On the broader global front, the campaign mobilized grassroots NGOs with an issue focus on women and peacebuilding to advocate at the local, regional, and national level. Approximately three hundred fifty of these organizations wrote to the international secretariat of the campaign requesting that their names be included on the list of campaign supporters. In order to manage communication with these different structures, campaign staff created e-mail listservs and a quarterly newsletter to update the groups on the campaign's progress on a monthly basis. IA also utilized support from their network partners, as well as their regional field programs for publicity and dissemination purposes.

NGOs in Attendance at the Beijing PFA

The Review of the Platform for Action[18] which had arisen out of the 1995 Fourth World Conference on Women held in Beijing was convened in New York in June 2000 to monitor how participating states had implemented agreements made at the Beijing Conference. This meeting provided another excellent opportunity for consolidating support among NGOs to ensure the adoption of a resolution by the Security Council in October 2000. The negotiating sessions in New York, at which governments debated the document that outlined achievements, challenges, and gaps to the implementation of the PFA, lasted long into the night and often into the early hours of the next day. On these occasions, friendships were forged and alliances cemented as representatives of NGOs, including IA's senior policy adviser, engaged in informal discussions and lobbying of government representatives about the proposed resolution as they emerged from formal negotiating sessions. Due to their activities at this PFA meeting, a loose grouping of NGOs, which became known as the NGOWG (NGO Working Group on Women, Peace and Security), articulated a shared resolve to work together on the campaign.[19] They quickly realized that support from United Nations agencies and key member states of the Security Council would be critical to the process, and they began to systematically and persistently engage United Nations Member States in dialogue. It was with these partners that the first draft of the United Nations Resolution was developed between May and July 2000.

United Nations Member States

Items can only be submitted for inclusion in the agenda of the United Nations Security Council by current member states of the Council or the Secretary-General. The campaign decided to lobby the Permanent Mission of Namibia, then presiding over the Council, to put the issue of women, peace, and security on the Council's agenda for October 2000. Namibia had an established interest in this area as, in May 2000, they hosted a conference on "Mainstreaming a Gender Perspective in Multi-Dimensional Peace Operations"; this resulted in the Windhoek Declaration, which suggested the Namibia Plan of Action.[20] Namibia agreed to become the primary sponsor of a draft Resolution on Women and Peacebuilding. A number of other member states also demonstrated their support. Jamaica and Ireland, for instance, convened Arria Formula debates on the issue,[21] while Bangladesh issued a press release on the importance of women and their role in peacebuilding and the consequent need for their inclusion in peace processes.[22] The governments of Canada and the Netherlands, which have always been very concerned about issues of civilian security, along with Slovenia, which in 1999 identified women and conflict as a priority during its presidency of the United Nations Security Council, also made marked contributions to the debate. The government of the United Kingdom provided financial support for the international conference that had taken place in May 1999. The Government of Finland supported the campaign by organizing a parliamentary hearing on the issue of "Women, Peace and Security: A New Paradigm."[23] It was attended by a wide spectrum of senior officials from such organizations as the European Commission, ANC, DFID, the Gender Desk of the Netherlands Ministry of Foreign Affairs, and the Greek Ministry for Equality, as well as notable NGOs from various regions. The Netherlands government assisted the launch of the campaign in other global forums.

EU Member States

By engaging in extensive research, the campaign staff mapped the women and peace policies of fifteen EU member states and recorded the information in an active database which would facilitate follow-up and future communication. This database established the basis for a targeted distribution list so that research papers, newsletters, and documents produced by the campaign could be widely disseminated to essential parties. These were also disseminated to women's organizations, policymakers, United Kingdom and EU parliamentarians, and other civil society groups. Initial start-up funding for this was provided by the United Kingdom National Lottery Commission Board and United Kingdom DFID.

United Nations Agencies

Support for the proposal was also gained via policy dialogues on the key campaign issues with UNIFEM, UNICEF (United Nations Children's Fund), DAW (United Nations Division for the Advancement of Women), OSAGI (Office of the Special Adviser to the Secretary-General on Gender Issues and Advancement of Women), the WFP (World Food Programme), the DDA (Department for Disarmament Affairs), the DPKO (Department of Peacekeeping Operations), and other key agencies and departments within the United Nations. These dialogues consisted of formal and informal meetings to cultivate personal relationships and understandings. The discussions focused not only on the critical cross-cutting issues that could be placed on the agenda of the international community, but were directed toward identifying the key United Nations agencies that could lend support and exercise influential leverage from within policymaking circles. In general, campaign staff found policymakers to be sympathetic and amenable to the proposals. Differences in opinion were minor and not on the substantive issue of the Women Building Peace campaign. The support of UNIFEM in particular, with its many years of experience in supporting women in armed conflict situations and its collaboration with NGOs in different constituencies, was vital. This relationship building with policy officials assisted in keeping the campaign relevant and realistic to the concerns and issues in the policy world and informed campaign staff of the appropriate language in which policy papers should be worded.

These policy dialogues resulted in a multilevel partnership between representatives from IA, UNIFEM, and the Namibian Mission to the United Nations, who engaged in a coordinated effort to facilitate women representatives from conflict countries to participate in a scheduled open debate at the United Nations Security Council in October 2000. This partnership worked hard to ensure that the women had the necessary documentation to give informal testimony to the United Nations Security Council members concerning crimes committed against women and girls in conflict countries, and to outline the efforts that women worldwide were undertaking to demand an end to war and a place for themselves at peace negotiating tables. Furthermore, this partnership enabled campaign staff to disseminate relevant material to United Nations officials and diplomats present at the debate, in order to foster informed dialogue. This effort identified and facilitated the participation of women peace advocates from Guatemala, Zambia, Somalia, and Sierra Leone in these noteworthy debates.[24]

Tactics

The campaign employed a variety of tactics to achieve its goals. These included policy dialogues, local and global campaigning, policy research and resultant recommendations, awareness raising and resource sharing, and the strategic use of leverage.

Policy Dialogues
   The IA believes that informed dialogue between campaigners and targets is crucial to successful advocacy, and therefore engaged in persistent, vigilant, and informed policy dialogue. Following the dissemination of policy products such as research documents highlighting specific policy recommendations, campaign personnel would contact policymakers to elicit their response; where appropriate, round-table discussions and bilateral meetings were organized to further discuss the issues. For example, following the production and dissemination of IA's policy briefing on "Gender and Peace Support Operations," staff contacted the relevant United Nations agencies to arrange for follow-up discussions.[25] The campaign staff have found this strategy of proactive engagement and constructive discussion to be a particularly effective campaign device.

Local to Global Campaigning
   It was important to demonstrate to the United Nations the existence of extensive grassroots support for the campaign. The participation and inclusion of women's groups at the local level generated much of the momentum of the campaign. Women from over three hundred fifty supporting NGOs translated the campaign's five demands into local languages such as French, Nepali, Spanish, Bahasa Indonesian, and Portuguese. They produced postcards and leaflets advocating for the United Nations resolution. The campaign work in Portugal provides an example of this local engagement. Women's groups worked with the local government authorities to produce billboards and very large posters publicizing the campaign. Pivotal regional NGOs followed a similar format in

the production of their campaign leaflets, an initiative that was self-funded by the local, regional, and national organizations. These coordinated activities generated increased visibility and support for the campaign, simultaneously enhancing its legitimacy and credibility in policymaking circles.

In order to further demonstrate this momentous grassroots support, the campaign organized a global petition, addressed to the United Nations Secretary-General, calling for the implementation of the five demands. Thirty thousand leaflets and postcards incorporating the petition were distributed in ten different languages to more than eight thousand individuals and over three hundred and fifty organizations around the world. The petition was disseminated electronically on the campaign website and provided a link to a form that people could download, sign, and return to the campaign headquarters. The petition was also circulated amongst the campaign's extensive networks. It proved to be an enormous success, with over a hundred thousand signatures collected. Helen Hakena, the winner of the Millennium Peace Prize, formally presented it to Angela King, the special adviser to the United Nations on Gender Issues and Advancement of Women on International Women's Day 2001.[26]

Policy Research and Recommendations

The campaign utilized a methodology of research and dissemination of policy recommendations that were produced in-house by the campaign's policy team or commissioned externally from issue experts. Since the campaign's inception, policy documents such as briefings, research papers, reports, and letters have been disseminated to a wide variety of targets including policymakers, parliamentarians, women's groups, church leaders, the media, and other interested constituencies, in order to stimulate and cultivate support for the five demands and the United Nations resolution.

Awareness Raising and Resource Sharing

The production and dissemination of an electronic and print quarterly newsletter, produced in English and Portuguese, enabled the geographically diverse focal points to share campaign information and knowledge. The production of an interactive CD-ROM, along with campaign packs and leaflets, contributed to raising the profile of women's organizations and their peacebuilding activities. The dissemination of informational resources secured IA's credibility in the debate and assisted the process of informed constructive dialogue and collective action at the United Nations and EU.

Use of Leverage

The importance of leverage with key targets cannot be overstated. The IA's location in the United Kingdom and its leadership on conflict prevention and conflict management issues, as well as its history of engagement with women and peacebuilding, has resulted in a cordial relationship and a degree of leverage with the United Kingdom's Department for International Development and the Foreign and Commonwealth Office (FCO). This relationship helped in the strategic and targeted engagement with key member states at both the United Nations and EU. Thus, during the preparations for the Beijing +5, and the subsequent period of lobbying for the United Nations resolution, the NGOWG employed a specific tactic in their targeting of member states. Based on an NGO's knowledge of the general policy position of a particular country or region, combined with the degree of leverage that existed, an NGO from the group would engage in a concerted lobbying effort with that state.

Outcomes of the Campaign

Adoption of United Nations Security Council Resolution 1325
The campaign requested that both UNIFEM and the Namibian delegation take the lead on furthering the draft of the resolution. UNIFEM redrafted the document in line with wording acceptable to the member states. Namibia presented a draft resolution on 24 October 2000 for discussion and debate. This was circulated to Security Council members in New York and in country capitals for amendments. The resolution was accepted by the United Nations Security Council and passed on 31 October 2000.

The unanimous adoption of a Security Council resolution which outlined the need for explicit gender mainstreaming in the peace and security policies of the United Nations system was the major success of the campaign. The resolution is testimony to the achievement of the campaign in its overarching goal of influencing and impacting United Nations policy. The swift, unanimous endorsement of the resolution by the Security Council, particularly its incorporation of the sentiments expressed in the five demands, surpassed even the expectations of those advocating and lobbying for its passage. Following the adoption of resolution 1325, the campaign has facilitated a number of national and regional consultations with women's organizations to inform them of the Resolution and to elicit their perspectives on the relevance and utility of the tool to advance women's peace and security in specific conflict and postconflict contexts. Such consultations have taken place in the Caucasus region (early March 2002) and East Africa (late March 2002); national consultations have taken place in Nepal (January 2002) and Nigeria (August/September 2002); and, most recently, a regional consultation took place in South Asia (February 2003). There are plans for further regional consultations in the future.[27] The campaign is also conducting peace audits that will undertake the mapping of potential instruments and mechanisms in each geographical area through which the resolution could become operational.

Additional Arria Formula Meetings
Preparation for the debate on Resolution 1325 included an Arria Formula dialogue to which women activists and experts from conflict regions were invited. The campaign succeeded in achieving additional Arria Formula meetings. Another such meeting was organized on the first anniversary of the resolution in 2001, and there are now plans for additional meetings that will continue to include women drawn from different geographical conflict and post-

conflict areas. These meetings have been reported on in depth by IA and the other members of the NGOWG and are publicized on their various websites.[28]

European Parliament Resolution on Gender Aspects of Conflict Resolution and Peacebuilding (2000/2025INI)

The work with the United Nations and particularly EU member states significantly assisted the passing of the European Parliament Resolution on Gender Aspects of Conflict Resolution and Peacebuilding (2000/2025 [INI])[29] in November of the same year. This resolution recognized the significance and necessity of the participation of women in peace negotiations, conflict resolution, and postconflict reconstruction processes.

Requests for Further Activities Focused on the Role of Women in Peacebuilding

There is little doubt that the global campaign, which stressed the horrors suffered by women in war as well as addressing their underused capacity as peacemakers, has generated requests for further activities focused on the role of women in peacebuilding. The campaign team have been asked to provide support to the Brussels-based Afghan Women Leaders Fund and associated working groups in preparation for the transitional government and postconflict reconstruction activities in Afghanistan. The campaign team has also been approached by the United Kingdom and other governments for assistance on specific issues related to women, peace, and security.

Challenges Faced by the Campaign

Lack of Resources

A lack of human and financial resources during the campaign's initial months resulted in considerable strain and overwork for its single full-time staff member. The short time period between the initiation of the campaign in May 1999 and the Security Council meeting in October 2000, while also preparing for the Review of the Beijing Platform for Action in June 2000, meant it was crucial that the campaign was able to efficiently and effectively capitalize on all opportunities to raise awareness of the need for a United Nations resolution at both Security Council and European Parliament levels. This resulted in a significant amount of travel to various regions of the world, particularly Asia, Scandinavia, Africa, and the United States, within a short time frame. The workload pressures were eased only when the campaign succeeded in raising funds by 2000, enabling the employment of additional staff. The campaign hired a consultant to act as a senior policy adviser, who spent 75 percent of her time attending meetings in New York, liaising with government officials and relevant United Nations agencies, and building a secure relationship with the NGOWG members. This consistent and permanent representative established continuity, allowing for the development of trusting relationships with key stakeholders, and became a significant contributing factor to the success of the campaign.

Based upon their experiences of the Women Building Peace campaign, however, IA would not now undertake another global campaign without first ensuring that it had secured adequate funding and had sufficient numbers of experienced staff.

Insufficient Knowledge of the Key Target Constituencies

Despite IA's previous work during 1996 and 1997 in engaging with the EU to put conflict prevention onto the agenda as part of the Lome Agreement,[30] there was very little systematic information on the two constituencies of the United Nations and the EU in terms of their stances on women and conflict issues. It was therefore necessary to undertake a systematic and time-consuming mapping of United Nations and EU target agencies, key departments, and personnel within the United Nations and EU secretariats in order to identify key personnel to target in the campaign.

Lack of Campaigning Expertise and Institutional Knowledge

The global campaign, Women Building Peace: From the Village Council to the Negotiating Table, was the first initiative of this kind engaged in by IA. Prior to its inception, there was a lack of institutional expertise on how to impact and shape policy through a campaign of this kind. Documenting the campaign as a case study for this book will provide an opportunity to contribute to organizational learning and an institutional memory that will inform and shape future program development.

Translating Complex Ideas into Simple and Effective Messages

A campaign such as Women Building Peace is constructed around complex issues and themes that require the buy-in of multiple constituencies. The success of such an initiative depends on the degree of understanding of the issues in the public domain, amongst the target constituencies, and within the campaign team itself. The ability to translate the ideas into simple but effective messages is crucial and depends on experienced staff. This posed a challenge to the campaign during its initial stages, but the problem was gradually alleviated as funding was secured and staff with the necessary experience were appointed.

Managing Relationships with Diverse Organizations

In many environments, networking has proved to be a very powerful and important tool for furthering organizational goals and policy impact. There are, however, disadvantages to such networking. Working in a coalition can be cumbersome, time-consuming, and frustrating, especially when negotiating issues of profile, contribution of resources, and definition of roles and responsibilities. A great deal of compromise is necessary, and there is often a need for skillful coordination and leadership and the subsuming of an organization's own particular priorities for the greater good of the whole. This was evident during the activities to secure the resolution. Each organization had specific goals and priority issues that it wanted to put on the agenda of the Security Council, but compromise was necessary in order to ensure that the group maximized the opportunities presented and the scarce resources that were available. Additionally, NGOs working with United Nations agencies and governments need to be aware of the fine line that exists between maintaining good relationships with these bodies and the lobbying and pressurizing that is often so necessary in progressing partnerships to achieve the desired results.

Lessons Learned

The campaign has identified some crucial steps and "must do" actions that can assist interested organizations when initiating similar campaigns.

Devise a Coherent Strategy

Develop a coherent strategy including elements of research, dialogue, dissemination, and follow-up. Ensure that the strategy is thoroughly discussed and agreed upon by all members of the coalition. Within your strategy, define roles and responsibilities and identify the lead person or organization from the group for each activity or block of activities. Include a list of stakeholders that you intend to target, divided into those that are sympathetic and those that are not. Undertake good research—a campaign that shows itself to be ignorant of the facts around the issues is likely to fail. Ensure that research informs your dialogue and the dissemination of your key message and choose a politically opportune time in which to engage in lobbying and advocacy activities.

Secure Sufficient Resources

It is imperative to secure sufficient financial and human resources before launching your strategy and undertaking campaign initiatives. Without such resources, personnel can become frustrated and demoralized, opportunities will be missed, and the overall dynamic of the campaign will suffer.

Know Your Stakeholders

Be clear on the key stakeholders in the process. The Women Building Peace campaign identified key stakeholders as active women in conflict NGOs, United Nations agencies, certain influential and interested governments, and member states of the Security Council and the EU. Within these groups of stakeholders, it is important to ensure that you have the name of the correct individual responsible for the subject of your concern. For example, when dealing with UNIFEM, the person to target is the Senior Officer on Governance, while within a member state at the United Nations, the crucial contact is the Second or Third Secretary responsible for dealing with the General Assembly. A well-constructed and repeatedly updated database is essential for the management of contacts. Its creation enhances the process of communicating effectively.

Undertake Systematic and Widespread Consultations with
Multiple Stakeholders

Throughout the life of the campaign, IA has found that systematic consultation with all relevant stakeholders, particularly communities directly affected by conflict, is very effective. This should include regular communication in a two-way channel that disseminates the results of consultations, developments at the policy level, and news of unfolding events to the stakeholders. The systematic consultations IA undertook with the different constituencies in South Asia, Europe, the Caucasus, West and South Africa, and the United States facilitated the refinement of aims and themes and helped to frame the women's demands.

Network and Build Alliances

A single organization is unlikely to make as much impact as a tightly constructed coalition of NGOs that possess a well-developed, coherent strategy, adequate resources, consensus on objectives, accountability to diverse constituencies, well-defined roles and responsibilities with effective leadership, and agile decision-making structures. Coalitions and networks are stronger than individuals or individual organizations. The larger and more diverse the network, the more compelling the message. A network of diverse organizations from a multitude of regions across the world presents a more potent and powerful message than a merely European organization, for example, making a similar recommendation. The mutual benefit of networks is created via the exchange of information, the building of coalitions, the development of common strategies, the increasing of the size of the network, and the linking of various groups with one another. Although cross-constituency relationships need to be managed with tact and diplomacy, the Women Building Peace campaign shows that a collective voice expressing a common concern is a powerful tool for effecting change. To maximize this potential, it is vital that the channels of communication between organizations working for peace enhance the capacity for efficient dissemination of information in order to amplify and strengthen these diverse voices. It is also essential to give credit to all stakeholders who are involved in campaigning.

Make Use of the Media

The media can be a powerful ally if targeted in the right way. Conduct research to identify journalists sympathetic to the issue. Pool knowledge of media contacts by creating a database. Ensure that journalists are informed through regular, targeted, and concise briefings that communicate the issues clearly. Press releases that are short, sharp, and to the point are critical and effective. Appoint one or two people within the group to be spokespersons and ensure that they are available as necessary. Consider developing an electronic list of media targets concerned and interested in the issue. Provide information to journalists in a timely manner. Where possible, introduce the human interest angle by offering interviews with women engaged in conflict and peace issues on the ground.

Be Persistent, Vigilant, and Informed

Be persistent and vigilant. NGOs and other organizations employ different methods for advocacy and lobbying. IA and the global campaign do not believe in aggressive campaigning, but rather in utilizing persistent, informative, and vigilant engagement in dialogue. The experience of the campaign as a whole demonstrated the value of such dialogue. Constant attention and vigilance through systematic consultations will enable coalitions, alliances, and groups to recognize and capitalize on windows of opportunity as they arise.

Conclusion

Women, who represent about half of any population, are an underused resource in postconflict reconstruction and peace processes. The global campaign, Women Building Peace: From the Village Council to the Negotiating Table, was established with the belief that peacebuilding is a process requiring the equal contribution of both men and women, and that the inclusion of women from the planning stages to implementation will improve the impact of local and international interventions, making the development of peace more just and sustainable.

Ensuring women's participation will also enhance the legitimacy of the process by making it more democratic and responsive to the priorities of all sectors of the population. The IA's engagement in the Women Building Peace campaign sought to address this challenge. The results have been multifarious, ranging from the unanimous endorsement of Resolution 1325 to an increased profile for the organization, its global issues department, and the issues in question, as well as many further opportunities for engagement with women's organizations and other groups in regions throughout the globe. We believe the campaign has given new hope and new opportunities to many women who wish to have their voices heard in the arduous process of postconflict peacebuilding that is facing so many communities on our planet today.

Notes

1. This chapter has been written by Ancil Adrian-Paul, campaign manager of IA's Gender and Peacebuilding Programme, with contributions, feedback, and editing from Kevin Clements (Secretary-General, IA), Eugenia Piza-Lopez (formerly head of the Policy and Advocacy Department), and Nicola Johnston (senior policy adviser).

2. The IA is an international NGO based in London and dedicated to the nonviolent prevention, management, and transformation of violent conflict. The IA works at national, regional, and global levels in order to enhance the capacity of individuals, peace networks, constituencies, and organizations to build sustainable peace. See www.international-alert.org.

3. The campaign was designed and led by Eugenia Piza-Lopez, Ancil Adrian-Paul (Programme Manager, IA), and Sanam Anderlini (senior policy advisor, IA).

4. The European Parliament is the parliament of the EU, and consists of the 626 representatives of the current fifteen countries which are members of the EU. See Appendix 1 for the successful resolution of the United Nations in 2000.

5. Created to promote the implementation of global policies that address the root causes of conflict, drawn from the agenda of global policymakers.

6. CEDAW was adopted in 1979 by the United Nations General Assembly and is often described as an international bill of rights for women. Consisting of a Pream-

ble and thirty Articles, it defines what constitutes discrimination against women and sets up an agenda for national action to end such discrimination.

7. In September 1995, more than one hundred eighty governments signed the *Beijing Platform for Action* at the Fourth World United Nations Conference on Women. Five years later, in 2000, at a special session of the United Nations General Assembly, a review of progress known as Beijing +5 addressed the obstacles encountered in implementing the platform.

8. See www.incore.ulst.ac.uk/cds/themes/women.htm.

9. The designation by the United Nations of rape as a crime against humanity within international law, in February 2001, represented a major step forward in achieving recognition for the traumas that women suffer in wartime. Many believe that such a move should also be recognized in women's experiences as refugees and internally displaced peoples. See C. Levine, "The Gender Dimensions of Peacebuilding," NPSIA Conference on Human Security: Policy Implications for the Twenty-First Century (1999).

10. *The Fourth World Conference on Women Platform for Action: Women and Armed Conflict.* See www.un.org/womenwatch/daw/beijing/platform/armed.htm.

11. Consultation on Resolution 1325 with women's groups in East Africa (March 2002).

12. For a report of the conference, see www.international-alert.org/women/confrep.pdf and www.womenbuildingpeace.org.

13. Five demands drawn, from the issues addressed by the United Nations Fourth Conference on Women, 1995, which issued two resolutions: The Bejing Declaration and the Platform for Action.

14. The Hague Appeal for Peace is an international network of peace and justice organizations which has produced fifty recommendations for the global promotion of peace. See www.haguepeace.org/index.php?name=aboutus.

15. Subsequent launches occurred at several international forums, including the 1999 Association of Women in Development annual conference (Virginia, United States, October 1999), the regional preparatory conferences for the Beijing +5 review organized in 1999 and 2000 (Bangkok, Addis Ababa, Geneva), the Finnish Parliament, and numerous meetings in the United Kingdom. Additionally, the forty-third session of the Commission for the Status of Women (CSW) and the International Women's Day celebrations in 1999 provided further opportunities to launch the initiative. This consisted of round-table discussions with high-profile speakers such as Dr. Noeleen Heyzerr (UNIFEM), along with representatives of well-known NGOs such as Femmes Africa Solidarite (Geneva) and support from the Women's Desk of the Netherlands Ministry of Foreign Affairs.

16. The members of the Security Council at that time were the United States, Jamaica, Tunisia, Argentina, United Kingdom, China, Bangladesh, Russia, Netherlands, Canada, France, Malaysia, Ukraine, Mali, and Namibia.

17. Financial support for this work came from IA out of its own core funding.

18. This conference, also referred to as Bejing +5, was convened under the title of "Women 2000: Gender Equality, Development and Peace for the Twenty-First Century." It redirected world attention to the progress made by governments toward implementing the Beijing Platform for Action, a twelve-point global agenda for achieving gender equality.

19. The group consisted of IA, the Hague Appeal for Peace, the Women's Commission on Refugee Women and Children, Amnesty International, and the Women's International League for Peace and Freedom. Subsequently, Amnesty has withdrawn from the group and the International Women's Tribune Centre and the Gender Caucus for the ICC have joined.

20. The findings of a gender mainstreaming study started in 1997 on the role of women in five multidimensional peacekeeping operations (in Bosnia-Herzegovina, Cambodia, El Salvador, Namibia, and South Africa) showed that women peacemakers working with local women's groups have much to contribute to the alleviation of a conflict situation. This study led to the powerful Windhoek Declaration and the resultant Namibia Plan of Action on Mainstreaming a Gender Perspective in Multidimensional Peace Support Operations of 31 May 2000.

21. Arria Formula meetings are open debates held by the Security Council to discuss issues of interest to their mandate. Members can invite anyone they choose to speak at these meetings.

22. On International Women's Day, 8 March 2000.

23. Held in the Finnish Parliament and hosted by the Speaker of the Parliament (Helsinki, November 1999).

24. Subsequently, these women electrified Council members with their personal testimonies, reflections, and perspectives on women, conflict, and peacebuilding at an Arria Formula meeting in October 2002.

25. This policy briefing was edited by Nicola Johnston, senior policy adviser, Gender and Peacebuilding Programme, IA.

26. Leitana Nehan, the conflict and development agency from Bougainville, presented the signatures to the Secretary-General's representative during the International Women's Day celebrations on 8 March 2000.

27. The work has been initially undertaken by Ancil Adrian-Paul, Dessy Roussanova, and Feyzi Ismail, and subsequently by Nicola Johnston and Bethan Cobley.

28. The campaign's website address is www.womenbuildingpeace.org; the NGOWG's website can be found at www.peacewomen.org.

29. See Appendix 1 for the successful affirmation by the United Nations in 2000.

30. This agreement is now known as the Cotonou Agreement. This is a comprehensive aid and trade agreement concluded between seventy-seven ACP (African, Caribbean, and Pacific) countries and the EU which was signed in June 2000 in Cotonou.

References

Anderlini, S., R. Manchanda, and K. Karmali, eds. 2000. "Women, Violent Conflict and Peacebuilding: Global Perspectives." Report of the International Conference, IA, London, 5-7 May 1999.

International Alert, with comments from Mazurana, D. 2000. *Gender and Multidimensional Peace Support Operations*. International Alert.

Karame, K., and G. Bertinussen. 2000. "Gendering Human Security: From Marginalisation to Integration of Women in Peacebuilding." NUPI Report No. 261.

Manchanda, R. 2001 (June). "Redefining and Feminising Security." *Perspectives, Economic and Political Weekly*.

UNICEF and UNIFEM. 2000. *War Affected Children*. The Machel Review (1996 to 2000). Canada and Norway: UNICEF and UNIFEM

Chapter 7
Impacting on Community Policing Policy: South Africa

UMAC—Sean Tait

In 1993, with the end of apartheid and the transition to multiparty democracy, policing in South Africa underwent a radical transformation, shifting away from a militaristic, authoritarian approach to policing, to one that aspired to greater community involvement. This community partnership approach to policing was advocated in the 1996 National Crime Prevention Strategy[1] and the 1999 White Paper on Safety and Security.[2] However, in spite of these legislative initiatives designed to stimulate community involvement in policing and greater trust in the police as impartial protectors of law and order, crime rates continued to dramatically increase. The growing disorder contributed to heightened fears about security and safety which predisposed politicians, the police, and the general public to favor implementing stringent law and order tactics rather than aspirationalist community policing strategies. By 1999, the reality of policing in South Africa differed from the legislative framework and it was evident that quite an extensive gulf had emerged between suggested policy and its implementation.

Recognizing this gap, in 1999, the South African NGO U Managing Conflict (UMAC) instigated a project which sought to illustrate that the advocated national policy of community policing could be an effective and feasible option, if only it were properly and fully implemented. Their strategy to ensure such implementation is the subject of this case study. This chapter explores the way in which UMAC worked to bridge the gap between legislation and implementation by assuming a leadership role on an issue where policymakers were reluctant and uncertain. The chapter outlines the background to the South African policing debate, explains the history to UMAC's strategy and the tactics it employed, as well as describing how UMAC sparked a NGO reaffirmation of the benefits of community policing and in particular crime prevention. The chapter also assesses the lessons learned by UMAC from this initiative.

Background to the Intervention: The Policing Debate

In many deeply divided societies, the police are regarded as emblematic of societal discord, with their actions often deepening, perpetuating, and exacerbating the division. Often, the police force will be staffed by a particular ethnic or political group who are operationally repressive, partial, unaccountable, and highly militarized, and whose activities are carried out with scant regard for human rights, the rule of law, and due legal process (Brewer, 1991: 183-85).

The South African police force, during the apartheid regime, conformed to this characterization, and their modus operandi was the violent suppression of nonwhite political movements. Discrimination, repression, and subjugation were the policies practiced by the police, with violence and brutality as their weapons of choice. In the absence of a just and impartial policing service, township communities enacted their own system of law and order. Community courts, self-defense units, self-protection units, and task forces were established within the townships both to defend against official police attacks and to provide basic safety services. At their height, in the mid-1980s, some four hundred people's courts were thought to be operating throughout the country (Scharf, 1992). They had become such a feature of the South African landscape that one of the central debates in the transformation of policing in South Africa at the time of the 1994 elections, was the extent to which nonstate ordering could be accommodated into the new political system.

A reformed, effective, legitimate security apparatus was deemed to be crucial to the enduring social, political, and economic transformation of South African society, as popular acceptance of a police service can often be a litmus test for the successful progression of political transition. In 1995, the South African Police Service Act[3] marked this new service-oriented approach by renaming the force the South African Police Service. It also adopted community policing as its major approach to involving the community in law and order issues. Community policing is deemed to be service-oriented rather than force-oriented, and is based on providing victim support and protecting citizens' rights in crime prevention. A key component of the transformation to community policing is the requirement that a secretive militaristic police force is replaced by an institution under inclusive civilian oversight.

Community policing emphasizes the establishment of police-community partnerships and a problem-solving, transparent, client-centered approach to policing. It is essentially a bottom-up approach to security needs, with local communities involved in setting community policing priorities and partnering with the police in developing programs for crime prevention. With community policing, the state would no longer be the most important actor in South African policing. Community Police Forums were the legislative answer to community policing.

Community Policing Forums (1995)

The functions of the Community Policing Forums included promoting local accountability and cooperation between the South African Police Service and the community, monitoring the effectiveness and efficiency of the service, advising the police service about local policing priorities, evaluating the provision of visible police services, and requesting enquiries into policing matters. The implementation of these forums proved an arduous process. Operating against a backdrop of decades of mistrust and abuse suffered by the nonwhite population at the hands of the police, the forum sessions often descended into tit-for-tat battlegrounds about community politics, thus impeding opportunities for constructive dialogue over issues of security and crime. A correlating and debilitating factor was that the community policing experiment appeared to be having no effect on the dangerously high crime rates.

National Crime Prevention Strategy (1996)

In 1996, the National Crime Prevention Strategy was introduced in response to rising crime rates. This strategy advocated the broadening of the safety and security partnership beyond the criminal justice system to fields such as education and local government and advocated crime prevention as a national government priority. Sole responsibility for crime and public safety was removed from the police and distributed across government institutions, civil society, and individuals. The Strategy advocated a variety of activities, each of which reaffirmed the use of community policing as the ethos to be adopted:

- community education with a view to improved participation in the criminal justice system;
- a program on reengineering key components of the criminal justice system for improved effectiveness;
- the systemic introduction of a system of victim empowerment and support;
- designing out crime through environmental design and an acknowledgment of the role of urban planning in the creation of safer communities; and
- specific mechanisms to address international crime, extending the partnership beyond the country's borders.

Implementation of this strategy proved extremely difficult as the legislation faced similar problems to those encountered by the community policing initiative, primarily an environment of rampant crime which was not conducive to the nurturing of an experimental project dependent upon long-term provincial commitment, cooperation, and support. The establishment of a national committee to initiate and structure provincial interactions met with varying success. In the Western Cape, a Multi-Agency Delivery Action Mechanism (MADAM) was established to spearhead their Provincial Crime Prevention Strategy, but this proved to be the exception. Rauch and Simpson[4] primarily attributed the implementation difficulties to a lack of resources, skills, and technical capacity on the part of the community and the police. This gap in implementation was a major reason behind the failure to popularize and galvanize support for community policing at the grassroots level and served to reinforce the domination of law enforcement agencies in the policing debate. It is not surprising, therefore, that community policing became restricted to the more commonly understood and easier to apply notion of highly visible proactive patrols, to the detriment of a long-term investment in community crime prevention strategies.

White Paper on Safety and Security (1999)

Legislation continued to outpace implementation with key recommendations from the 1996 National Crime Prevention Strategy adopted into the White Paper on Safety and Security (1999). This established a framework for the evolution of policing over a five-year period. The paper advocated a dual approach to policing, suggesting a return to the core duties of detection, investigation, and prosecution, with increased training and information technology highlighted as core investment areas. Also, the development of a crime prevention strategy involving local and provincial governments and the establishment of local crime prevention forums to enable grassroots community participation. Opposition to these suggestions, although not unified or directed, was extensive. Local government, itself in the midst of upheaval and political transition, balked at the idea of additional responsibility. The public, annoyed and disgruntled with continually high crime, were cynical of new gimmicks, and were nostalgic for an era when the police had effectively maintained societal order.

Support for community policing reached a low ebb. This was eventually mirrored in the national government with the appointment of ANC member Steve Tshwete as Minister of Police in 1999, who all but shelved the National Crime Prevention Strategy and absorbed resources into the general police budget. A "get tough on crime" or "zero tolerance" approach was introduced. Dubbed Operation Crackdown, it identified national crime hot spots and centrally directed a tough security response to those areas, independent from local police stations and local communities. Minimum sentences, more stringent bail procedures, random searches, and roadblocks were introduced, and resources were diverted away from local community policing. The vision of a community partnership approach to policing all but disappeared. At the same time, the crime figures remained worryingly high, with murder rates in South Africa in the 1995-1998 period at 64.5 per one hundred thousand—eight times higher than the United States (SAPS Crime Information Center, 1999: 3; ISS, 1998: 6).

Intervention by UMAC

It was against this background of continuing high crime rates and a failure to establish community policing, that UMAC decided to act. Established in 1985, UMAC is a South African NGO which advances peacebuilding and undertakes work to strengthen the South African transition to democracy. Previously known as the Urban Monitoring and Awareness Committee, its activities prior to the 1994 elections focused on exposing state abuses during the height of apartheid. Capitalizing on the grassroots knowledge, capacity, and network of trust built up over the years, UMAC's role expanded into conflict resolution activities during South Africa's transition from apartheid to democracy. It was a key resource in monitoring the conflict resolution processes during the 1994 elections. Currently, its strategic priorities are in the area of human safety and security, with a concentration on developing approaches to criminal and social justice issues in an integrated and holistic manner.

UMAC has offices in Cape Town, Port Elizabeth, and East London and has twenty staff consisting of four administrators, six managers, including both director and project managers, and ten staff located in the field. A central aim of the organization is the integration and implementation of credible and legitimate policing based on the philosophy of community involvement. This experience and commitment has resulted in UMAC accumulating a wealth of expertise in community-police relations, stemming from 1985 until the present. The organization is firmly committed to the promotion of problem solving, community partnership, conflict resolution strategies, and crime prevention procedures in addressing the root causes of crime. Rather than forceful methods of controlling crime, including vigilantism, with its inherent dangers of infringement on human rights and a return to an incremental militarization of South African society.

With the passing of the South African Police Service Act in 1995, UMAC was centrally involved in establishing Community Policing Forums throughout the Western Cape and later transferring this knowledge to the Eastern Cape. Although legislation had established a framework for community policing, the difficulties and challenges of implementation had undermined momentum and innovation. Even in areas where community policing structures had been implemented, such as the Western Cape Community Policing Project, fundamental problems emerged which limited the overall effectiveness of the project. UMAC were acutely aware of the shortcomings of the Community Policing Forums, which had mass grassroots participation but a narrow focus in terms of connected personnel, in the criminal justice system. The forum's primary agenda was therefore directed by policing issues of criminal detection, rather than crime prevention or victim-related issues. The Department of Social Services, for example, created a number of transformative committees on children, which examined issues such as child support grants and street children; despite the obvious implications of these issues in the crime prevention arena, this agency was given no role in the Community Policing Forums. UMAC decided that they did not want simply to advocate for structural reform of the Community Policing Forums, but to look at alternative models which would better facilitate community policing approaches and complement the forums.

Community Safety Forums

UMAC decided to develop a new local partnership model to illustrate the easibility of a fully implemented and operationalized crime prevention partnership as envisaged by the National Crime Prevention Strategy (1996) and the White Paper on Safety and Security (1999). The effort was to demonstrate the tangible benefits that could be derived from the existing legislation. These new partnerships were called Community Safety Forums, and the challenge that faced UMAC was to develop, implement, and maintain these as an effective policy strategy through which to implement community policing in South African society. An additional goal would be to demonstrate the potential of the pilot in terms of both process and impact, and thus enable UMAC to adopt an advocacy role to expand the intervention nationally.

Development of the Strategy

UMAC had a well-established reputation and credibility among South African policymakers, academics, and the NGO sector, placing it in a powerful position to begin the campaign. Its organizational knowledge and experience enabled it to articulate a reliable and authoritative voice in the crime prevention debate. This process was assisted by UMAC's range of established networks and linkages, both at the community level among fellow NGOs, and with the state.

The Community Safety Forums Project was launched in early 1999, with a feasibility study examining the idea of multidisciplinary forums at a local level as a mechanism toward both enhancing the effectiveness of the criminal justice system and facilitating the identification and implementation of crime prevention initiatives.[5] The study increased the credibility of the initiative with policymakers, which facilitated UMAC's efforts to garner political support for the implementation of the forums as well as generating legitimacy for the intervention. It also established an administrative and political platform for future debate on the potential for national expansion.

UMAC subsequently began to develop a strategy and a workable business plan for the development of the Community Safety Forums, and proposed these to key players for their endorsement. This stage of the strategy took over eighteen months of development, and required extensive consultations with various parties, mainly national and provincial government officials. UMAC also engaged in dialogue with existing Community Policing Forums personnel to try and ensure their support for the initiative. Simultaneous to the UMAC consultations on the development of a new model of police-community partnerships, public consultations were being held regarding the White Paper on Safety and Security (1999). UMAC enthusiastically engaged in the public discourse and presented practical options for the implementation of some of the policy ideas. The culmination of this stage in the strategy was a three-year plan which outlined pilot areas for the implementation of Community Safety Forums, suggested the functions of the forums, and outlined the stakeholders whom UMAC believed should be involved to ensure their value and effectiveness.

Intentions

The aim of UMAC in launching the Community Safety Forum project was to assist the implementation of the recommendations from the National Crime Prevention Strategy (1996) and the White Paper on Safety and Security (1999), which highlighted the utilization of local solutions in crime prevention. The objectives of the forums were to break down barriers between government and community and assist the involvement of civil society in taking control in their own areas in issues of crime prevention and management. It was intended that each Community Safety Forum would be a single, multidisciplinary forum where actors from local government and criminal justice agencies, community leaders, NGOs, and various government departments such as those of education and labor could meet to debate issues and pursue cooperative solutions to prevent and manage crime. The forums also were intended to address those additional causes of crime, such as housing, education, restorative justice, and urban planning needs, which were not traditionally within the purview of the South African Police Service and the existing Community Policing Forums. It was hoped that this broad frame of reference and the involvement of diverse policy actors could enable complex projects such as the Victim Empowerment Program or the Rape and Child Abuse Protocols to be debated and developed through partnership approaches with the communities. It was also hoped that the forums could save time and bureaucratic processing by having key personnel debating the salient issues under one roof.

It was anticipated that, although UMAC's project staff would be essential to the establishment of the Community Safety Forums, they would gradually decrease their direct operational involvement, with the state assuming greater ownership of the process. This would ultimately enable UMAC to relinquish primary responsibility for the forums.

Making It Happen

In the Western Cape, seven pilot communities, offering an urban/rural split, were selected for the introduction of a Community Safety Forum.[6] Khayelitsha, just outside Cape Town, is an example of an urban pilot. It is a predominantly black community of four hundred thousand people which is afflicted by steep levels of overcrowding and high crime rates. Robertson, located three hundred kilometers from Cape Town and with a population of approximately one hundred thousand people, was chosen as a rural pilot area. It is a typical rural locale, where there is a stark dichotomy between the townspeople and those who inhabit the surrounding farms. Situated in the heart of the South African wine producing region, it has significant problems of alcohol abuse which are a legacy of the notorious DOP system.[7] This in turn has exacerbated problems of violent assault, domestic abuse, and an expanding drug trafficking trade which has contributed to a burgeoning gang problem.

The Community Safety Forum project was launched in the Western Cape under the guidance and full endorsement of the MADAM, the province's highest decision-making body at the time for crime prevention. Its membership consisted of individuals such as the Provincial Commissioner of Police, the Regional Manager of Justice, and the Provincial Head for Correctional Services, and it was chaired by the director general of the province. A MADAM subcommittee assumed responsibility for steering the project, ensuring that the government-backed project would have credibility from the outset. In addition to overseeing the project, the Community Safety Forums could utilize this provincial body for referrals, mandating, and problem solving. A similar process was followed in the Eastern Cape, where the establishment of a project steering committee was linked to the Provincial Crime Prevention Strategy. Provincial and senior policymakers were critically involved in the development and guidance of the project and as such provided a sense of ownership and legitimacy that was invaluable to the anticipated outcome of the project.

Project Implementation

The project plan consisted of three phases. Phase 1 involved identifying and securing commitment from the key stakeholders. Phase 2 was the implementation of a UMAC-directed training program of prospective participants in the Community Safety Forums. Phase 3 was to focus on reviewing and auditing current governmental and civil society projects, so that they could be included in a holistic Safety Plan for Crime Prevention.

Nine staff members were responsible for implementing the pilot projects. Two project managers were assigned, one for each of the East and West Cape Provinces. In the latter, one field staff member was responsible for two pilot forums, while in the Eastern Cape, where distances between project sites are far greater, each staff member was responsible for one forum.

Field staff were in charge of actively facilitating the creation, development, and promotion of the Community Safety Forums. They spearheaded Phase 1 of the project by identifying relevant stakeholders and gaining their commitment to participate in the project through a series of bilateral meetings. These stakeholders generally included the station commissioner, chief magistrate, senior public prosecutor, local government officer, and NGOs working in criminal justice projects. UMAC also involved nontraditional stakeholders from outside the criminal justice sector such as the Departments of Health and Education, as it was believed that they too would have a role in this holistic crime prevention intervention.

Stakeholders were initially cynical and wary of the Community Safety Forum project. Time and relationship building on the part of field staff was necessary to assure actors of the efficacy of the project. Identification of influential stakeholders was conducted in a comprehensive manner by scanning the crime prevention arena, matching inputs against the facilitative and administrative arrangements in the local context, and then approaching these agencies, departments, and competencies. Once an agency had been identified as having a need or role in the safety and security environment, a field officer would attempt to make a presentation on the Community Safety Forum to the most senior individual. Generally, a preliminary introductory meeting was arranged, followed by a more detailed presentation.

UMAC mapped the progress of the current legislation, highlighted local and international trends, and debated the transformation of the criminal justice system in South Africa in terms of the law enforcement versus crime prevention discourse. The merits of a partnership approach were strongly articulated, with the aim of accumulating support for the initiative. The credibility of the facilitators and their knowledge of the field proved invaluable, as did the advantage of being able to draw upon existing provincial government support. Mature, skilled facilitators proved to be the most successful, but UMAC had to balance the skill-based allocation of resources against a geographical consideration which enabled facilitators to become immersed in the local dynamics, cultivate a network of relationships, and identify problem issues and crime patterns.

Among the more reluctant partners were the Community Policing Forums, who initially saw the Community Safety Forums as a duplication of their work. UMAC used the workshop interactions to dispel ignorance, fears, and rumors about such duplication. In recognition of this suspicion, a compromise was negotiated whereby the Community Safety Forums publicly recognized the Community Policing Forums as the primary community representative body. They agreed to work together where possible. In a station area like Khayelitsha, for instance, political power play amongst community leaders was inhibiting progress in the Community Policing Forums, so the Community Safety Forums offered to help with the long-term repercussions and micromanagement of the problems. UMAC's decision to work with the Community Policing Forums was not simple expediency (although it did create a bulwark against widespread political criticism), but was derived from UMAC's principles to support and reinforce the existing process aimed at the positive transformation of South Africa.

Phase 2 of the strategy involved building on this emerging partnership through a series of capacity-building training sessions held on the subjects of crime prevention and cooperative governance. These introductory workshops were initially held on a monthly basis to clarify the aims of the Community Safety Forum, and to enable participants to build relationships as well as focusing on information sharing and forging understandings amongst participants. Training concentrated on four areas:

1. the differences between social crime prevention and law enforcement techniques;
2. structures and systems within the criminal justice and policing system;
3. the need for victim empowerment programs; and
4. project management and how to apply these skills to community safety programs.

Phase 3 of the strategy involved examining and auditing current govern-mental and civil society projects and interventions to identify areas of potential cooperation. The aim was to catalogue established projects with a crime prevention function and foster integration and cooperation. A matrix of current interventions would provide clearer insights into the needs of a particular com-munity, providing a partnership platform for future initiatives. It would also enable allocation of activities and responsibilities to participants in order to begin implementation of the safety plan and effect the initiation of projects to address the issues identified in the safety plan.

UMAC's advocacy for the Community Safety Forum project was also accompanied by an ongoing media campaign to raise awareness about their ac-tivities. The campaign included a communication component which engaged stakeholders in recording their role and contribution to crime prevention. These inputs were translated into a media campaign which included, for example, a competition for primary schools to design a poster about Community Safety Forum activities.

Outcomes

The initial goal of each Community Safety Forum was the production of a Safety Plan for Crime Prevention. This framework document outlined potential crime prevention initiatives and defined roles and responsibilities specific to the requirements of a particular area. These often varied, as the Community Safety Forums addressed the local safety and security needs of individual communities. Consequently, plans needed to be adaptable and diverse in operation. For exam-ple, in Khayelitsha, the vigilante issue is a pressing concern, whereas in Robert-son it is the growing drugs trade.

A second essential feature of the Community Safety Forum is its ability to improve the effectiveness of a variety of initiatives by, for example, ensuring that government processes are accessible for community input, fostering partner-ships between relevant community and policy bodies, and actioning and imple-menting measures where possible. The Lay Assessor Project serves as an exam-ple of an initiative whereby the Community Safety Forum identified a gap and proposed action to improve the operation of an already existing policy. Lay as-sessors are individuals appointed as assistants to magistrates to advise on the local dynamics and context of crimes committed in township communities. Previous to the Community Safety Forum intervention, lay assessors were appointed on an individual basis regardless of their linkages to organized com-munity structures. Hence, they may have been civilians, but not necessarily community representatives. The Community Safety Forum was able to facilitate an improvement to this process by enabling community participation in the election and administration of the lay assessors so that community organizations were properly represented alongside representatives from the Department of Justice and Constitutional Development.

Another area where the Community Safety Forum enhanced the operation of policy was in improving the linkages between citizens and state justice. For instance, after the first court[8] was established in a South African township in Nyanga/Philippi, the Community Safety Forum assisted in the smooth operation of this resource by educating the community about legal processes. They aided in the smooth implementation of court-distributed child support payments, thus easing tensions between the Justice Department and the community. This has been further promoted via regular information sessions regarding proposed changes to bail conditions, community sentencing, and the transformation of the child and youth care system.

Improved communication and interaction between state and nonstate actors in these Community Safety Forum pilot areas is demonstrated in the number of community structures that are now formally interacting with departments previously out of reach, such as the Department of Justice and Correctional Services. A number of interventions promoting increased partnership between the state and community structures have been actively facilitated through the Community Safety Forum process. These include the development of victim empowerment programs and the development of protocols on rape and child abuse to promote better service delivery in respect to crimes against women and children.

Community Training Programs on issues such as child support and domestic violence were also promoted in the Community Safety Forums. Their success was facilitated by the fact that there were a greater range of stakeholders who could contribute to the content and implementation of programs through the establishment of the forums. New partnerships were established between schools and police for regular patrolling as well as lectures on crime prevention and safety. The Community Safety Forums thus became a mechanism for past, present, and future initiatives to develop in an integrated fashion.

Was the Project a Success?

In 2001, UMAC commissioned an external evaluation of the Community Safety Forums, to assess the strengths, weaknesses, and overall effectiveness of the project (Pelser and Louw, 2001: 7).[9]

The evaluators noted the project had successfully achieved the following:

1. the forums had developed a better understanding of crime prevention amongst a range of actors within and outside the local and provincial spheres of government;
2. government departments had been assisted to receive input from a range of civil society organizations that might otherwise not have had such an opportunity if the forums had not existed;
3. there was a better understanding amongst government and civil society actors regarding the relationships between their various roles and activities;
4. the project had enabled agreement to be developed amongst these actors on priority issues to be addressed; and
5. the project had enabled these actors to develop a better coordinated response to these priority issues.

Lessons Learned

The process of assisting the implementation of previously unsuccessful government policy has been a useful and interesting learning experience for UMAC. A number of critical lessons have emerged: the importance of utilizing existing policy, guidelines and legislation, achieving ownership of the implementation process, demonstrating success, relationship building, managing institutional agendas, and dealing with political fluidity and resistance to change.

Utilizing Existing Policy

Critical to gaining support from state and civil society actors was the ability to demonstrate the clear link between the UMAC initiative and existing government policy. This linkage provided an impetus to state actors to participate in the programs even in the face of limited budgets, narrow job descriptions, and hectic schedules. In this case, the Community Safety Forum initiative was drawn from the government's White Paper on Safety and Security, the National Crime Prevention Strategy, and most fundamentally the new South African Constitution. The Community Safety Forums thus created a working model at the local level which assisted the implementation of these policies, thereby creating justification for the participation of a range of state actors in the continuing policing debate.

Ownership

Ownership has been another important lesson. There are few visible victories in the arena of crime prevention—hence the popularity of stringent law enforcement measures. It was therefore crucial for the continued operation of the Community Safety Forums that stakeholders were able to partner with and claim ownership of the initiative so that it did not become singularly associated with UMAC or seen as an externally imposed experiment.

Demonstrating Success

Demonstrating success is perhaps one of the most important activities to plan for in an intervention of this nature, and has enormous value in terms of advocacy for further development and supporting participants, especially state actors, to justify continued involvement in the project when pressured to disengage and reprioritize. The formal evaluation undertaken by UMAC became a key tool in responding to critics and doubters. The experience of an effective working model was paramount in convincing key decision makers of the viability of pursuing its development. It is also helpful if the project can organize a conspicuous media strategy which communicates the results of the project both internally within departments and agencies and externally to the public at large.

Relationship Building

Developing strong and productive relationships with the diversity of individuals in a joint NGO-government project is essential to its long-term success. It is important to recognize and accommodate different perspectives, assumptions, priorities, and personalities. The NGO initiating the project has a crucial role to play in building, strengthening, and maintaining these relationships through the use of professional facilitation and conflict resolution training processes. For UMAC, the cultivation of trusting relationships has been at the core of the project's success. This has been achieved by a combination of the methodology of facilitation along with extensive knowledge and expertise of the subject matter gained via consultations and discourse.

Managing Institutional Agendas

Smooth interaction between the actors involved in the Community Safety Forums was and continues to be difficult, for it requires transcending the boundaries of current disciplines and finding the space within busy schedules and strict performance contracts to work together in an ongoing and structured manner. Although there is little doubt that the project's functioning is dependent on the multistakeholder approach, the presence of multiple actors, claiming multiple agendas, is a constant hurdle. At times, the stakeholders are absorbed in lobbying for their own individual agendas, and there lies the danger that the overall aim of project—providing safety and security for the community—will be lost in this trend of individual agenda setting. Here, the active conflict resolution and facilitation abilities of UMAC proved indispensable in facilitating consensual outcomes. Flexibility and patience were essential, as UMAC had to adapt to a variety of institutional agendas and priorities. UMAC also had to facilitate procedures for transcending strict government boundaries in order for a variety of agencies to work together.

Resistance to Change

There is a vital need to be conscious of the insecurity and the fear of change that is inherent amongst stakeholders. To allay such fears, NGOs need to demonstrate a coherent strategy with clear achievable goals and to involve themselves in continual dialogue with key stakeholders.

Political Fluidity

Successful conflict resolution projects are generally characterized by their long-term commitment to the issue at stake. Conversely, success in politics is most commonly characterized by the exact opposite—short-term actions that maximize immediate gain for political advantage. Consequently, when NGOs attempt to instigate a long-term project that overlaps with political institutions, they need to be prepared for political fluidity. This can occur in many forms: civil servants swapping posts, elections changing the government, or policy shifts in reaction to a crisis. Regardless of the impetus, NGOs need to be ready for the changes and handle them constructively.

UMAC worked amidst the institutional flux and change common to all countries emerging from protracted conflict. During the initial phase of the project, three changes in the Western Cape's political leadership occurred, each bringing with it a change in priority for the institutions participating in the Community Safety Forums. For instance, the MADAM is no longer in existence, and in its place a crime prevention partnership called the Cape Renewal Strategy was created. This new strategy dovetailed with the Community Safety

Forum in some ways but contradicted it in others, and two years later, MADAM seems to be making a comeback. Managing these changes has been part of the facilitation role and shows the resilience of the Community Safety Forum model.

The project's long-term answer to local political fluidity and dynamics was to pilot the intervention in different locales, thereby providing a counterbalance to potential political risks as well as demonstrating the feasibility of the approach across a range of conditions. The intention was to provide national policymakers with a number of clear-cut examples of the operationalization of crime prevention across different dynamics, but with as much standardization as possible to allow for a national recommendation.

Conclusion

The Community Safety Forums have resulted in many accomplishments and benefits in the area of human safety and security. Probably the most important, however, has been the expanding recognition and openness on the part of the state and the public concerning the merits of a community-state partnership approach to crime prevention measures. As a measure of such recognition, the Western Cape provincial government has now made a definitive financial commitment to the project. Similarly, in the Eastern Cape, the project is formally linked to the provincial strategy on crime prevention. At a national level, a current review of the Police Act includes an investigation of the Community Safety Forums as a means of promoting broader community-state partnerships in the crime prevention field. Contrary to the disillusionment with community policing that existed in 1999, there is now an observable enthusiasm for continued state and community collaboration on issues of policing as a result of UMAC's initiative, which has demonstrated that community policing can indeed be successful, if effectively implemented.

Notes

1. The National Crime Prevention Strategy was initiated by the South African Executive in 1995. It aims to provide a comprehensive framework for coordinated governmental and civil society measures to tackle crime. It emphasizes wider responsibility for crime, not just limited to the criminal justice process but involving community values and education. It represents a significant paradigm shift which advocates proactive crime prevention rather than reactive crime control. See www.gov.za/reports/1996/crime1.htm.

2. The White Paper on Safety and Security outlines a five-year plan for the Department of Safety and Security. It adopts a dual approach to crime reduction, combining law enforcement (policing) and social crime prevention. See www.polity. org.za/html/govdocs/whitepapers/safetydwp.html?rebookmark=1.

3. See www.polity.org.za/html/govdocs/legislation/1995/act95-068.html.

4. Unpublished paper on the National Crime Prevention Strategy.

5. The study was funded by the UK Department for International Development (DFID) and the Open Society Foundation.

6. In addition to the initial seven sites, a year later, three were initiated in the Eastern Cape followed a year after that with a further three in KwaZulu Natal, and one in the Durban area.

7. The DOP System in the Western Cape involved the payment of alcohol to farm laborers as a condition of their service. The system is no longer legal.

8. Previously, black citizens had to travel considerable distance outside of the townships, to attend court proceedings.

9. This was conducted by the research company, Insideout, and the Institute for Security Studies.

References

Brewer, John D. 1991. *Inside the RUC: Routine Policing in a Divided Society.* Oxford: Clarendon.

Catholic Institute for International Relations. 1988. *Now Everyone Is Afraid: The Changing Face of Policing in South Africa.* Cape Town, South Africa: Allies Press.

Interdepartmental Strategy Task Team of Department for Safety and Security. (Department of Correctional Services, Department of Justice, Department of Welfare.) 1996. *National Crime Prevention Strategy.* Pretoria Republic of South Africa: Government Printer.

Louw, A. and M. Shaw. 1988. "Dubious Distinctions: Comparing Crime across Countries." *Crime Index* 2. Pretoria Republic of South Africa: ISS/Nedcor.

Ministry for Safety and Security. 1999. In *Service of Safety and Security 1999-2004.* Pretoria Republic of South Africa: Department for Safety and Security.

Nina, D. 1994. "Reorganising People's Power in the New South Africa: Working on Peace, Safety and Justice with a Gugulethu Street Committee." *Imbizo* 1.

Parliament of South Africa. South African Police Service Act (68, 1995). 1995. Pretoria, Republic of South Africa: Government Printer.

———. South African Constitution (108, 1996). 1999. Pretoria, Republic of South Africa: Government printer.

Pelser, E. 1999. "Can Community Police Fora Work? Revisiting Key Police Strategy." *Crime and Conflict* 18.

Pelser, E., and A. Louw. 2001. *Evaluation of Community Safety Forums.* Pretoria Republic of South Africa: ISS, 2001.

Rauch, J. 1988. "Police Reform and South Africa's Transition." Unpublished paper.

Rauch, J., and Simpson, G. Undated. *Reflections on the National Crime Prevention Strategy.* Johannesburg Republic of South Africa: Centre for the Study of Violence and Reconciliation.

SAPS Crime Information Analysis Centre. 1999. Crime Statistics, Pretoria, Republic of South Africa.

Scharf,W.1992."CommunityPolicinginPost-ApartheidSouthAfrica:TheViewsof some Black TownshipCivic Associationsin Cape Town." Paper presented to the InternationalPerspectivesConferenceonCrime,JusticeandPublicOrder,Leningrad.

———. 1996, (7 May). "Community Policing: A Preliminary Critical Analysis." Paper presented to a Workshop on Community Policing, Techikon South Africa.

Shearing, C. 1998 (August). "Changing Paradigms in Policing: The Significance of Community Policing for the Governance of Security." Occasional Paper 34, Institute for Security Studies.

Tait, S. 2000 (October). "Gugulethu South African Police Service Transformation: A Case Study of the Challenges and Complexities Facing Transformation of State Policing in South Africa." Dissertation in Criminology, University of Cape Town, South Africa.

————. 2001 (23 May). "Vigilantism." Paper presented to South African Police Service Western Cape Workshop on Vigilantism.

————. 2001 (September). "Crime Prevention and Peacebuilding." Paper presented to South African Association for Conflict Intervention, Biannual Conference.

UMAC. 2002. Project Proposal and Report Documentation on Community Safety Forums. Cape Town, South Africa: UMAC.

Chapter 8
Multifaceted Programming: Influencing Policies in Burundi

Search for Common Ground—Amr Abdalla and Susan Collin Marks

Search for Common Ground (SFCG) has been engaged on the ground in Burundi since 1995. The intricacies of this conflict require a multifaceted engagement on the ground and include international actors and foreign policy. Through this experience, SFCG has developed significant insight into the dual meaning of policy and the overarching challenges with which NGOs seeking to engage at a policy level must grapple. This chapter addresses one of these overarching challenges through the specific features of the Great Lakes Policy Forum (GLPF), which is a strategic coalition of international organizations, governmental, and nongovernmental agencies, business leaders, and the media, with the shared goal of building sustainable peace and preventing further bloodshed in the Great Lakes region of Africa. The learning generated from this work is reflected upon in the concluding section of the chapter.

History of the Conflict

Since 1993, civil war in Burundi between Hutu rebels and the minority Tutsi government has claimed the lives of more than two hundred thousand people. While the conflict in Burundi is perceived to be mainly political, its ethnic dimension, whether real or manipulated, has profoundly affected the Burundian population. Tutsis live in extreme fear of being exterminated should Hutus take a large share of power in the country. Past events, and the example of what happened in Rwanda when Hutus took over power, fuel their concerns. As a result,

Tutsis are sometimes resistant to efforts to distribute power between the two ethnic groups. On the other hand, Hutus, despite being the vast majority of the population, continue to feel disenfranchised on all levels. They suffer from poor access to resources, education, employment, health, and political participation. The resistance they feel coming from the Tutsis to efforts to share power and resources only reaffirms the Hutus's sense of oppression and resentment.

Since the outbreak of violence, there have been continual attempts—formal and informal—at negotiations. High profile, secret talks held in 1994, 1997, and 1998, have been equally unable to bring together all the fighting factions in an inclusive agreement. In 2000, the Arusha Accords, mediated by Nelson Mandela and signed by seventeen political parties, secured a political agreement and established a transitional government, but the parties were unable to maintain a ceasefire among hard-liners and military groups who had withdrawn from the negotiations. In 2001, the process continued with an attempt at dialogue in South Africa; again, the meeting dissolved with no face-to-face contact between rebel and government leaders. Another attempt at inclusive formal talks between the government and all three rebel groups began in August 2002, in the Tanzanian capital of Dar-es-Salaam. A ceasefire agreement between the transitional government and the larger of the two main Hutu rebel groups, the Conseil national pour la defense de la democratic-Forces nationals de liberation (CNDD-FDD), was signed on 3 December 2002, and took effect on 30 December. Efforts to enforce this agreement continued through February 2003, and numerous violations occurred on both sides. Nonetheless, there is reason for optimism, as important players including the former CNDD-FDD leader, Jean-Bosco Ndayikengurukiye, have returned to Burundi to assume seats in the transitional government.

Search for Common Ground

In 1995, in the wake of the genocide in Rwanda the previous year, SFCG and the European Centre for Common Ground (ECCG)[1] launched SFCG in Burundi to help stop the horrors of Rwanda being repeated in Burundi. Following an assessment in conjunction with Refugees International and the United Nations Secretary-General's Special Representative, and with funding from USAID, an office was established in Bujumbura in early February.

SFCG in Burundi began its Burundian activities with the establishment of Studio Ijambo, initially a mechanism to counter hate radio. The activities diversified from there, and over the intervening years SFCG has utilized multiple approaches to address various aspects of the conflict. The goals and objectives of the Burundi program have been continuously refined as the context has changed, though the overall goal of reducing ethnic violence remains. The current activities operate within the framework of four distinct projects within the country.

The inaugural project, Studio Ijambo, which in Kirundi means "wise words," produces a wide mix of radio programs that address the daily problems and issues confronting Burundians in a manner that promotes dialogue, reconciliation, and peacebuilding, using common ground journalism techniques.[2] The quality of Studio Ijambo has been recognized internationally through a number of prestigious awards. The next project established was the Women's Peace Centre (WPC) in 1996. The center promotes dialogue between Burundian women of all backgrounds to enable them to play an active and independent role in peace-building. It offers multiple trainings, disseminates information through radio programming, and facilitates communication and interaction among women's associations, as well as between associations and government and funding bodies. The Youth Project has since 1999 carried out interethnic youth events, dialogues, and conflict resolution trainings to promote unity among Burundian young adults and children, and to reduce instances of ethnic violence. Finally, the Integration Initiative seeks to maximize the synergies between SFCG's Burundi projects, and between SFCG and other organizations, agencies, and NGOs working in Burundi.

SFCG's work on the Burundi conflict is not limited to projects within Burundi. Recognizing the lack of engagement by the international community which had characterized the run-up to the Rwandan crisis, SFCG initiated policy forums to draw attention to Burundi on the international level. The GLPF was established to secure a high profile on the foreign policy agenda of the United States.[3] Established simultaneously with the office in Burundi, the GLPF has convened monthly in Washington, D.C., since February 1995 to share information and approaches amongst a diverse range of actors. The projects in the Burundi program support and reinforce each other's efforts, particularly for the GLPF, as the field projects provide both credibility and an essential link to the ground situation in Burundi. This connection, in terms of real-time information, local perspective, and access to a wide range of actors, is critical to the successful functioning of the GLPF.

The program of work in Burundi is only one illustration of the efforts of SFCG. Currently consisting of three hundred seventy-five staff and offices in thirteen countries on four continents, SFCG has grown rapidly since its foundation in 1982 with two employees. The vision, then as now, is to transform the way the world deals with conflict, away from adversarial approaches toward co-operative solutions. In order to effect change, SFCG applies its resources and attention to reaching millions of people through its media outreach, to multilevel programming directly addressing conflict issues on the ground, and, where it can, to work at the highest levels. A number of SFCG's projects either directly engage with the policy process or have a policy element integral to the project.

This chapter focuses on the latter type of SFCG work, that which directly engages with the policy process. However, before one introduces the specifics of this case, understandings of key notions need to be articulated, as they can differ from case study to case study. The discussion begins by looking at the dual meaning of policy impact; formulated policy and institutional practice. From there the authors, based on their Burundi experience, outline three challenges that NGOs seeking to influence policy can encounter. Each of these challenges has been faced by the spectrum of work that SFCG conducts within its Burundian program. Only a brief outline of the approach to the first two of the challenges is given, owing to the length and scope constraints of this chapter. Two more detailed case studies are included as appendices.

The third challenge and SFCG's strategy in response are considered in detail through an analysis of the strategy and implementation of the GLPF. The wisdom gained through these experiences has been summarized as a checklist of "rules of thumb for policy engagement," which concludes the chapter.

The impact of the SFCG projects outlined in this chapter has been determined by means of formal evaluations of the Burundi work and interviews conducted specifically for this purpose. The primary source is an independent evaluation mission conducted in October and November 2001.[4] This evaluation considered both process and outcomes and utilized a number of research methods ranging from focus groups to interviews with key stakeholders. Additional information was gathered between February and August 2002 to assess the policy impact of the policy forums based in Washington, D.C., and Brussels. This assessment included interviews with individuals who have been actively involved with the policy forums over the past few years, including representatives of the U.S. and Belgian governments, NGOs, the Burundian government, academics, international organizations, and donors. The focus of the interviews was on their participation in the GLPF and the impact the forum has had on various aspects of policy and institutional practices in their and others' organizations.

What Is Policy Impact?

This chapter describes one way in which SFCG has sought to have an impact on policy. It is recognized, however, that policy impact is a very vague phrase that can be used in a multitude of ways. Therefore it is necessary to clarify some concepts related to policy impact as it is used in this chapter. First, *policy* here refers to both the institutional practices and the formulated policies influencing the actions of various actors in society: governments, NGOs, civic organizations, international organizations, and community groups. By *institutional practices* we mean the processes and methods of conducting the work of any of these organizations, which do not necessarily reflect formal rules or regulations, but are more informal and reflective of an organizational culture. By *formulated policies* we refer to the more formal avenues of decision making that often result in legislation, white papers, party platforms, or policy proposals.

The distinction between the two types of policy is important. Impact on formulated policies is easier to detect and assess because it usually requires making changes to existing rules or regulations or introducing new ones. Impact on institutional practices may be less visible, as it relates to changing or introducing practices that are part of informal culture. However, both are significant in terms of their contribution to peacebuilding and conflict resolution.

Policy Challenges and Responses

In the process of establishing themselves in a conflict zone and delivering services, NGOs face numerous challenges on many fronts. Engaging at the policy level is no different. This section outlines three of the overarching policy challenges that can face NGOs, regardless of the specifics of the case or conflict. The first two challenges—policies and institutional practices that exacerbate conflict and the nonimplementation of progressive policies—and the associated strategies developed by SFCG, are briefly discussed as they specifically relate to Burundi. The third policy challenge—the struggle for realignment of power relationships between governments, multilaterals, and NGOs—and SFCG's associated strategy of long-term enlightenment is the overarching policy challenge and strategy that is the focus of this case.

Policies and Institutional Practices that Exacerbate Conflict

Many NGOs working to resolve conflicts on the ground are challenged by the existence of policies that discourage communication and accentuate division between conflicting groups. Changes in perceptions of difference and conflict on the ground are made increasingly difficult to achieve when division is being demanded and exacerbated from the top, either through formal policy or institutional practice. When these policies are in the form of official decrees or Acts, in addition to the negative consequences to the citizens of the conflict area, they make illegal many crucial projects that NGOs could instigate. Informal policies of division can have an equally debilitating effect on people and NGOs alike.

The division, chronic mistrust, and enmity among political factions and ethnic groups in Burundi were solidified by the political instability and the ensuing violence and war which erupted in 1993. As a result, policies were put in place by the government to contain various forms of opposition, as they were regarded as a threat to the stability of the country. At one point, according to several key government and NGO officials interviewed during the 2002 evaluation, it was strictly forbidden to broadcast the voices of rebel leaders on radio or television within the country, exemplifying the government policy of no communication between conflict parties. In parallel, the rebel groups cut off contact with the government. Coupled with the existing ethnic tension, the policy of division and separation reverberated into the day-to-day relationships between members of the two major ethnic groups, the Tutsi and the Hutu. These policies also made NGO initiatives difficult to implement, particularly those involving media projects.

In order to address policies that discouraged communication between contending groups in Burundi, SFCG assumed a strategy of indirect mediation. Capitalizing on Studio Ijambo's reputation for credible, unbiased reporting by journalists from both ethnic groups, SFCG developed a type of mediation via on-radio dialogue between warring factions, which significantly opened dialogue channels. This strategy facilitated the essential first steps in establishing a dialogue without requiring either side to take the potentially face-losing step of rescinding their no-communication policy. Further information about this approach may be found in appendix 2.

Nonimplementation of Progressive Policies

In contrast to the implementation and subsequent enforcement of divisive policies, in many situations positive, forward-looking policies are developed but are
not enacted by the government, for many reasons including lack of political
will, lack of resources, or significant resistance in the populace. Often, existing
institutional practices fly in the face of new written policies and laws, usually in
cases where cultural norms and customs are incompatible with modern formulated policies. This lack of implementation of a new policy can as a minimum
result in no change on the ground and at most cause or continue discrimination
against certain groups. In Burundi, institutional practices related to marriage,
inheritance, and independence reflected norms and customs which set severe
limitations on women's rights and well-being. These practices did not necessarily reflect the policies articulated in the legal code but were dominant and perva-
sive because they were grounded in tradition.

In order to address the continuing discrimination against women caused by
the lack of implementation of the aspects of the legal code that support women's
legal rights, SFCG developed an implementation strategy for the existing policy. This multipronged strategy informed women of their rights and supported
them in taking action to achieve those rights. In a joint project between the
Women's Peace Centre and Studio Ijambo, workshops, radio programming, and
information packs were used to help these policies to become realities with their
originally intended beneficiaries. The project has resulted in positive societal
changes at local government, community, and individual levels. An overview of
this strategy may be found in appendix 3.

The Struggle to Realign Power Relationships

We now turn our attention to the third and most important policy challenge
addressed in this chapter. Governments have traditionally perceived themselves
as the primary arbiters and holders of power, and have developed structures,
systems, and cultures that support this position. With the development of multilateral institutions and NGOs as significant players at both national and international levels, governments have had to review these relationships. To date, all
three sectors are still learning the symbiotic nature of their particular strengths
and weaknesses and the value of learning to live together as a "three-legged
stool." A major challenge for many NGOs is their acceptance by governments
and multilaterals as significant players who have value to contribute to the policy process. Since NGOs have access to communities, information, and knowledge which is often denied to officials who are far removed from and distrusted
at the grassroots level, and since they are relatively flexible and informal, NGOs
can and should play a vital and complementary role in full partnership with the
other two sectors. However, not all policymakers understand this new and
evolving relationship. In fact, in many cases institutional practices have developed which support their separation and introversion.

In the mid-1990s many American and European foreign policymakers had not yet reviewed their relationships with civil society, keeping the traditional policy hierarchy of actors. When and if attention turned to Burundi or the Great Lakes region as a whole, information was garnered from the "usual suspects" and the decision-making process consisted solely of official actors. With little or no interaction with the organizations involved on the ground, policymakers did not have access to grassroots sentiment or real-life events outside the urban centers. The lack of understanding of what was happening on the ground was reflected in Burundi's low priority on the policy agenda.

In order to address the lack of consistent interaction between governments, multilaterals, and NGOs, SFCG adopted a strategy to create systematic and respectful engagement amongst all types of policy actors in Washington, D.C. While simultaneously redefining roles and relationships within the D.C. policy hierarchy of actors, this strategy of engagement enabled SFCG to help place Burundi and the region on the foreign policy agenda. Central to the effectiveness of this strategy was the establishment of the GLPF. The purpose of the forum is to create a safe environment for a diverse group of interested individuals to exchange knowledge and ideas regarding the Great Lakes area, thereby placing the NGO sector firmly within the policy dialogue. The usefulness of the forum and its effectiveness in altering roles instigated the creation of a similar forum by the ECCG in Brussels in December 1998.

Policy Forums in the United States and Europe

Although addressing the overarching policy challenge was essential for success, it was not the focus of SFCG's daily activities, which was the impending crisis in Burundi. Though the civil war in Burundi raged on, in 1995 the topic seldom appeared on the U.S. foreign policy agenda. This was of particular concern in light of the recent tragedy of the genocide in Rwanda. Many who were familiar with the region were identifying parallels between 1995 Burundi and the recent past in Rwanda, in terms both of the internal turmoil and the lack of attention from the international community. These parallels had not gone unnoticed by some in the U.S. policy world. On the other hand, the NGO community recognized that their past approaches to policymakers, especially in the Rwanda context, had not been effective. A growing realization that a coordinated approach, not only among NGOs but also with policy agencies, was needed in order to avert future tragedies.

At the same time, as a result of its newly established office in Burundi, SFCG was acutely aware of the crisis situation existing in the country. It was also conscious of the lack of awareness and attention this crisis was receiving on the U.S. foreign policy agenda. Although seemingly ideally placed to be a conduit of information and analysis to government decision makers, the norm of minimal engagement between different types of actors severely limited the actions that SFCG felt they could effectively take.

SFCG adopted a long-term engagement strategy which sought to expand the actors involved in decision making beyond the traditional policy hierarchy, thereby increasing the range of options considered and improving the amount of information on hand. The desire to put Burundi onto the foreign policy agenda, so that it would receive the international attention it needed, would be achieved through the successful translation of this strategy into action.

The action took the form of the Burundi Policy Forum, subsequently renamed the GLPF. Initiated in February 1995 in Washington, D.C., the GLPF is an ongoing, informal problem-solving forum that acts as a mechanism for sharing information and coordinating strategies for the region. The purpose of the GLPF was summed up by a participant at the initial forum as "to expand and maintain a steady dialogue and exchange among all those entities and institutions that can advance the peace process."

After a successful implementation in D.C. and recognition of the same policy challenge and issue in Europe, the European Great Lakes Forum (EGLF) was established in December 1998 in Brussels. As with the U.S. forum, its goals are information exchange, debate, and dialogue facilitation between different partners, with a focus on the Great Lakes region. It aims to keep the European authorities interested in the region, serving the special relationship between the two areas due to Belgium's colonial past and the huge diaspora of the Great Lakes region in Belgium.

Putting the Strategy into Action

The GLPF was founded and prospers on the principle of partnership. It was originally constructed around the ability of each partner to access different audiences; with the Center for Preventative Action at the Council on Foreign Relations accessing the policy world, SFCG covering the conflict resolution NGO sector, the Africa-America Institute[5] reaching the diaspora communities and Refugees International the humanitarian actors. School of Advanced International Studies (SAIS) also joined the consortium. The partners shared strategy implementation, such as identification of speakers, recruitment and retention of participants, neutral facilitation, regularity of meetings, and logistics and coordination.

Speakers

Obviously a key element to the forum is the quality of the speakers. They come to the forum in one of three ways. First, speakers who have been identified through a coordinated effort by the partner organizations as having strong credentials are invited to give presentations on topics that directly address current issues in the Great Lakes. Alternatively, participants may suggest relevant individuals. Finally, speakers may request a place on the agenda. As a forum organizer stated, "because NGOs and others know we have the experience and we have access [to government officials] they come to us and ask us to organize a forum on an experience they want to share with others."

Over time the forum has become recognized by those involved in the Great Lakes as an effective means for reaching a broad and diverse audience of concerned sectors. For example, the Minister for Public Information of the Democratic Republic of Congo (DRC), shortly after signing the Pretoria Accords in the summer of 2002, asked to address the forum as a means of presenting his government's position on the peace process. Often, information made available to the forum will be receiving its first public airing. When Dr. Reginald Moreels, former minister of cooperation in Belgium, presented the report from his mission to the Great Lakes region, Forum attendees heard the conclusions before the report was officially submitted to the Belgian foreign minister, Louis Michel.

Every effort is made to have speakers who represent all sectors and positions on the issues. This, however, has proven to be one of the most difficult aspects of the forum. Upon reflection the organizers have recognized that sometimes they have not been as diligent as possible in seeking out new voices and have tended to invite the people they knew or who were easily accessible. However, a new initiative to widen the array of voices given space has been instigated, with a particular emphasis on those who previously have not been systematically included. For instance, in early 2003 a private security firm spoke on a platform with American government officials about military peacemaking options in the DRC. Although their inclusion was controversial, SFCG felt that this strengthened the credibility of the forum as a space for all voices.

Participants

Such high-quality speakers and presentations usually attract seventy to eighty participants from various NGOs, multilaterals, and government agencies. The Washington and Brussels forums differ somewhat in their participants, and this has some impact on the dynamics of the meetings. Although open to the public, each forum has a natural constituency. In Washington, this includes government representatives from the State Department, USAID, DOD, and other U.S. government agencies; a wide range of NGOs; diplomats from the Great Lakes region and other interested countries; academics; and the World Bank and United Nations. One participant commented that "this diversity is what makes the forum very effective."

Participant outreach has also been extended beyond these communities to include the private sector, such as consulting groups or industry associations. Although they are commonly disregarded by the NGO sector, their inclusion is essential owing to the critical role the private sector plays in the U.S. policy process. At present it is recognized that this constituency primarily attends for the information and does not actively engage in the discussion or networking aspects of the forum. As of early 2003 efforts are under way to develop a strategy by which this key audience can be further integrated into the forum.

The process of identifying potential participants has remained largely the same since the forum's inception, when the organizers identified and invited all agencies, organizations, and individuals interested and engaged in the region. They accessed government and NGO lists, which are available as public information and are even more accessible nowadays through the internet, made personal contact with high-level individuals, contacted relevant African embassies as well as potential donor governments, notified academics institutions, and expanded the invitation list by word of mouth. The principle was inclusivity. Anyone who wanted to come was invited. In a short time, the forum became the accepted meeting place for the Great Lakes community in Washington, D.C.

EGLF attendance, on the other hand, caters to the large diaspora population in Brussels, as well as to policymakers. Due to the inclusion of so many nationals with a deep emotional connection to the conflict, the discussions tend to be emotionally charged. Additionally, the strategic location of the European forum in the building of the European Parliament in Brussels draws many policymakers from the EU, furthering the goals of placing the Great Lakes on the international agenda and attracting a diverse group of stakeholders. With both forums, the organizers will also invite participants strategically so as to ensure that all key stakeholders are aware of the meetings. Each partner organization draws from its experience and contacts to bring participants from different milieux.

Facilitation

Given that forum participants represent diverse interests, views, and goals, a neutral facilitator is crucial for ensuring a successful dialogue, and for building participants' trust in the process. "They [SFCG] maintain a posture of strict professional facilitation, they are not advocates, but facilitators," commented one participant. Neutral, professional facilitation ensures an atmosphere of shared respect and interest among participants. Another participant confirmed the achievement of this, stating that "the leadership of Search and other players created a safe space to express views."

Regular versus Ad Hoc Meetings

The GLPF meets the first Thursday of every month, allowing for ongoing contact and interaction between participants. This regularity helps to strengthen relationships between participants, build trust, establish networks, and develop actions for the benefit of the Great Lakes region. The date is a fixture in people's calendars and lives. Participants cite this consistency as a trust-builder; one participant commented that "people have been coming for a while, which makes it very collegial." In contrast, the EGLF meets irregularly, gearing its meetings to relevant and interesting speakers and topics. Both models have their advantages and disadvantages. One interviewee valued the GLPF model for the relationships it establishes, but was eager to experience "fresh eyes and new voices . . . it is always the same people and same views wherever you go to attend an event related to the Great Lakes area." With the ongoing commitment to increase the inclusion of a broad range of sectors, SFCG hopes to address this concern.

Logistics and Operations

Behind the scenes, staff at each of the partner organizations is responsible for the functioning of the forums. With Refugees International handling the invitations, SAIS aiding with the provision of a meeting place, and SFCG coordinating the organizational issues, each institution contributes according to its abilities. All three, together with the Center for Preventive Action at the Council on Foreign Relations, contribute to the design and content of the program. The joint effort signals the collaborative and unbiased nature of this endeavor.

Specific activities include:

- maintaining an up-to-date list of key persons in government, think tanks and other policy-level institutions, NGOs, Great Lakes associations, and members of the diaspora;[6]
- meeting with them to introduce the forum;
- calling to remind them about upcoming forum meetings;
- making sure they get something from the forum by choosing topics that are "hot" or, conversely, have not been covered by the media, by having interesting speakers, and by inviting speakers from the field (for example, when the EGLF invited a bishop from Kindu who was a delegate at the Inter-Congolese Dialogue (ICD), the forum participants were keen to hear what happened from a delegate point of view, how he experienced the ICD, what he reported to his people, and what his people's comments were);
- responding to their suggestions for interesting speakers, and where possible inviting them to speak; and
- providing regular, written reports of the meetings.

The time and effort necessary to initiate and maintain this project should not be underestimated. Being active in the policy community is significant to the successful implementation of an engagement strategy. This involves being aware of current issues and actors in the region, through which the SFCG projects in Burundi play a significant contributing role, but also being familiar with the U.S. policy context. Supporting this effort, within SFCG alone, requires a part-time position.

Principles

Just as important to success as the operational aspects are the principles upon which the forums are based. These aim at increasing interaction, dialogue, and trust between members of various organizations and agencies. Inclusivity, value added, professional conduct, and attendance as individuals are central to the forums' ability to address the policy challenge and thus the Burundi issue.

Principle 1: Inclusivity

The forums are inclusive, bringing together well-informed, engaged, and interested individuals from agencies and organizations involved in the Great Lakes region. This principle is a primary step in creating a new atmosphere for joint problem solving between groups and individuals who have not been listening to each other, or in cases where only certain groups have been given a voice. SFCG's approach assumes that all voices must be heard and allowed to present themselves safely to others. The balancing act of ensuring that all sides are represented occurs over the long term. While every panel may not have a perfect balance of participants, the program for the year is equitable. Though the speakers may be controversial at times, this is mitigated by the extensive question and answer period that is the focus of every meeting. Therefore, speakers act as catalysts for discussion rather than lecturers. In response to the accusations of bias which are sometimes made, SFCG finds it essential to communicate the long-term equity of the program and to remain steadfast rather than shifting position to accommodate critics.

Participants in the Forums recognize that there are many benefits to this approach. First and foremost, access to stakeholders outside of those with which the participants normally engage was seen to be of great value. As one NGO representative noted, "ordinarily . . . especially those representing NGOs, do not get to meet people such as UN representatives, and other government administrators on a regular basis. For NGOs and nongovernmental agencies in general, this is an incredible opportunity to meet those people on an ongoing basis." In addition, due to the inclusivity principle, a wealth of viewpoints and perspectives are offered during these discussions, and this in turn serves to enrich and augment the viewpoints and perspectives of all participants. Another NGO participant was surprised to discover that "at times there was a sharp diversion in views between NGOs and those from government. The forum allowed for exchange to narrow down perspectives in a civil manner. So the NGO and government perceptions both improved."

Principle 2: Value Added

The organizers of both forums ensure that they stay abreast of developments in the region, keeping themselves updated and informed, via offices in the fields, contacts in the Great Lakes region, Great Lakes embassies, diaspora, and NGOs. The networks of each of the on-the-ground SFCG projects provide an invaluable source of real-time information and nuance. With this knowledge, the organizers are able to insure that each forum adds value to the overall policy debate in order to maintain the momentum and dedication of participants to the forum. Over time, this principle has meant that the forum has developed a reputation as an event not to be missed. In Washington, D.C., many perceive the GLPF as the venue for discussion about the region. During the Clinton administration, the president's special envoy regularly used the forum to communicate his findings, views, and dilemmas, as it provided him with access to the entire Great Lakes constituency in one go.

Principle 3: Professional Conduct

The manner in which the forums are implemented contributes significantly to the way in which they are perceived and the importance attributed by participants to making the time to attend the meetings. As one participant noted, "organizing the forum, being efficient and timely in sending invitations and informational documents . . . dealing with sensitive actors representing three countries at war and the choice of the place to hold the forum, the European Parliament, has a special meaning in Europe and Brussels." Implementing the forums consistently in a professional and efficient manner sends the message that this is a serious and thoughtful event. Maintaining the principle of professional conduct at all times requires time, attention to detail, and a sense of pride in the work on the part of the organizations and their staff.

Principle 4: Individual Representation

Participants represent themselves as individuals; their views are not attributed to their organizations or agencies. This allows them to operate more effectively within an informal setting, without being limited by their roles as representatives of specific organizations. They share ideas more freely, and engage in frank discussion.

Many of the participants interviewed recognized the significance of this principle to the effectiveness of the forum. One participant stated: "Sometimes when you have people representing government and parties it is important that they feel that they will not be liable for what they say. I personally said things from my own point of view which were not necessarily reflecting my organization's policies." In order to maintain this level of freedom and honesty, video cameras are not permitted in the forums and journalists must agree to a non-attribution policy for any quotes they may publish. Although there have been no specific, serious instances of misrepresentation of a member's comments, it is important to note that the content of the discussions generally reaches Burundi and the other Great Lakes countries almost immediately.

Results

The GLPF not only contributes to the establishment of NGOs as players with expertise, it also has a number of other important effects. Significantly, however, the GLPF has been instrumental in the slow shift of U.S. government and multilateral institutional practices with relation to the inclusion of NGO views and perspectives. Participants provided several examples illustrating that the forum discussions and interactions have contributed to this end. One government individual recounted an instance where an interagency working group made up of the State Department, USAID, National Security Council, and the Department of Defense, which was developing policy on the Congo, turned to the vice president of an NGO and asked to be briefed on his findings from a recent trip. The impetus for this invitation as well as the relationship with the invitee was based on the experience that many members of the working group had had with the forum as a source of credible and "important information."

In another instance, an NGO who was involved in preparing the ICD recounted a scenario in which their information countered that which was generally accepted by government agencies. In this case, the press was expressing the view that the process of selecting civic society delegates had been very successful; however, the information from the NGO's field offices indicated that the process was not running that smoothly and was in fact proving quite controversial. This information was shared with the forum, after which USAID contacted them to gather more information. Interestingly, the NGO discovered that their information was further validated by a report from the USAID team that was in the Congo. In both examples, NGOs were seen as credible actors to be included in the discussion on these pressing policy issues—a significant shift in institutional policy.

Becoming recognized as a credible and valuable stakeholder is not the only benefit to be gained from working with the GLPF. Time and time again, government participants indicate that the information that they receive during these forums is instrumental in assisting them to develop their understanding and formulate decisions. One participant noted: "I . . . came away frequently with insights and information from others [human rights organizations and the UN, for example]. This helped with suggesting ways to do things or crafting an approach. Sometimes it helped us to communicate differently based on what we learned from interacting with others in the forum."

This result was not limited to the Washington-based forum. Government participants in Brussels also commented on the effect that information garnered through the forums plays in their decision making. A member of the European Parliament who had recently returned from a trip in the DRC was invited to speak at the Brussels forum about his experiences. He later commented that "it was fortunate that I came to the forum just after my trip to the DRC and before the case of the DRC was discussed at parliament. The information I brought in from my trip and the forum were valuable for the recommendations of what to do in the DRC, and I was the only one to have such information."

Clearly, when information is shared, new lenses or perspectives are also presented. Several of the participants voiced their appreciation of the exposure to these alternative viewpoints that the forum provides. As one U.S. official noted, "this gives us lenses to evaluate others and our work. It takes us into another realm which we do not have being a government only." The opportunity to present and discuss different perspectives on an issue is essential if paradigm shifts in approaches are to happen in terms of government policy in conflict areas.

A second outcome of this work is the building of relationships between forum participants. These relationships provide the cornerstone for ongoing engagement and discussion between the various sectors in attendance. One such example of the forum establishing a relationship that went on to work independently occurred when the Ministry of Cooperation in Belgium decided to establish a new department to promote African arts and artists. The head of the new department was a regular member of the forum, and one of their first acts was to contact the Brussels office to discuss how SFCG uses the arts to bring people together. The working relationship has continued and the departmental head consults SFCG staff whenever she gets a proposal from Burundi or the Great Lakes diaspora. An ECCG staff member later observed that this influence on government decision making would never have occurred "if we didn't meet at the forum and if I didn't keep in touch with her." Irrespective of the significant results that both forums have played a role in achieving, an essential outcome is the perspective of the value of the forums in the eyes of their participants. These tend to be individuals with high-pressure, time-demanding jobs, and their presence is testament to the importance they place on the forums. In fact, several of the participants had such high praise for the forums that they suggested replicating the model to address conflicts in other parts of the world.

Operational Challenges

As with any long-term project, there is the potential for the forum to become stagnant over time. Through rehashing topics and speakers or circulating the same participants over and over again, the mechanism can lose its appeal and function. Keeping the forum relevant and consistently offering something new was identified as a major issue after the forum had been running for several years. In mid-2000, efforts began to look at the basic assumptions of the forum to see if they still held relevance five years from inception. As one organizer stated, "keeping it relevant is a constant struggle."

A related problem is the risk of inadvertently being perceived to be aligned with the government of the day. The GLPF faced this when the Clinton administration changed; it discovered that, practically overnight, it had gone from being truly connected to a wide and diverse set of policy actors to being connected to no one in the new government.

Rules of Thumb for Policy Impact

1. Understand the importance and power of relationships. People will be more open to you if they know you. Relationships are built through consistency and action. Woody Allen said: "Most of life is showing up." Show up, and do what you say you will do; these are rare qualities that will set you apart.
2. As an NGO, be there for the long term. Do not assume that you can accomplish much by simply parachuting in, and flying out just as quickly. Working in conflict zones requires the establishment of trust, credibility, and more significantly, human connectedness. Those who suffer in war zones need to feel that those who come to their aid really care. This can happen only if these latter parties stay the course and get involved in the communities affected by the conflict. Again, relationships are key to effectiveness.
3. Credibility, respect, and trust as a peacemaker and peacebuilder are earned. Meet with people from all sides of the conflict, listen respectfully to all perspectives, hold confidences, stand in the shoes of everyone you talk to, and try to understand the forces that shape their positions. Only then can you address the real issues as they are, rather than as you would like them to be, and in doing so, have some influence on events, attitudes, and policies.[7]
4. Give everyone a voice. A national-level conflict affects everyone, not only those who control the army, government, or economy, yet policies and traditions of exclusion and hierarchy tend to limit the scope of voices that can be heard. One crucial aspect of SFCG's work both in Burundi and in the GLPF has been to facilitate dialogue in a safe, neutral environment. Such exchanges bring people together, expand their horizons, and show them multiple ways to peacebuilding.
5. Ask high-level officials to engage—you will be surprised at how many agree. Request an interview and speak concisely and briefly to make your

point. Recognize them as human beings! Provide half a page of talking points—most officials are too busy to deal with more. Provide a safe space where they can talk to others they would not normally meet; when they see that you offer something of benefit, they are likely to participate. When one high-powered person accepts, use his or her acceptance to leverage the participation of others.

6. The parties to a conflict often need a third party as an interlocutor, though they may be unwilling to admit it. By assuming this role, and building the legitimacy to enact it as in Principle 6 of the Policy Forum, you can provide the opportunity, excuse, and safety for the parties to shift their positions.

7. Be proud of being a member of an NGO. You have a right to talk as an equal with policymakers and other "high-ups," who are, after all, people just like you. Think of the relationship as synergistic—governments have power, multilaterals have credibility and a mandate by virtue of their diverse base, and NGOs have flexibility and access. Each sector has something to offer that the others (should) want, but they don't always know it—yet! Show them.

8. Recognize that peacebuilding is multipronged. The more diverse the approaches, the greater the chance of impact. Neutral facilitation helps maintain the GLPF as an effective medium for communication between various agencies and organizations. Mediation, via radio programs, contributed to ending hostilities between the government and rebel groups. Advocacy for the implementation of a legal code advantageous to women has helped ameliorate the impact of traditional, discriminatory practices.

9. When targeting programs to government officials as an audience, it may be advantageous to first approach individuals other than the officials themselves, such as former public servants, think tank founders, business leaders, and so on. Such allies grant the agency/organization credibility when it becomes appropriate to work directly with public officials and serve as conduits to communicate informal conversations back to official channels. Moreover, these influential figures are less constrained by regime policy. Be particularly considerate of former political figures—they often have direct and immediate contact with the current policymakers. That said, be careful to ensure that they still have a good relationship with the new government.

10. Identify internal champions: having someone on board who is within the policy agency can be very helpful in both designing and enacting a policy strategy.

11. Advocating for a process is possible: most policy advocacy focuses on developing new policy for a specific issue at a specific time. However, advocating for a process, as illustrated by the forum, is possible and potentially more sustainable as the process can be applied to multiple issues.

12. Do not become complacent: periodically reevaluate the partners and network to ensure relevance over the long term. Pay attention to nontraditional policymakers—they have a role to play, with interests and concerns that shouldn't be ignored.

Notes

Appreciation is extended to Nicole S. Bennet, who conducted substantial research to support the writing of this case study.

1. SFCG was founded twenty-one years ago to transform the way the world deals with conflict, away from adversarial approaches toward cooperative solutions. In 1995, SFCG established a full partnership with the ECCG.

2. SFCG establishes radio production studios, not stations, so as to provide nonpartisan programming to all local broadcasters; it has a highly competent and factionally and ethnically balanced staff. A politically balanced work environment allows the staff to gain perspectives on various sides of the conflict; SFCG works with all sectors; and the journalists are trained in interviewing and reporting techniques that include representing the perspectives of all sides to the conflict, carefully defining the problem, and generating solution-oriented discussions.

3. A second forum, the EGLF, was established in Brussels.

4. This evaluation mission was headed by one of the coauthors, Dr. Amr Abdalla. The evaluation team included Dr. Noa Davenport and Leslie McTyre.

5. The Africa–America Institute was a founding partner but is no longer involved in this project.

6. According to SFCG officials, "at times it was not easy to maintain such contacts. For example, when the administration in Washington, D.C. changed, virtually all government positions changed, and it took a while to catch up."

7. For example, according to an SFCG official, "one African rebel leader told me that he trusted me personally because of the way I facilitated a discussion at the GLPF between him and the other factions. He subsequently sought my advice on a number of occasions as a result."

Chapter 9
Reframing the Problem: An Approach to the Kurdish Question in Turkey

TOSAM—Dogu Ergil

The Republic of Turkey was established in 1923, after a difficult struggle of nation and state building which left it burdened by interstate conflict. As the heir of the Ottoman Empire, it inherited both an ethnically mixed population and a state-centric government which was instituted to control the country's diverse citizenry. At the Republic's inception, the bureaucracy at the center of the state apparatus took control of all institutional spheres of public life and monopolized it through its hegemony over politics. The main determinant of statecraft and politics, which are indistinguishable in Turkey, therefore appears to be the security of the state, not that of the nation. For instance, the preamble of the Constitution talks about the "indivisible unity of the state with its motherland and nation," thus establishing a hierarchical relationship in which both land and nation are secured under the auspices of the state.

The Ottoman Empire's tradition of playing on the mutual fears of "competing" ethnicities to justify a repressive state is still the norm in present-day Turkey. This power play of an autocratic state system has perpetuated violent unrest, mainly between the Turkish identity groups and the Kurdish minority, claiming tens of thousands of lives since the mid-1980s.[1] The people of Turkey have become victims of state propaganda, being made to believe that the ethnic "other" is a threat to their national and personal security. The result is that both ethnicities suffer when their country is stigmatized as a conflicted, economically stagnant, and immature democracy with little respect for the rule of law.

The country remains basically agrarian, which has retarded the emergence of a strong and influential bourgeoisie and working class. In the absence of these classes, industrialization has failed to develop in any significant way, and the political system has not yet been transformed into a full democracy. Civil society is generally very weak, and thus is unable to challenge the formidable power of the state or to influence its policies. This case study will attempt to show, however, how one civil society group, the Center for the Research of Societal Problems (TOSAM), set out to challenge the status quo in Turkey, and to transform the perception of the Turkish-Kurdish issue from one of interethnic strife to one which addressed the democratic accountability of the state. Specifically, this case study will show:

- how the perception of the so-called "Kurdish problem" was reframed, despite a very repressive and security-conscious state;
- the initial strategy employed to develop discussion on the issue amongst the local intelligentsia, which led to the formation of TOSAM; and
- how the development of TOSAM transformed the "Kurdish problem" into an issue that brought domestic and international pressure to bear on the government of Turkey to reform its policies so that they conformed with the rule of law and international standards of democracy.

In order to draw lessons from this experience in influencing policy, an account will be given of the challenges TOSAM faced in moving its policy objectives forward. Some suggestions will also be offered for those who wish to replicate such a strategy in other situations of state repression.

The "Kurdish Problem"

The issue that had previously been labeled the "Kurdish problem" was first publicly aired in Turkish society in August 1995, with the publication of a research study entitled *The Eastern Question: Observations and Diagnosis*.[2] Led by Professor Dogu Ergil of Ankara University (later president of TOSAM), the study was commissioned by the Turkish Union of Chambers of Commerce and Industry (TOBB). A team of ten researchers/interviewers conducted a field survey on the attitudes of the Kurds in order to understand their relationships within their families, in their indigenous community, and in society at large. Their identity constructs were treated with the utmost importance because their insistence on recognition of their ethnic identity, Kurdish, openly clashes with the official Turkish identity that is nurtured by the state. The study also investigated the Kurds's attitude toward the state and the outlawed armed insurgent organization, the Workers Party of Kurdistan (PKK).

The study appears to have been groundbreaking on a number of levels. Most importantly, a subject hitherto taboo, which challenged the ideological and moral foundations on which existing policies and institutions were built, was opened to discussion. The study also gained immediate public attention not only because of the sensitive nature of the issue but also because the sponsoring organization, TOBB, was supposedly a bastion of conservatism, representing the small and medium business class. TOBB is the most influential economic body and the largest business organization in Turkey, with a membership of more than seven hundred thousand business persons.[3] With its employees and family members, it has been estimated that it could mobilize one-sixth of the Turkish population.[4] It has significant local influence, with branches in every corner of Turkey and a wide-ranging informal network. As it services the local commercial elite, it is influential in the electoral process both through its influence in the determination of candidates and by its determination of party political delegations. As the largest of the NGOs in Turkey, whose official duty is to represent the business community, it is perceived as part of the "establishment," and its president has a place in the protocol of the state.

Despite this backing, both the motivation behind the report and its scientific findings were challenged by the state, who declared it to be a CIA plot to divide the country. However, whereas previously it had been officially taboo to speak about the "Kurdish problem," subsequent to the report the issue was debated on every TV channel and radio station and commented on in every paper for an entire month.[5] Many columnists, broadcasters, and commentators used the publication of *The Eastern Question: Observations and Diagnosis* as an opportunity to air their previously suppressed views.

Data obtained from the research proved that the official suspicion of the Kurds as subversive elements was unfounded. Ninety percent of the Kurds interviewed responded that they did not want an independent Kurdistan. They wanted to remain in Turkey as equal citizens, but respected as Kurds. Hence, Kurdishness was not found to be contradictory to holding citizenship of the Republic of Turkey, and the official position of labeling as subversive everyone who does not deem herself/himself as ethnically or politically Turkish was shown to reflect an archaic and unjust attitude. At the same time, it was discovered that the PKK had wide-ranging psychological support amongst the Kurds of Southeastern Turkey, not because they supported its terrorist methods, but rather because it represented Kurdish dignity by protesting against adverse or unjust conditions. It was also discovered that the PKK had become the only available political body for dissenting Kurds, because the government had repressed all democratic Kurdish organizations that had the ability to pool the energies of the Kurds living in the cities. Although few would accept living under the tutelage of a Marxist-Leninist—and very authoritarian—organization like the PKK, in the absence of any other Kurdish organization that represented Kurdish dissent and pride, this organization acquired representative status by default. The study named the PKK "the illegitimate child of the system in Turkey." These findings and many others shattered the official view concerning the Kurds and the definition of nationhood, which was not based on a social agreement by the people but imposed from above for the citizens to obey.

The head researcher and author, Professor Dogu Ergil, together with a handful of supporting liberal intellectuals, was accused by the security institutions of being an accessory to the "alien powers that want to partition our country." The study was condemned by the state, the author's advisory services were terminated by the TOBB administration, and Professor Ergil was taken to the State

Security Court, which was not a regular court but a political one, created to deal with crimes such as terrorism and treason.

International Assistance and the Formation of the Foundation for the Research of Societal Problems (TOSAV)

Convinced that the reaction to the research study held out an opportunity for further progress on the "Kurdish problem," Professor Ergil decided to appeal to those international organizations that he personally knew, and that had expertise in conflict resolution and reconciliation techniques, to assist in taking the dialogue further. These appeals, to the Peace Research Institute of Oslo (PRIO) and an American NGO in Washington, D.C., called Search for Common Ground (SFCG) bore fruit.[6] These organizations sent their representatives to meet with Professor Ergil in late 1995.

Subsequently, a team of experts from these organizations, together with Professor Ergil, formulated a strategy which was designed to gain agreement on the exact nature of the problem and explore it in a safe environment, and to expand the discussion further throughout Turkey. Participants were recruited to form two groups, one representative of Kurds and the other of Turks, to take part in the initial dialogue. It was deemed essential that each individual chosen to represent one group had his or her counterpart in the other group, so as to ensure that the major social and professional strata of each "ethnic" group were fairly represented. Fourteen highly representative persons were selected through a series of interviews conducted in Ankara, which aimed to make sure all members of the respective negotiation teams met the same criteria. Of the fourteen, two were women, one in each team. Another important criterion for selection was that each member of each negotiation team would have a following in his or her community or professional sphere. The groups included staunch nationalists on either side representing the hard-core, difficult-to-convince part of the population.[7] Everything was open to debate except two principles: (1) condoning violence as a way of politics or problem solving, and (2) questioning the territorial integrity of Turkey.

The next step was to identify likely sponsors. Organizations such as the Winston Foundation for World Peace and the National Endowment for Democracy from the United States, and PRIO from Norway were approached. These organizations subsequently helped put together a group of international experts to facilitate the dialogue, clarify procedures, and try to ensure agreement on certain terms and concepts that were interpreted differently by each group. Among this consortium of worldwide foundations and institutions that sponsor and work on efforts for peace-building and conflict resolution were SFCG and the Center for Strategic and International Studies (CSIS), who contributed their expertise and their experts. William Ury, director of the Global Negotiation Project, a principal research project of the Program on Negotiation at Harvard Law School, and coauthor of a classic text on negotiation,[8] was appointed as the mediator-facilitator and facilitated all three of the four-day discussion-deliberation meetings. David Phillips of SFCG, Dan Smith of PRIO, and Joseph Montville of the CSIS constituted the brains trust (advisory group), which designed the *modus operandi.* The advisory group facilitated the smooth progression of the deliberations and helped with the clarification of equivocal concepts such as "self-determination," "minority," "minority rights," "people," "deliberative democracy," "cultural rights," "multiculturalism," "collective or group identity," and "civil society versus the state."

Throughout 1996, the group of fourteen, seven Turks and seven Kurds from different professions with varying social and institutional affiliations, met discreetly in politically neutral locations including France, Switzerland, and Belgium. Each meeting held in these countries went on for four working days. Including travel and leisure time, the groups remained together for a whole week during each meeting. The debates were very contentious. On some days, progress was made, but on other days a single word could turn the tide on any agreement that appeared to be developing and take the group back to their starting positions. It was therefore felt necessary to design a strategy to alleviate misunderstandings and clarify the intentions of the participants. The following processes were implemented by both Bill Ury and members of the advisory group:

- In the discussion, expectations and goals were clarified and misconceptions cleared over and over again.
- Methods for achieving these goals were discussed. Both sides agreed that democratization of the political institutions and liberalization of the constitution would provide enough leverage to transform the conflictual nature of the relationship between the state and society. These responses provided enough confidence for the groups to continue to work together.
- Efforts were made to increase awareness and understanding of both groups' experiences of the conflict. Each person was asked how they lived and how they perceived the conflict that had torn their country asunder. The accounts were very emotional. Through them the Turks came to understand how the Kurds were deeply hurt, humiliated, and disappointed, and the Kurds came to understand how the Kurdish rebellion had created a deep distrust among the Turks about the intentions of the Kurds, and how their violent protest was expediently used by the state to legitimize their repression. Both sides came to understand that without reconciliation, the basic instinct or reflex of the state would be to satisfy its own security needs, and this in turn would sustain the predominance of the military strategy over a political one.

Relationships between the groups continued to improve rapidly. This process strengthened the foundations of mutual trust and the will to work together to transform the authoritarian nature of their country's political system. Both sides came to understand that they were not each other's enemy, and that the real problem lay with the authoritarian and exclusivist political and legal system, which victimized both groups by denying them basic liberal democratic rights and freedoms. The groups concluded that this system had to change. Instead of expending their energies bickering with each other, they directed them in synergy toward strategic targets, namely systems change and planning for the further democratization of the Turkish political-legal system.

After this mutual agreement, there was little deviation from the agreed targets. Subsequently, the participants began to meet inside Turkey, rather than outside of it. Relationships continued to improve rapidly between the parties, who were literally beginning to walk arm in arm by the end of the year. Having agreed on the nature of the problem and many of the remedies, the groups decided to write down the points on which they had agreed. When these points were compared, this document, which started out as a search for a solution to the "Kurdish problem," became a framework for a program to democratize the Turkish political system. Everyone involved began to see that the "Kurdish problem" could be solved by expanding the agreement generated between these two small but representative groups outward to the larger society, thereby persuading the larger society to transform the system that carried the seeds of conflict. The document was called the *Document of Mutual Understanding* (DOMU).[9]

The participants and facilitators agreed that this was a healthy and exciting outcome. The excitement, however, soon turned into concerns about the future. Could this agreement, reached in "an oxygen tent," survive in the real world? Could it be transformed into a national consensus? Could a new constitutional system be built, based on this consensus and reflecting new qualities like pluralism, multiculturalism, and rule of law? It was decided that an organizational instrument was necessary to carry the group's consensus to the society at large and to solicit its support. After long deliberations, a foundation was established in 1997 to take on this mission. In order to give a wider perspective to its activities and to secure the endorsement of the authorities, the group decided to give a name to the new institution, namely, TOSAV.[10]

TOSAV: Strategy into Action

In February 1997 TOSAV was founded. The founders were members of the original negotiation teams, except for a few who had official employment or who were expecting new appointments that would compromise their desire to be directly associated with TOSAV. After a series of interviews TOSAV recruited qualified staff who had higher education in the social sciences. The organizational structure of TOSAV reflected the "mirror strategy" from which it was conceived. The core personnel numbered only four, consisting of two representatives of the Turkish community and two of the Kurdish community. The Foundation perceived its mission as threefold: to seek conciliation between the Turkish and Kurdish citizens of the Republic of Turkey along the principles in the DOMU, to disseminate the culture of democracy, and to sensitize the society and administration to the multicultural reality of the country and its management.

Objectives

This foundation was the result of a strategy that sought to define the exact nature of the "Kurdish problem" clearly and to gain consensus on the crux of that problem as viewed by principal opinion leaders in the Turkish and Kurdish communities. The outcome of that exercise, embodied in the DOMU, was the discovery that state policies needed reforming. In essence, the "Kurdish problem" was reconceptualized: from being defined as a question of interethnic strife, it became seen as a problem of manipulative, authoritarian state policy. With this consensus achieved amongst representative intelligentsia of Turkey, the objectives of TOSAV as an organizational instrument were clear:

- To develop the DOMU further and expand the basis of consensus amongst opinion leaders in Turkey;
- To reframe the international community's perception of the conflict, with particular attention to the implications of the conflict for Turkey's acceptance into the EU; and
- To expand the issue of democratic policy reform to a structured public debate amongst the people of Turkey.

Strategy

The strategy of TOSAV was threefold:

- To *build empathy* by bringing together representatives of the conflicting sides to tell their stories and communicate the ways in which they perceive and live through the problem.
- To *build confidence and understanding* between the communities by way of regional meetings in areas where Turks and Kurds live side by side—within and outside Turkish borders. In these meetings, facilitated by international experts, local opinion leaders of both sides first developed a mutual understanding regarding the nature of the problem and then identified both their specific group needs and also their mutual needs and concerns.
- To *frame and paraphrase, domestically and internationally,* the reconceptualization of the problem in such a way as to transform the political, legal and economic institutional structure whereby the "Kurdish problem" could be solved through the greater process of Turkey's democratization.

Tactics

The tactics employed by TOSAV to ensure the implementation of its objectives were as follows:

- The publication of the DOMU. This consensual document symbolized the determination, achievement, and vision of the representative groups.
- Disseminating the DOMU to every multiethnic community in Turkey and encouraging discussion so as to ensure that it was considered and incorporated into their understanding, and the understanding of their public opinion makers, of what was required to bring peace to Turkey. The hope was that the ideals of DOMU would act as a catalyst for policymakers in undertaking the development of programs.
- Utilization of every academic, journalistic, legal, civic, and international medium or venue to assist discussion of the DOMU in every corner of the country, so as to build pressure on the system to adopt the principles and consensual propositions in the DOMU.
- Disseminating the DOMU to every influential international decision-making body, including the European Parliament and Commission, the United Nations General Assembly and General Secretariat, the parliaments of all democratic countries, Turkish embassies in those countries and their embassies in Turkey so as to bring international pressure to bear on Turkish decision-making circles in order to turn the principles of the DOMU into policy.

The core of the public outreach and consensus-building program was to organize regional meetings across Turkey to open the DOMU to wider public discussion and support. Each region was studied and public opinion leaders selected. The DOMU was sent to each with a request to study it, develop new ideas, and then disseminate these views in their social "hinterland" community. To each regional meeting TOSAV invited people who were representative of the local population and equipped with new ideas or constructive criticism.

Seven regional meetings were organized in Turkey, as well as one meeting in Europe. The latter took place in June 1998 in Switzerland and was a groundbreaking event. Twenty-five leaders living in the diaspora in six different countries in Europe, all of whom had been declared persona non grata by authorities for their political activities, were invited by TOSAV. Through discussion of the DOMU, they came to realize that resisting Turkey's candidacy to the EU would condemn Turkey to its own darkness. Neither the Turks nor the Kurds would benefit from the continuation of the current authoritarian regime, and the Kurds would suffer even more. At the end of the meeting, the group declared their support for Turkey's accession to the EU, something they had previously opposed vehemently. Events that followed proved the commitment of the participants to their new understanding of what was required for Turkey to move toward a more peaceful society, as they subsequently engaged in petitioning civil society organizations in Europe about Turkey's candidacy to the EU.

After each meeting the DOMU grew richer with new inputs and criticisms and developed as a framework for a new democratic constitutional system. The final form of the document emerged after the last meeting, which was held in Istanbul in May 1999 and to which other, non-Muslim, minority members of Turkey were invited. Only those proposals or principles on which there was unanimous agreement were included in the final version of the DOMU.

Unfortunately, both Turkey's principal power centers, the Turkish government and the PKK, viewed TOSAV's work on the Kurdish issue and its efforts to develop peaceful ways of finding a solution as deviant, because they had positioned themselves as "warriors" in the conflict rather than as political actors. Both appeared to want to dominate their respective political domains, to eliminate their adversary and take away its strategic capability, rather than allow their constituencies to reconcile. They appeared to opt for war rather than for conciliation, and therefore saw organizations such as TOSAV and their efforts as suspicious. Hence, the power centers' efforts aimed at preventing the creation of a middle ground in which conciliation could take place.

Aware of the urgent need to disseminate the culture of democracy to promote their efforts of conciliation, the Board of Directors of TOSAV launched two complementary programs. One of these, established in 1997, was Democracy Radio. Buying primetime slots on Saturdays between 11:30 a.m. and 1:00 p.m. TOSAV worked through three radio stations in Ankara Opening each of these ninety-minute programs, two or three TOSAV members and relevant experts presented a topic concerning democracy, such as "Democracy and the Rule of Law," "Democracy and Women," or "Democracy and Environmental Issues." In the final thirty-forty minutes, listeners called in and either gave comments or engaged in a question-and-answer session. This interactive program has been so successful that fifteen radio stations from all over Turkey have subsequently demanded recorded programs from TOSAV in order to rebroadcast them to their local listeners and open up a debate in their own community. Also upon the demand of its radio audience, TOSAV published in 1999 a book of its radio programs, called *Talking Democracy 1*, and through the Ministry of Culture distributed thirteen hundred copies to all the existing public libraries in Turkey. Books are also given away by the radio stations as prizes to quiz solvers. The radio programs were funded by the National Endowment for Democracy, by the PRIO and by the Westminster Foundation for World Peace in Britain.[11] The first two of these institutions also funded the publishing of the books.

The second program TOSAV launched was a quarterly journal, the *Tosav Newsletter*, published in three languages, Turkish, Kurdish, and English, through which ideas of democracy and conciliation were disseminated. The journal accepted views and analyses from different individuals and groups with something to say about building peace and creating a democratic order in which all ethnic and cultural groups would find an equal place and opportunity. The aim of the journal was to emphasize the importance of effective citizenship and the power of the people to solve their own problems without the arbitration of a higher authority. As there are strict rules in Turkey which require the contents of journals to be cleared by the police, the journal was given the guise of an internal company newsletter in order to bypass these regulations. Newsletters are commonly irregular and are not subject to constant police scrutiny unless they are brought to the attention of the authorities. Paid experts translated the Turkish edition of the *Newsletter* into English and Kurdish, and the trilingual *Newsletter* was distributed around the world, creating a substantial readership. The cost of the journal was met by a grant from the Democracy Programme of the European Commission.

Unfortunately, in June 1999, when the finalized version of the DOMU was printed in three languages, the Ankara State Security Court No. 1 suspended TOSAV's activities. Although the ban on publishing in Kurdish had been lifted in 1991, the authorities often made it difficult when something political was printed in Kurdish. The court found the document "subversive" and "supportive of separatism." Not only was the DOMU banned and confiscated, but TOSAV's activities were also halted. Faced with this fait accompli, a group of TOSAV founders, who wanted to follow their unfinished mission to its end, joined with new people from academia and the labor movement to create TOSAM in July 1999.

Immediately TOSAM shouldered all of the activities of TOSAV, while developing more. Raising public awareness concerning further democratization, establishing the rule of law, and meeting the Copenhagen Criteria[12] as necessary conditions for impending EU membership became the first priorities of the organization. Achieving this aim was facilitated by half a dozen of the new organization's members or advisers who are renowned newspaper columnists and frequently write articles promoting the ideals and aims of the Center. The academic members disseminate democratic and pluralist ideas to younger generations, teaching political theory that is consonant with the aims of TOSAM, and this also attracts young volunteers to the organization's cause. Moreover, many of TOSAM's members are frequent speakers and commentators on television talk shows or news programs that require commentaries on political reform, liberalization, and empowering citizens and civil society.

In addition, TOSAM has continued publishing its journal. However, owing to funding constraints, the formerly "quarterly" journal was reduced to a biannual publication, financed by PRIO. The new name of the journal is *New Horizons*, and it is published in Turkish and English only, for fear that production of a Kurdish-language edition might lead to the journal's termination. The organization has produced another book of its later radio programs, *Talking Democracy 2*, which has been distributed to all public libraries throughout Turkey by the Ministry of Culture.

The reborn organization developed two new programs. The first, an educational-cultural activity, consists of conferences and panels throughout Turkey, dealing with matters of democratic transition, the rule of law, multiculturalism, and political pluralism. Every year, TOSAM organizes a series of two-day panels and conferences in different cities of Turkey, in the belief that strategic groups of this kind can have a multiplier effect in their respective communities, such as local businessmen, trade unions, and professional organizations such as the bar associations.

The second new program goes beyond public outreach by the power of the spoken and written word. Training courses for trainers, including groups of community and institutional leaders are organized by TOSAM. Since its inception in the summer of 1999, TOSAM has organized close to thirty multiday courses in conflict resolution, problem solving, effective communication, change and crisis management, strategic planning, good governance, and leadership. Guest instructors have been invited, including experts from Norway, South Africa, the United States, Israel, Lebanon, India, Belgium, and Palestine. Additionally, local trainers have received further training on conflict resolution, problem solving, change management, effective communication and leadership in the United States, Israel, Ireland, Switzerland, and Finland. All these activities have not only created a pool of highly qualified trainers under TOSAM's roof but have enhanced its reputation as an expert organization in these fields, winning it national acknowledgment.

Also TOSAM takes advantage of every opportunity to engage directly with members of government or the official apparatus. Testifying before a parliamentary commission in late 1999 is only one example. In this case TOSAM advocated for the State to take on board human security issues in its approach to the conflict. It is emphasized in TOSAM's testimony that without addressing "soft" security measures such as basic freedoms, justice and fair trial, work, food, shelter, and education, as well as freedom from forced participation in violent confrontations, "hard" security measures neither solve problems nor fully satisfy people's need for security. Organizational activities of TOSAM, such as seminars, conferences, and symposiums, as well as its members' writings, radio and TV talks, have contributed to a broadening of approach by the political and military establishment.

Outcomes of TOSAV/TOSAM's Policy Engagement

Events that have taken place since the publishing of the DOMU in late spring of 1999 have shown that the general strategy, and many of the associated tactics employed by TOSAM, have succeeded. A major achievement of TOSAM's policy intervention has been to reframe an issue throughout Turkey in such a way that a seemingly intractable ethnic and cultural conflict, deemed as terrorist by the state and security apparatus, became a question of state constitution/policy reform. This shift in definition from terrorism to social conflict[13] has brought about a new rationale in the state's approach to the "Kurdish problem". For the first time the state has started to consider the need to include "soft" or "human" security measures in its approach to the problem. Recent improvements in Turkish laws emphasizing human rights, more humane procedures in prosecution, detention, and interrogation under custody, and modifications in the internal structure of the State Security Courts brought about by dropping the military judges, all attest to the changes that have been taking place since the summer of 2002.

A second shift in Turkey's political discourse that was largely instigated by TOSAM was the transformation to the concept of "national unity." The work of TOSAM has made the public aware that what had been in existence was "uniformity," not "unity," and that unity should be created out of diversity. The Turkish political culture and its educational and legal systems have imposed political, ideological Turkish nationalism, and the cultural Turkish identity on citizens who were born into different ethnic and religious groups. The efforts of TOSAM have helped public opinion to redefine these concepts by pointing out their authoritarian character and their misleading interpretation of solidarity and camaraderie. The political rhetoric in Turkey today is based much more on a mind-set that promotes the creation of unity out of diversity and pluralism than on one that denies cultural, ethnic, or political diversity. Furthermore, the official understanding of pluralism has now been redefined by TOSAM[14] as multiculturalism, a concept which, although already in circulation in international circles, was first introduced to Turkey by the writings and conferences of TOSAM members.

The end result of these paradigm shift is that the basic principles and concepts on which Turkish politics relating to the Kurdish question have been based in the past have been transformed into more democratic forms or annulled altogether. Because of TOSAM's work, the language of politics has changed considerably to fit the requirements of substantial reform, and this has helped the country to comply with the standards it must meet to become a member of the EU.

Movement has been achieved in the international arena as well. The Copenhagen and Maastricht criteria, which require Turkey to raise its political, legal and social standards, are in perfect tune with what TOSAM has advocated. In fact, many of the key notions that have been outlined in the DOMU, but not as yet accepted by the system in Turkey, have been reintroduced by the European Commission as necessary conditions to qualify for membership of the EU. Concrete examples of such conditions include the lifting of bans on non-Muslim minority organizations (for example, a ban on property acquisition by non-Muslim foundations and endowments) and adoption of laws allowing public use of ethnic languages and education in these languages. All of these laws were adopted by the Turkish Parliament in August and December 2002. Together with other factors, such as international dynamics, this process, in a matter of two years, has led to the change of more than one-fourth of the Constitution created by the military in 1981, as well as changes in other critical codes which were either authoritarian or archaic, such as the Law of Associations and Foundations (applying to NGOs in general) and Law on Procedures of Litigation Involving Civil Servants.[15]

Challenges to TOSAM's Policy Engagement

Although much work still needs to be done, the above-mentioned results of TOSAM's activities are encouraging. They were not, however, achieved without encountering significant challenges of which the reader should be made aware. One of the results of the authoritarian, state-heavy structure in Turkey is the restrictive legal system. It limits many basic rights, individual freedoms, and collective initiatives, no matter how peaceful. A concrete example of such restrictions is the rules outlined in the Law of Associations and Foundations, which was created on 6 October 1983 under military rule as Law #2908. According to this law, no Turkish NGO can cooperate with similar foreign civic organizations and/or receive project funds without the special permission of the Council of Ministers. What is "good" and "safe" for the society is determined by official authorities and this makes it practically impossible to establish partnerships and to receive project funds. If the law is breached, the "perpetrators" face a prison sentence ranging from one to three years.

Another restriction emanates from the unlimited veto power of the bureaucracy. If an organization decides to organize a conference or training seminar in a hotel or in the meeting hall of a public or private institution, it has to apply to the governor of the relevant province for permission. The governor's office studies the motivations behind the event and the content material, which is given in the application form. It examines the identities of the organizers, speakers and trainers, and requires a statement for each person from the local public prosecutor's office, to prove they have no criminal record. If permission is obtained after a number of weeks, then the meetings are video and audiotaped by the police with prosecution and court cases often following such meetings. For example, the activities of the TOSAM/TOSAV president, such as speeches, published articles or conferences, have resulted in four cases at the State Security Court, which deals with crimes of terrorism and treason, and another four cases at the Heavy Penalty Court, which deals with crimes against the state.

Another difficulty is the problem of reaching the people and mobilizing society in support of certain goals, ideals, and concrete programs. The central and deterring role of the state has caused huge societal apathy and passivity. This apathy is also caused by the majority's acceptance of a passive role in public affairs whereby they refrain from participating in decision making in return for support and protection from the power elite in particular and the state in general. This passivity is largely due to socioeconomic factors. The GNP in Turkey has declined from US$3,300 per annum in the past two years to US$2,160 in 2002,[16] and the inflation rate has been 60 percent on average since the 1980s.[17] In addition, the average length of education is 3.6 years for men and 2.4 years for women.[18] Hence, one can easily appreciate the precarious position of most citizens in terms of actual survival, and their difficulty in having a perspective that goes beyond their sheer struggle for daily existence.

This combination of apathy and passivity on the part of the majority and the authoritarian and deterrent attitude of the state toward any civic action leaves little room for NGOs and civic initiatives. Therefore TOSAM tried to reach the active community elite, to mobilize the urban intelligentsia, and to convince the liberal elements in the bureaucracy and politics of the usefulness of their cause. This strategic internal alliance was supported by international organizations who assisted with financial resources, expertise, training services, and program partnerships.

Conclusion

Drawing from the experience presented in this case study, TOSAM has identified a number of key issue areas to which NGOs need to direct their attention if they hope to be successful in affecting policy in areas of conflict. The key areas involve issues of preparation, legitimacy, timing, international support, and relationship building.

Preparation

Understanding the landscape of public opinion on your policy issue is mandatory preparatory work for anyone intending to embark on a public campaign. Engage in a "force field analysis" before initiating a public campaign. Find out who supports your cause and who is against it and why. Rally those who are in favor and make them your partners or fellow travelers. You may not win the support of the opposing groups or organizations, but do keep them informed. Find mutual interests and at least try to persuade your opponents not to put formidable roadblocks in your way.

Legitimacy

It is also essential in a divided society to choose the right public or popular instrument to bring the cause into the open or to champion its realization. The most appropriate and most effective group or organization (NGO) must shoulder the cause or take up the issue under consideration. That group or organization must be acceptable to, or have representation in, wider strategic social groups that are pressing for a demand or expectations to be met. The championing group or organization must have legitimacy in order to bridge the gap between the demanding social groups and the policymakers dealing with the problem or issue that has acquired urgency.

Timing

Timing your policy initiative appropriately greatly enhances the chances of success. This means detecting the importance of an issue and the need to address it at the right time and sensing the density of public demand for its realization or solution. There may be a problem that needs to be solved or a task to be accomplished, but if it is not a burning issue at the time, or if public demand in support of its solution or realization is not widespread, the individual or collective agents championing it are likely to fail to reach the people and acquire the representation necessary to pursue the desired goal. Hence the importance of choosing the right issue and finding out whether there is enough public support or demand for its solution at a particular time are of critical importance for the success of the campaign.

International Support

Rallying international support is a distinct advantage to policy change in an area deemed to be in conflict. It gives the NGO an importance and weight which cannot be mustered domestically. Foreign support can also provide a shield, which can often partially protect the NGO from unrestricted official pressures and arbitrary legal prosecution. In addition, foreign support often comes in the form of financial or project aid. Because of the lack of civic initiative and the lack of sources of domestic funding, NGOs are often starved out of business despite their enthusiasm.

Relationship Building

Above all, relationship building is the foundation of any continuing policy program. This does not mean solely building relationships with like-minded organizations. Building a relationship with the institution you are aiming to influence is extremely important to making real progress in the policy process. It is important to be principled, but also flexible in cooperation. Resources and aid mechanisms are often in the hands of central or local governments, and cooperation and the development of a working relationship with them can make life and a successful outcome easier. At TOSAM, when we tour less-developed parts of Turkey where civil society is not organized and the economy is too weak to sustain an active city elite, we apply to the provincial governor, or to his office, to ask for his support in, for example, attracting participants to our "Effective Citizenship and Increasing the Problem-solving Capacity of the Local Elite" training seminars. These offices sometimes do extend support, and when they do, they open many doors for us. Once this rapport is developed, conducting similar activities in adjacent provinces become much easier, as intelligence and police reports often circulate between provinces and governors communicate with each other informally, which can at times be to our advantage.

The Strategy of TOSAM for policy change is predominantly one of bringing an issue into focus, reframing it through constructive and shared discussions, and thus assisting the Turkish people in addressing their problems and moving their country forward. The foundation believes that without a new generation of leaders who are independent-minded citizens, who are ardent defenders of the rule of law, fair play in business, participatory government, and an administration devoid of corruption and nepotism, and who are cognizant of their country's need to be a part of the democratic and developed world, Turkey is doomed to underdevelopment and instability.[19] However, TOSAM also believes that, through its work in the dissemination of democratic culture and its activities as an agent of peace and reconciliation, it has made a significant contribution to building Turkey's capacity to move forward into democracy and, increasingly, out of conflict.

Notes

1. Some thirty-five thousand people have been killed as a result of such conflict from 1984 to 1999. See Human Rights Watch, Annual Report 1999: Turkey www.hrw.org/worldreport99/europe/turkey.html.

2. Ankara: TOBB Special Issue, 1995. "Eastern Question" is a euphemism for the "Kurdish question," as most of the Kurds live in Eastern Turkey.

3. See "Problems of small and medium sized enterprise development in Turkey," www.home.gwu.edu/cigdem/SMEDevelopment.doc.

4. Statement by Yalim Erez, President of TOBB, in his reelection speech, 2 July 1995.

5. As recorded by Ajans Pres, a media company which monitors and provides news records.

6. Further information on these organizations can be found at www.prio.no and www.sfcg.org.

7. The only member on the ethnic Turkish side who had no counterpart on the Kurdish team was a newly retired, fairly young high-ranking army officer. Also, a Kurdish semi-feudal large landowner, who had no equivalent in the Turkish group, was included in the Kurdish group.

8. William Ury and Roger Fisher, *Getting to Yes* (New York: Penguin, 1991).

9. This document can be reached at the www.tosav.org website.

10. TOSAV became the only NGO carrying out research and working to create public awareness concerning the "Kurdish problem." However, without losing its primary focus, it began to develop projects and programs to empower civil society and help build a democratic dialogue between different segments of society in Turkey. The International Advisory Board served until TOSAV was banned by the authorities in June 1999. Most of its members took part in the International Advisory Board of TOSAM, created after the demise of TOSAV.

11. It is now funded partly by the U.S. Information Program and partly by private sources.

12. These were the criteria established for accession to the European Community in 1993, at the European Council meeting in Copenhagen.

13. In TOSAM's view, any conflict which involves unarmed millions ought to be called a social conflict, even if the use of violence is part of that conflict.

14. The political party AK Parti (Justice and Development Party), which adopted this rhetoric and philosophy, won the majority of the parliamentary seats in the November 2002 national elections.

15. This law made it practically impossible to prosecute officials accused of torturing suspects in custody.

16. www.ekutub.dpt.gov.tr/ekonomi/gosterge/tr/1950-01 section 1, "National Income and Production," tables 1.4-1.9.

17. www.ekutub.dpt.gov.tr/eg/2002/tr/10.pdf (inflation rate in 2002 was 63 percent).

18. Website of State Institute of Statistics: http://www.die.gov.tr/english/istatis/esg/00turkey/egitim3.htm

19. TOSAM's efforts and achievements in the field of democracy, good governance, and human rights have been reflected by the award to the TOSAM president in 2000 of the University in Exile Award, given by the New School for Social Research University (New York). TOSAM has also been invited to be one of the sixteen founding members of the International Forum on Democracy.

Chapter 10
Lessons Learned in Conflict-Related Policy Engagement

Mari Fitzduff and Cheyanne Church

Although conflict resolution NGOs are relative newcomers to the field of policy engagement, the case studies outlined in this book show that their influence is becoming substantial. They exemplify the growing confidence of conflict NGOs throughout the world in their attempts to influence policymakers at all levels of society from the local to the global level. Increasingly, there is also a recognition by governmental and international organizations of the need to take NGO capacities into account when trying to address issues of conflict management and resolution. For most NGOs, however, influencing policymaking is still a relatively new role that requires taking up different responsibilities, using different methodologies, and altering their positions in relation to the policymakers they wish to influence. This book will hopefully be of use to those who wish to expand their capacity in this sphere, as well as to policymakers who wish to gain a better understanding of the potential contribution of NGOs in conflict situations.

NGOs come in many guises, and in setting out to achieve their goals, the organizations in this book showed considerable variety in terms of the strategies they adopted. For one organization, an international and comprehensive campaign tightly targeted at governments and international institutions was necessary to achieve their objective of the adoption of legislation at the United Nations and the EU. For another, a multilevel, multifaceted program that focused on influencing international policy and practice approaches to a particular country (Burundi, for example) was important. Others, such as the projects in South Africa and Northern Ireland, focused on particular dilemmas around the implementation of policies designed to address issues in conflict and postconflict situations, working closely with the policy organizations responsible for such implementation. The case study on the Caucasus shows an NGO taking the specific decision to engage explicitly in influencing the quality of political dialogue and political consensus building by working at all levels, including the most senior political levels. The final case study demonstrates the attempts of a relatively small but highly vocal NGO in Turkey to advise and influence a redefinition of the historical problems of the Kurds within Turkey, and thus allow for new perspectives on this conflict issue.

Aware that the development of an effective and appropriate strategy is the key to success, all of the NGOs outlined in this book tailored their strategies according to the desired objectives, while taking into account the capacity and ethos of their organizations, the issue to be addressed, and the particular conflict context. The NGOs in the case studies varied significantly in size. While some organizations had many hundreds of staff, others had less than twenty, thus exemplifying the possible effectiveness of even the smallest of organizations in the field. What has emerged from the case studies, the chapters by Ross and Assefa, and the Foreword by McDonald, is the general consensus that work in influencing policymaking can be effectively undertaken by NGOs in the conflict field who are prepared to pursue the following measures.

Prepare Well

Each chapter illustrates the benefits of rigorous preparation both before and during a policy-engagement. A set of core themes have emerged which translate into the following guidelines for NGOs: be an informed advocate; channeling expertise, know your stakeholders; develop a coherent strategy; and secure adequate resources.

Be an Informed Advocate

Dedicating time, energy, and resources to becoming an informed advocate is a measure that the majority of the case studies found to be invaluable. Becoming informed is not narrowly limited to knowing only one's own argument on an issue—one must understand all perspectives in the policy debate, the history of the issue, and the current status of new thinking or positions. Knowledge of the current legislation on the issue, if it exists, is crucial, as is an understanding of the mechanisms and procedures that may already have been utilized in attempting implementation. The evidence indicates that sometimes it is not a change in a policy that should be targeted, but rather a change in the way in which it is operationalized. Being in tune with the prevailing mood of public opinion is also very important, as this knowledge can be essential to identifying opportune times for successful action.

A second important aspect to becoming an informed policy advocate, and the driver behind an effective NGO policy engagement strategy, is knowledge of the systems and structures in which an NGO seeks to effect change. A crucial lesson that has emerged from all of the case studies is that if NGOs do not understand the hierarchy and internal system of their target organization, they may be unable to affect it. To the best of their ability, NGOs need to become familiar with the intricacies and peculiarities of a particular system, to capitalize on detailed knowledge of the policy and legislative process in order to understand the obstacles and challenges which need to be overcome.

Channeling Expertise

The NGOs studied in this volume found that acquiring knowledge and channeling it into a utilizable format within the organization is a crucial factor in any successful project. For some it involved developing a database used for updating contacts, identifying and mapping targets, and the management of an effective communications strategy. Others hired the requisite expertise in the form of consultants to fill in the gaps in knowledge within the organization, and almost all the NGOs relied upon their staff to engage in rigorous desk research to build a sustainable knowledge base.

Identify the Key Stakeholders

All the NGOs from the case studies realized that identifying key stakeholders, either existing or potential, was an essential step in developing effective policy work. It was important to include as part of a strategy not only actors who were naturally sympathetic to the cause, but also those who may be hostile to the suggested policy. One NGO suggested utilizing a "force field analysis" before initiating a public campaign; this would aid an NGO in recognizing possible supporters and detractors along with the motivations behind such positions. Stakeholders will vary according to the particular issue and objectives of a campaign, but the list generally includes local community groups, national politicians, international organizations, civil servants, local politicians, diplomats, NGOs, and retired elected officials. Knowledge of personnel in the policy community can be augmented by developing an awareness of the particular interests or positions of each stakeholder group and strategizing how the campaign objectives will affect their interests.

Within the governmental stakeholder groups, the NGOs found it highly useful to understand which actors were responsible for different aspects of policymaking. It is important to target the pivotal individual within an organization who is capable of taking decisive action in advancing campaign objectives, and to cultivate a good working relationship with them. Furthermore, by personally arranging your own appointments to meet with senior policy individuals, an NGO representative can develop a personal relationship with the potential "gatekeepers"—namely the personal assistants, appointments secretaries, or scheduler. Additionally, in allocating time and energy to building relationships with policymakers, an NGO should seek to understand the constraints put upon these policymakers, such as budgets, hierarchies, and the party political platforms that policymakers often have to adhere to. Where possible, it is also useful to identify individuals within the policy structures that are sympathetic to your position and work to establish them as "champions" for the cause. These people can also be very useful as strategists and advisers and can help to tailor the policy project so that it can be more effective in achieving its objectives.

Throughout the life of a policy project, it is vital to maintain systematic consultations with all relevant stakeholders, particularly the affected communities. This can include disseminating the results of consultations, alerting people to new developments at the policy level, or circulating new information of unfolding events that are relevant to the project or campaign.

Develop a Coherent Strategy

Developing a coherent strategy is a fundamental step in policy work. The experience of those conflict resolution NGOs who have been pioneers in policy engagement has illustrated a number of lessons in this area. One of the first considerations many NGOs embarking upon policy engagement face is whether an "insider" or "outsider" strategy will be most effective. Those adopting insider strategies seek to work within the halls of power. They align closely with those who have significant power to influence decisions or guide behavior in the policy area. Such strategies call for relationship building with key actors, stimulating empathy with these organizations and individuals, and creating a space for dialogue and reflection whereby ideas and methods can be devised and debated which will help to address issues of conflicts. Such insider alliances often take considerable time and require coalition building which not only involves building trust and confidence with key individuals but often also requires a compromise on behalf of the NGO to respect confidentiality and demonstrate loyalty to those within the halls of power. Outsider strategies, on the other hand, operate from outside of the policy community, and attempt to externally drive policy actors and public opinion in specified directions through pressure tactics of issue advocacy, lobbying, and the use of the media to exert influence.

Both approaches have merit, with their appropriateness depending upon context, resources, and the particular policy issue under review. Yet they do require different strategies, tactics, and orientations on the part of an organization. Many NGOs are better suited to outsider strategies, particularly if their ethos is to operate in an advocacy or oppositional mode to the policy actor in question, such as the government or an IGO. Indeed, these NGOs may perceive the use of insider strategies as "selling out." Yet, for many other NGOs, the insider approach is a logical development of their desire to have a more profound impact on governmental and institutional policymaking. Every NGO needs to make a measured judgment about which strategy is most appropriate, bearing in mind their objectives and their constituency.

A second strategy lesson that can be drawn from the scenarios outlined is the need for clarity and coherency on the exact changes one is seeking to effect. Most NGOs in the case studies were able to organize their policy objectives into short- and long-term goals, and were prepared to adapt these strategies according to need. They also learned to avoid "agenda creep"—the creeping expansion of the policy agenda—realizing that this can lead to the gradual disengagement of policymakers from the cooperative process. In doing so, they addressed one of the main paucities often referred to by those who are cynical of conflict resolution work: that the field is rich in terms of its idealism, but often suffers from thinking that is vague in terms of its focus.

One final consideration when devising a strategy is to determine whether there is a need for an alteration or addition to legislative policy, or alternatively, if improved mechanisms of policy implementation will produce the necessary benefits of change by redressing the problem at hand. Some NGOs found that using existing legislative instruments as leverage and devising realistic and practical tactics to fill a policy vacuum was easier and more practical than trying to create additional legislation.

Secure Sufficient Resources

Many of the NGOs illustrated in this volume suggested that it was important to secure sufficient financial and human resources prior to the full-scale launch of the policy project. Without such resources, personnel can become demoralized and opportunities may be missed, which could prove detrimental to the overall project. Such a suggestion is all too frequently unrealized of course, given the precarious state of most NGOs' funding. However, as some NGOs found, initiating a pilot program which demonstrated the possibilities for both the success and further development of the project was crucial to securing the long-term funding required to successfully develop their policy impact work.

Build Success through Cooperation

What is clear from these case studies is that it is a rare advocate who achieves policy success through unilateral efforts. A range of cooperative initiatives were illustrated in this book, developed and based on the context, actors, issue, strategy, and agency involved. For all the organizations, their sense of competency and therefore the success of the initiative was integrally connected to their cooperative efforts with other organizations.

One NGO at the more independent end of the spectrum sought just a few international partners as strategists, symbols, technical support, and fundraisers, while remaining securely at the fulcrum of the strategy. Another NGO found literally hundreds of partner and supportive organizations, at both local and international levels, to help them in their campaign.

It is obvious from the case studies that those NGOs who succeeded in rallying international support for their cause were often at a distinct advantage when effecting policy change, as such support can give an NGO an importance and weight which often cannot be mustered domestically. Foreign stakeholders can provide financial and other resources as well as acting as a shield, offering partial protection to the organization from unrestricted official pressures and legal prosecution. Such support, however, needs to be carefully undertaken and managed, lest it be perceived as biasing the work of an organization or deskilling the work of local participants to the conflict.

Formal partnerships between NGOs ranged from just two agencies working together on a common issue to large-scale, intricate networks and alliances. Coalitions and networks are beneficial as they build on the differing strengths and legitimacy of each partner. Often, the larger and more diverse the network, the more compelling its message is to policymakers. These networks can be used to exchange information, develop common strategies, and enhance capabilities for linking diverse actors with one another. Essential to the viability of a network partnership are coherency of goals, cooperation on strategies, an effective and agile decision making structure, and most importantly, accountability to partner organizations as well as the affected communities in general. As some of the case studies highlighted, developing a policy coalition is not without its own challenges. An NGO following this path needs to allocate sufficient time and resources to managing coalition relationships in order to ensure effective and efficient operation. Efforts need to be made to create a smooth interaction between agencies with different cultures and contrasting approaches, and to find adequate space within busy schedules in order to work together in a productive and structured manner. The presence of a multitude of actors claiming multiple agendas is a constant hurdle. At times, stakeholders can be absorbed into lobbying for their own individual agendas, and there is a danger that the overall aim of a project can be lost in this trend of individual agenda setting. Therefore, for many NGOs, the temptation to go it alone is ever present, although often tempered by the recognition of what can be better achieved through the building of wider and more powerful alliances. What was important in managing such varied agendas was ensuring adequate facilitation and conflict resolution abilities to facilitate consensual outcomes for the project.

Other key elements in creating effective partnerships of any size are fostering ownership, being generous with credit, equitably sharing resources, and clearly communicating roles and responsibilities. In order to increase ownership, openness to formal evaluations of the project, where possible, is perhaps one of the most important factors to plan for in an intervention. Demonstrated success has enormous value in terms of ensuring the further development and expansion of the project. It provides tangible evidence for supporting participants, especially governmental and state actors, to justify continued involvement in the project if they come under pressure to disengage and reprioritize. It is essential to give credit to all the stakeholders involved in campaigning, especially in times of success. Finally, significant time should be allocated to open communication regarding roles and responsibilities within a partnership, without which confusion and cleavages in the operation of a policy strategy can result in the loss of opportunity and credibility.

Securing Access to Officials

Once an NGO has made decisions on strategy and the framework for coopera-tion, implementation of the strategy is the next logical step. One of their first steps will inevitably be to approach official actors. The NGOs studied here used a number of methods to secure access to officials. Some found it advantageous to use an indirect approach by seeking out "connected" individuals such as for-mer public servants, think tank founders, or business leaders and enlisting their assistance in developing influential and credible positions. Former political fig-ures are often particularly useful to target, as they often have direct and immedi-ate contact with the current policymakers. Such allies can not only enlighten the NGO about institutional and cultural necessities within official institutions, but can also grant the agency or organization credibility when it becomes appropriate to directly approach public officials. These connected individuals can also serve as conduits to communicate informal conversations back to official channels and are often less constrained by current regime policy.

Some NGOs also suggested that one should consider approaching local po-litical leaders who may be interested in the positive public relations potential of aligning with a worthy cause. These individuals can also be excellent strategy advisers, and will certainly have connections at higher levels within the political system. Utilizing existing personal relationships so as to "open doors" was also seen as important, and some of the NGOs found this to be an ideal way of gain-ing important introductions. Finally, as discussed earlier, one should be con-scious of the key role that "gatekeepers" play; ensuring their support is vital, lest they block access to essential actors.

Relationships

Developing and maintaining strong and productive relationships with the diver-sity of policymaking and other stakeholders is essential to the long-term success of a policy-project. These relationships should not be limited to like-minded actors, as there is considerable value in establishing productive rapport with representatives from opposing sides. Many of the NGOs studied found that this was often best done through the development of personal contacts, and that, whatever the issue and at whatever level (local, national, or international), face-to-face meetings were often better than impersonal approaches such as letters or e-mails. Such meetings allowed for concerns to be raised and dealt with in a more informal and confidential manner, and this often facilitated increased flexi-bility of attitudes.

A few lessons were offered with regard to building solid and productive re-lationships. Firstly, as conflict issues are often contentious, particularly where group issues or identities are concerned, many NGOs found it useful to use pro-fessional facilitation and conflict resolution processes. These allowed for the recognition and accommodation of different perspectives, assumptions, priori-ties, and personalities on the part of various stakeholders, and ensured that these factors were not counterproductive in developing the necessary relationships between the NGOs and policymakers involved. Secondly, it was seen as important to build trust through consistency of position and action. This fosters an NGOs reputation as an agency that is reliable and professional. Finally, where possible, it was useful to be consistent in terms of representative personnel from the organization. This does not imply that there can only be one face for a policy-project, but rather that the different target actors should each have, if possible, one person within the organization that they can always connect with.

The Delicacies of Timing

Timing, in its practical and conceptual form, plays a significant role in any NGO policy engagement. The NGOs need to understand that the notions of time needs have a different meaning in policy circles, that not all times are opportune, and that political fluidity will have to be factored into those strategies that seek a long-term engagement. The NGOs in this book's case studies found that being able to capitalize on the "right time" for a policy initiative greatly enhances the chances of success. This means detecting the importance and/or necessity of an issue at the right time and sensing the extent of public demand for its realization or solution. As there are many extensive and complex conflict problems in existence at any time, if the problem an NGO seeks to address is not perceived to be a burning issue or lacks widespread public recognition, the individual or collective agents championing the issue will face an uphill struggle in directing attention to their campaign. Seizing an opportunistic moment to drive an issue is a critical tool of the NGO.

Another aspect of timing is the fact that most politicians want to start and finish something useful "on their watch"; thus, they look for policy initiatives that can achieve success in the short term in order to maximize the credit they receive. Recognition of such time pressures and the needs attendant upon them is therefore critically important. If you can help deliver on some "instant" successes for policymakers, for instance, you may get the support you need for longer-term measures. This is often problematic in that the adoption of a policy is normally a long-term process, and a lot of time may pass between the initial recognition of an issue and the ultimate policy solution, particularly if there is not a groundswell of public opinion demanding its immediate resolution. Experienced political advocates balance these notions of differing time needs in all their strategic decisions.

Despite the long-term nature often associated with generating complex policy, the exact opposite holds true for most civil servant postings, as fluidity and flexibility are inherent in the political and diplomatic arena. Personnel in some major IGOs change every six months, while the average time spent in a position in the United Kingdom government is only two years. This shifting of personnel is but one aspect of political fluidity which NGOs need to be cognizant of, and they must be prepared to handle such shifts constructively. Changes in local and national political staff brought about by elections, policy shifts in reaction to a crisis, and changes in international conventions are all possibilities which can alter the policy environment in terms of actors, direction, agenda, and importance. Whatever the cause, NGOs need to be prepared to switch tactics in the shifting political and policy landscapes, recognizing and exploiting favorable circumstances to their advantage.

Use the Power of the Media

Some of the NGOs studied found that the media can be a powerful ally if handled appropriately. One NGO from the case studies conducted research to identify journalists sympathetic to its cause and kept them informed of its work through regular, targeted, and concise briefings that communicated the issues clearly. This organization also noted the effectiveness of press releases that are short, sharp, and to the point and the importance of keeping an updated database of journalists. The appointment of specific people within a group to be spokespersons to the media and ensuring their availability for interviews is another effective strategy. Where possible, introducing a human-interest angle to stories by offering interviews with people engaged in conflict and peace issues is often a productive strategy to engage the interest of the media.

Electronic media such as e-mail listservs and websites are also valuable media to be considered if public outreach is an important aspect of the policy work. It is also particularly helpful if the project can organize a conspicuous and integrated media strategy which communicates results to official actors and externally to the public at large about the success of the project.

Adopt a Professional Approach

Being professional in all interactions with key stakeholders and being cognizant of the appropriate approach to policy institutions is vital when attempting to influence policymakers. As the case studies have illustrated, passionate and emotional advocacy is not considered acceptable behavior in the policymaking arena, and an overtly emotional attitude may be misinterpreted as aggression by policymakers, leading to a deteriorating relationship. Using facts and statistics to support arguments and understanding that reports that rely upon anecdotal evidence are generally dismissed by governmental and other policymaking agencies is an important lesson to be learned from the NGOs in this volume. It is essential not to publicly criticize or condemn an organization that one is trying to impact when attempting to effect changes in institutional thinking or operational procedures. It is also important to respect the time frames of officials, as most officials are too busy to sit down and read long documents. One method utilized was to provide a half-page of talking points for them to consider, rather than a lengthy and cumbersome document that would most likely go unread.

Finally

The conflict resolution NGOs exhibited in this volume are now experienced actors in the policy arena. They understand that there is no quick fix or magic wand for most conflict problems. They also know that to effectively transform a conflict, there is a need for their work to be more effectively developed through institutionalized actors that have both substantive and sustainable policy- and program-making power. Despite their usually limited resources, each of these NGOs were able to work alongside policymakers, ensuring that they were aware of alternative possibilities in changing, alleviating, and transforming many conflict situations throughout the world. The NGOs in this book represent the fact that increasingly, the relationship between many NGOs, the United Nations, and other policymakers is beginning to develop an essential mutuality in the processes of policy formulation and the execution of those policies on the ground in conflict areas. Each side may be cognizant of some losses in such developing partnerships. However, to have both sides moving together in common directions, complementing each other's visions and expertise, can only be of significant benefit to the areas of conflict in which they work—areas which are likely to continue to need such effective partnerships in the decades to come.

Appendix 1
United Nations Resolution 1325 (2000)

Adopted by the Security Council at its 4,213th meeting, on 31 October 2000

The Security Council,

Recalling its resolutions 1261 (1999) of 25 August 1999, 1265 (1999) of 17 September 1999, 1296 (2000) of 19 April 2000 and 1314 (2000) of 11 August 2000, as well as relevant statements of its President, and *recalling also* the statement of its President to the press on the occasion of the United Nations Day for Women's Rights and International Peace (International Women's Day) of 8 March 2000 (SC/6816),

Recalling also the commitments of the Beijing Declaration and Platform for Action (A/52/231) as well as those contained in the outcome document of the twenty-third Special Session of the United Nations General Assembly entitled "Women 2000: Gender Equality, Development and Peace for the Twenty-First Century" (A/S-23/10/Rev.1), in particular those concerning women and armed conflict,

Bearing in mind the purposes and principles of the Charter of the United Nations and the primary responsibility of the Security Council under the Charter for the maintenance of international peace and security,

Expressing concern that civilians, particularly women and children, account for the vast majority of those adversely affected by armed conflict, including as refugees and internally displaced persons, and increasingly are targeted by combatants and armed elements, and *recognizing* the consequent impact this has on durable peace and reconciliation,

Reaffirming the important role of women in the prevention and resolution of conflicts and in peacebuilding, and *stressing* the importance of their equal participation and full involvement in all efforts for the maintenance and promotion of peace and security, and the need to increase their role in decision making with regard to conflict prevention and resolution,

Reaffirming also the need to implement fully international humanitarian and human rights law that protects the rights of women and girls during and after conflicts,

Emphasizing the need for all parties to ensure that mine clearance and mine awareness programs take into account the special needs of women and girls,

Recognizing the urgent need to mainstream a gender perspective into peacekeeping operations, and in this regard *noting* the Windhoek Declaration and the Namibia Plan of Action on Mainstreaming a Gender Perspective in Multidimensional Peace Support Operations (S/2000/693),

Recognizing also the importance of the recommendation contained in the statement of its President to the press of 8 March 2000 for specialized training for all peacekeeping personnel on the protection, special needs and human rights of women and children in conflict situations,

Recognizing that an understanding of the impact of armed conflict on women and girls, effective institutional arrangements to guarantee their protection and full participation in the peace process can significantly contribute to the maintenance and promotion of international peace and security,

Noting the need to consolidate data on the impact of armed conflict on women and girls,

1. *Urges* Member States to ensure increased representation of women at all decision-making levels in national, regional and international institutions and mechanisms for the prevention, management, and resolution of conflict;

2. *Encourages* the Secretary-General to implement his strategic plan of action (A/49/587) calling for an increase in the participation of women at decision-making levels in conflict resolution and peace processes;

3. *Urges* the Secretary-General to appoint more women as special representatives and envoys to pursue good offices on his behalf, and in this regard *calls on* Member States to provide candidates to the Secretary-General, for inclusion in a regularly updated centralized roster;

4. *Further urges* the Secretary-General to seek to expand the role and contribution of women in United Nations field-based operations, and especially among military observers, civilian police, human rights and humanitarian personnel;

5. *Expresses* its willingness to incorporate a gender perspective into peacekeeping operations, and *urges* the Secretary-General to ensure that, where appropriate, field operations include a gender component;

6. *Requests* the Secretary-General to provide to Member States training guidelines and materials on the protection, rights and the particular needs of

women, as well as on the importance of involving women in all peacekeeping and peacebuilding measures, *invites* Member States to incorporate these elements as well as HIV/AIDS awareness training into their national training programmes for military and civilian police personnel in preparation for deployment, and *further requests* the Secretary-General to ensure that civilian personnel of peacekeeping operations receive similar training;

7. *Urges* Member States to increase their voluntary financial, technical and logistical support for gender-sensitive training efforts, including those undertaken by relevant funds and programmes, inter alia, the United Nations Fund for Women and United Nations Children's Fund, and by the Office of the United Nations High Commissioner for Refugees and other relevant bodies;

8. *Calls on* all actors involved, when negotiating and implementing peace agreements, to adopt a gender perspective, including, inter alia:

(a) The special needs of women and girls during repatriation and resettlement and for rehabilitation, reintegration and postconflict reconstruction;

(b) Measures that support local women's peace initiatives and indigenous processes for conflict resolution, and that involve women in all of the implementation mechanisms of the peace agreements; and

(c) Measures that ensure the protection of and respect for human rights of women and girls, particularly as they relate to the constitution, the electoral system, the police and the judiciary;

9. *Calls upon* all parties to armed conflict to respect fully international law applicable to the rights and protection of women and girls, especially as civilians, in particular the obligations applicable to them under the Geneva Conventions of 1949 and the additional Protocols thereto of 1977, the Refugee Convention of 1951 and the Protocol thereto of 1967, the Convention on the Elimination of All Forms of Discrimination against Women of 1979 and the Optional Protocol thereto of 1999 and the United Nations Convention on the Rights of the Child of 1989 and the two Optional Protocols thereto of 25 May 2000, and to bear in mind the relevant provisions of the Rome Statute of the International Criminal Court;

10. *Calls on* all parties to armed conflict to take special measures to protect women and girls from gender-based violence, particularly rape and other forms of sexual abuse, and all other forms of violence in situations of armed conflict;

11. *Emphasizes* the responsibility of all States to put an end to impunity and to prosecute those responsible for genocide, crimes against humanity, and warcrimes including those relating to sexual and other violence against women and girls, and in this regard *stresses* the need to exclude these crimes, where feasible from amnesty provisions;

12. *Calls upon* all parties to armed conflict to respect the civilian and humanitarian character of refugee camps and settlements, and to take into account the particular needs of women and girls, including in their design, and recalls its resolutions 1208 (1998) of 19 November 1998 and 1296 (2000) of 19 April 2000;

13. *Encourages* all those involved in the planning for disarmament, demobilization and reintegration to consider the different needs of female and male ex-combatants and to take into account the needs of their dependants;

14. *Reaffirms* its readiness, whenever measures are adopted under Article 41 of the Charter of the United Nations, to give consideration to their potential impact on the civilian population, bearing in mind the special needs of women and girls, in order to consider appropriate humanitarian exemptions;

15. *Expresses* its willingness to ensure that Security Council missions take into account gender considerations and the rights of women, including through consultation with local and international women's groups;

16. *Invites* the Secretary-General to carry out a study on the impact of armed conflict on women and girls, the role of women in peacebuilding and the gender dimensions of peace processes and conflict resolution, and *further invites* him to submit a report to the Security Council on the results of this study and to make this available to all Member States of the United Nations;

17. *Requests* the Secretary-General, where appropriate, to include in his reporting to the Security Council progress on gender mainstreaming throughout peacekeeping missions and all other aspects relating to women and girls;

18. *Decides* to remain actively seized of the matter.

References

Mitchell, C. 1981. *The Structure of International Conflict.* Basingstoke: Macmillan.

Moore, C. 1996. *The Mediation Process* (2nd ed.). San Francisco, CA: Jossey-Bass.

Rubin, J., and D. Pruitt. 1994. *Social Conflict: Escalation, Stalemate and Settlement.* New York: McGraw-Hill.

Appendix 2
Indirect Mediation via Radio—Dialogue between Rebels and Government

The war in Burundi has been brutal both in terms of its impact on civilians, and the division of the Burundian people along ethnic lines. This brutality and division reduced the ability of various fighting groups to communicate, and at the same time solidified each other's negative images of the enemy (Mitchell, 1981; Rubin, Pruitt, 1994).

Initially, Search for Common Ground established Studio Ijambo to counter hate radio such as Radio Mille Collines, which had served as one of the principal catalysts to the genocidal killing spree in Rwanda. In Burundi, this took the form of a radio station owned and operated by a rebel group, the CNDD-FDD, which broadcast hate messages from eastern Congo. When Studio Ijambo was launched in May 1995, Hutu and Tutsi populations across the Great Lakes region were at the lowest point in their bloody relationship. As a result, access to balanced information was at a premium. Studio Ijambo was founded "to produce balanced and non-inflammatory programs" with the specific goal of initiating dialogue between rebel leaders and the government. The founding idea was "to counter and transcend a culture of suspicion and hatred, often prompted by radio, which manipulates listeners and foments violence."

At that time it was the only ethnically mixed (Hutu and Tutsi) radio production facility in the country, a fact which provided its programs with a unique credibility throughout the country. When Studio Ijambo covers an event, people trust the report because it is not the product of one group or another, with bias inevitably built in, but of an ethnically mixed, professional team. This combination of ethnic mix and professionalism allows Studio Ijambo to fill the vacuum of reliable news, current affairs, and information dissemination in the country.

Policy Challenges and Responses

As a result of mutual feelings of threat and fear, government and rebel policies become strict in disallowing dialogue with the enemy, for fear that it may compromise their positions or give legitimacy to the other's position (Rubin and Pruitt, 1994).

In order to address the issue of lack of communication, and the delegitimization by the government of the rebels and vice versa, Studio Ijambo initiated media efforts aimed at making each party hear the other over the sound of guns and bombs. Typically, especially in the beginning of the conflict, the clear policy of both government and rebels was one of zero communication. Unwillingness to communicate, exemplified on the Tutu side by a policy of "no communication with those who had committed genocide" and a distrust of the government on the Hutu side, made the first step one of the most difficult in the peace process. Each party strongly believed in its cause and demonized the other,[1] as is always the case in violent conflict and war. Studio Ijambo's approach was to talk to warring factions with neutrality and impartiality. In other words, Studio Ijambo's journalists did not preoccupy themselves with judging the legitimacy of warring parties' positions; instead, they focused on bringing to the public, and at the same time to the rivals, the issues and interests of those fighting each other.

When stakeholders refuse to talk in direct negotiations, Studio Ijambo brings them together via radio and telephone. As one method, journalists at the studio call rebels directly, asking them to join a discussion of current problems with in-studio guests, who include members of political parties, government officials, or civil society leaders. This both develops a relationship between rebels and journalists and introduces a form of collaborative dialogue between adversaries.

This process of indirect mediation gave parties the type of face-saving (Moore, 1996) they needed in the early stages of the conflict. By talking to journalists on the radio, it did not appear that they were conducting a direct dialogue with their enemies, but each party heard the other. Eventually, this process helped warring factions to follow a type of indirect mediation process in which Studio Ijambo programs provided the medium for their discussion of issues and for generating options aimed at stopping the fighting.

Studio Ijambo was able to play the role of an indirect mediator with access to both the government and the rebels because of three factors:

1. Over the years, Studio Ijambo has established credibility, unprecedented popularity, and a reputation for fairness among all Burundians.
2. Studio Ijambo's staff reflects the ethnic and geographical diversity of Burundi, and presents a role model for peaceful coexistence.
3. Studio Ijambo's staff has actively traveled to where events were taking place, regardless of how inconvenient or even dangerous it was to go to such places. Being on the ground where events are happening has been a significant feature of Studio Ijambo's work, and gained them much respect

among Burundians who were not accustomed to seeing journalists operate in such places.

Policy Impact of SFCG's Indirect Mediation

Studio Ijambo developed a style of journalism that was new to the Burundian market—one of openness, in which interviews with stakeholders from all sides and all levels could be heard. In serving as a model for this approach, the project had a direct impact on the policies of the official radio station, RTNB. The government had forbidden the official station to broadcast any statements by the opposition. The Studio Ijambo programs, which gave a voice to the rebels, were often subjected to censorship on the government station. Studio Ijambo were undeterred, and the growing popularity of their programs made it more and more difficult for the government to justify their policies of non-recognition. Finally, Studio Ijambo and RTNB reconciled their opposing policies with an agreement that the rebel statements could be read or paraphrased by journalists, without the broadcast of the rebels' actual voices. The station changed its policy to allow these statements to be read on air. A high-ranking official of the Burundian government applauded the process: "Studio Ijambo helps them [fighting factions] hear each other's needs and issues; this facilitates negotiations, and puts an end to the fight." The relationship between the media and government, however, is in constant flux, and in June 2002, the Burundian Minister of Defense reverted to the former policies, disallowing "all media working on Burundi soil to broadcast any interview with a rebel."

These radio programs impact the formulated policies of both the government and the rebels, transforming established rules of zero communication, and successfully opening a medium for dialogue in which parties are able to discuss their needs and issues and eventually make a commitment to the peace process. In effect, this radio work establishes a safe medium for parties to express their aspirations and grievances, and to adjust their policies toward a more open expression of their views, even to their rivals.

Note

1. Print news sources were a primary conduit for spreading messages of hate and violence. *L'Aube de la Démocratie* for the Hutus and *Le Carrefour des Idées* for the Tutsis were the most widely read; the latter, owned by a well-known Tutsi hard-liner, offered rewards for the killing of Hutu leaders. The Burundian government later suppressed both of these newspapers under pressure from the international nonprofit organization Reporters sans Frontières.

Appendix 3
Implementing Existing Policies—Women's Rights and the Legal Code in Burundi

Despite the existence of legislation that promotes equality and fair practices for women and families, adequate resources to ensure implementation of laws and changes in customary practices often do not meet the ambitions of legislators. Furthermore, the government's development programs, many of which were designed to aid the condition of women, have been repeatedly interrupted over the last decade due to the ongoing crisis. The most recent changes in the legal code are part of an ongoing process of reform of the legal statutes concerning women which began in 1993 with the reform of the Code of the Person and the Family. However, some aspects of the traditional value system in Burundi dictate behaviors and practices that reinforce notions of male superiority and female subjection. Traditionally reinforced practices in the spheres of marriage, divorce, and inheritance hinder the implementation of the legal code that attempts to grant women equal rights and securities.

In order to address these issues, SFCG's Legal Code Project is conducted via three main methods: radio programming, community workshops, and information dissemination:

Radio Programming

Studio Ijambo produces a regular radio magazine program called Uko Bukeye Uko Bwije ("the law for every day"), concentrating on the legal code. Each week, a new program is produced and broadcast three times on two radio stations. The purpose of each program is to inform the public about an aspect of Burundian law. According to one interviewee, "in general the use of radio programs to transmit messages fits very well in the Burundian tradition of oral communication; in Burundi there is hardly a written tradition."

Subjects include explaining how to marry legally, what it means to marry legally, and what the differences are between being married versus living together without a legal marriage contract. This is a significant social problem in Burundi, as many women who are not married end up at a severe disadvantage once a relationship is terminated, and the effect on their children is devastating. Another critical issue is that of family assets, the importance of knowing how to use them, and how they should be divided among the family. This program discusses how assets are acquired from both the side of the husband and from the side of the wife, and emphasizes that children should be informed about inheritance laws.

The radio programs use personal testimony, in which someone tells a personal story about a legal issue, followed by a discussion about its implications. This allows the audience to understand and relate the law to a tangible situation they can identify with. Testimonies have included subjects such as polygamy, domestic violence, and illegal marriages. Individuals sometimes call Studio Ijambo asking for guidance on how to proceed in order to resolve a particular problem in a legal manner.

Community Workshops

The initial series of training workshops were held in Bujumbura and other communities in order to bring people together around the main subjects of the legal code. Two jurists (different in both gender and ethnicity) trained a selected group of twenty individuals, composed of equal numbers of men and women, Hutus and Tutsis, each with a background in education. The beneficiaries of the first workshop then became the trainers of several groups from a different background. Generally composed of three separate sessions (held consecutively or over a period of time depending on the needs of the community), the training events reached twenty different counties throughout the country in addition to numerous workshops in the capital. As word spread, the WPC began getting demands from community organizations as diverse as the boy scouts, schools, and women's organizations.

The community workshops, which focus on the main issues of the legal code, have resulted in regular meetings where women discuss issues that help them improve their living conditions. Commenting on the radio program and the community workshop approaches, a legal expert stated: "Their sketches are well performed; the information is impartial and very useful. I believe that an activity such as the translation in Kirundi and distribution of the legal code can impact the law. Also their work on the community level is of a great importance in this respect and has the potential to contribute to a change."

A unique aspect of this approach was the creation of a safe forum where issues that are often considered taboo can be discussed in a mixed group. The unprecedented mixture of genders and ethnicities was a radical step for many of the participants, one that had a face-to-face component unachievable via radio. SFCG informed the participants of modern legislation, of which many had no knowledge, and the group could then discuss these changes. Learning from one another's opinions and voicing their own, they began a dialogue in the classroom that would continue in the community.

Information Dissemination

In Kirundi, posters and small guidebooks are distributed by officers of local government agencies to explain the rule of the law in cases of disputes. In one instance, upon completion of a phase of community workshops, a total of one hundred thousand small guides were distributed.

Policy Impact of the Legal Code Project

The impact of this project is on the implementation of an existing policy, rather than on the policy itself. The legislation exists, but is poorly applied, if at all, to the everyday lives of Burundian citizens. The project has had a significant impact, as indicated by several interviewees, on three levels: governmental, organizational, and individual.

At the governmental level, administrators have been more active in advising couples to get married and utilizing the information resources of the project in their information campaigns and regular activities. Additionally, as one beneficiary of the project stated, "the local authorities are more willing to listen when a woman comes up with a complaint."

At the organizational level, the SFCG model for this project intrigued other organizations enough that they adapted and expanded it into other areas of the country. Several officials in other women's and media organizations affirmed that the WPC was the first organization to execute such a project, and that other associations, including the Association des Femmes Juristes du Burundi, followed this initiative. In particular, the participatory approach, and the willingness to invite and include people from other ethnic groups, are factors which are now much more integrated into the practices of other organizations. As one interviewee stated: "The Women's Peace Centre has prepared our path in a favorable manner."

Finally, at the level of the household and the individual, several couples that were living together decided to get married legally. This tendency seems to continue. In the community of Mirangara, for example, twenty couples got married formally in the first months after the information was provided. Normally this number is one or two.

Index

About the Contributors

Amr Abdalla is an affiliate assistant professor with the peace operations policy program at George Mason University. He has conducted numerous evaluation and research projects on conflict resolution programs in several countries.

Ancil Adrian-Paul is the program manager for International Alert's Women Building Peace campaign. He was born and raised in Guyana, South America, and has lived and conducted research in the United Kingdom and parts of Africa. Previously, Ancil acted as IA's liason officer and coordinator for the development and peacebuilding program.

Hizkias Assefa is professor of conflict studies at the conflict transformation program at Eastern Mennonite University in Virginia. He is the founder and coordinator of the Africa Peacebuilding and Reconciliation Resources located in Nairobi, Kenya, which is also the base for his peacebuilding practice in Africa, Asia, and Latin America.

Cheyanne Church is the director of institutional learning and research at Search for Common Ground in Washington, D.C. She is the former director of the policy and evaluation unit at UNU/INCORE in Northern Ireland. She has published on evaluation in conflict resolution, single-identity work, and conflict-related research impacting policy. Church received an MSc in International Relations from the London School of Economics and a BComm Honours from Queen's University in Canada.

Kevin Clements is professor and foundation director of the Australian Centre for Peace and Conflict Studies at the University of Queensland in Brisbane. He is the former secretary general of International Alert, where he acted as advisor to various European governments on conflict prevention and resolution and oversaw field programs in the Great Lakes of Africa, West Africa, the Caucasus, Asia, and Latin America.

Dogu Ergil is professor of political sociology and chairman of the political behavior department in Ankara University Turkey. He is the founder and president of the renowned Turkish NGO, TOSAM, which is dedicated to working toward conflict resolution and disseminating a culture of democracy throughout Turkish society.

Mari Fitzduff is currently professor and director of the master's program in coexistence and conflict at Brandeis University in Massachusetts (www.brandeis.edu/coexistence/masters). She is a former professor of conflict studies and former director of UNU/INCORE in Northern Ireland. From 1990-1997 she was director of the community relations council and has also worked as a program consultant on projects addressing conflict in the Middle East, Sri Lanka, Basque country, Indonesia, and the CIS states. Her previous publications include *Community Conflict Skills* and *Beyond Violence—Conflict Resolution Processes in Northern Ireland.*

Nicola Johnston is a gender and advocacy specialist with expertise in forced migration issues. She is senior policy advisor for International Alert's gender and peacebuilding program. She is the former head of the University of Witwatersrand Refugee Research Programme in South Africa, where she lead work on research and advocacy relating to the development of refugee and immigration policy in the country.

Susan Collin Marks is executive vice president of Search for Common Ground, an international conflict resolution and prevention NGO. A South African, her book *Watching the Wind*, chronicles her work under the auspices of the National Peace Accord during South Africa's transition to democracy.

Ambassador John W. McDonald is a lawyer, diplomat, former international civil servant, development expert, and peacebuilder concerned about world social, economic, and ethnic problems. He spent twenty years in Western Europe and the Middle East and worked on UN economic and social affairs for sixteen years. McDonald retired from the Foreign Service in 1987, after forty years as a diplomat and is co-founder of the Institute for Multi-Track Diplomacy in Washington, D.C. He holds B.A. and J.D. degrees from the University of Illinois and graduated from the National War College in 1967. McDonald was appointed ambassador four times to represent the United States at various UN World Conferences

Susan Allen Nan is currently working in School for International Service (SIS) at the American University. She is the former director of the Alliance for Conflict Transformation, Inc. (ACT) in Fairfax, Virginia. In 1999, she received a Ph.D. in conflict analysis and resolution from George Mason University. She received the Peace Scholar Award from the United States Institute of Peace. Dr. Nan's extensive practical international conflict resolution experience spans a wide variety of work from the head-of-state level to civil society dialogues to youth-based reconciliation.

Chris O'Donnell works as a demobilization officer for the United Nations Organization Mission in the Democratic Republic of Congo (MONUC) and is stationed in the South Kivu region of Eastern DRC. Before taking up this post, he was the project coordinator for the Making an Impact project at INCORE in Northern Ireland. O'Donnell has many years of experience as a management consultant and received an M.A. with honors in peace and conflict studies from the University of Ulster and a B.A. with honors in international relations from the University of Pennsylvania.

Eugenia Piza Lopez is the former head of the policy and advocacy department at International Alert. She is currently working in the conflict prevention and recovery unit of the UNDP in Jakarta, Indonesia.

Marc Howard Ross is William R. Kenan Jr. Professor of Political Science at Bryn Mawr College. He has written or edited six books, including *The Culture of Conflict* and *The Management of Conflict*. He has written over fifty articles that have appeared in a diverse range of academic books and journals.

Sean Tait is executive director of UMAC and regional coordinator of the Southern African Prevention Network. He has worked extensively in the field of peacebuilding both before and after the South African elections in 1994. He is an honors graduate in criminology from the University of Cape Town.